Learning
Microsoft®
PowerPoint® 97

Iris Blanc

To My Family
Alan, Pamela, and Jaime–*I.B.*

Special thanks to Julia Ingram,
for her multiple contributions to this project
and to Cathy Vesecky,
for going above and beyond the call of duty.

Managing Editors	**Project Manager**	**Technical Editor**	**Design and Layout**
Kathy Berkemeyer	Cathy Vesecky	Cathy Vesecky	Julia Ingram
Westmont, IL	Westmont, IL	Westmont, IL	Westmont, IL

Jennifer Frew
New York, NY

First DDC Publishing Inc. Printing

10 9 8 7 6

Printed in the United States of America.

Microsoft®, Excel® 97, Internet Explorer, MS-DOS®, PowerPoint® 97, Word 97®, and Windows® are registered trademarks of Microsoft Corporation.
Yahoo!™ and Yahoo™ logo are trademarks of Yahoo!™
LYCOS™, LYCOS™ logo are trademarks of LYCOS™.
AltaVista™ and the AltaVista™ logo are trademarks of AltaVista Technology, Inc.
Excite is a service mark of Excite Inc.
Infoseek^{SM} and infoseek^{SM} logo are trademarks of the Infoseek Corporation.
Some illustrations in this book and on the DDC Web site have been acquired from Web sites and are used for demonstration and educational purposes only. Online availability of text and images does not imply that they may be reused without the permission of the copyright holder, although the Copyright Act does permit certain unauthorized reuse as fair use under 17 U.S.C. Section 107. PowerPoint 97 Screen Shots reprinted with permission of Microsoft Corporation.

All registered trademarks, trademarks, and service marks mentioned in this book are the property of their respective companies.

Contents

Contents

About Microsoft® PowerPoint® 97

- **PowerPoint 97** is the presentation graphics component of Microsoft Office 97. It combines text, clip art, drawing objects, charts, tables and other objects to create visual presentations. Each file created by PowerPoint is called a presentation, and each presentation is made up of slides.

About this Book

Learning Microsoft PowerPoint 97 will teach you to use PowerPoint 97 on an IBM or PC compatible computer.

Each lesson in this book explains concepts, provides numerous exercises to apply those concepts, and illustrates the necessary keystrokes or mouse actions required to complete the exercises.

Lesson summary exercises are provided at the end of each lesson to challenge and reinforce the concepts learned.

After completing the exercises in this book, you will be able to use the basic features of PowerPoint 97 with ease.

How to Use this Book

Each exercise contains four parts:

- **NOTES** explain the concept and application being introduced.

- **EXERCISE DIRECTIONS** explain how to complete the exercise.

- **EXERCISES** allow you to apply the new concept.

- **KEYSTROKES** outline the keystroke shortcuts and mouse actions required for completing an exercise.

✔ *Keystrokes and mouse actions are only provided when a new concept is being introduced. Therefore, if you forget the keystroke or mouse action required to perform a task, you can use the either the Help feature (explained in the Basics section) or the index of this book to find the procedure.*

Before you begin working on the exercises in PowerPoint 97, you should read the first introductory section entitled Basics. This section will explain the PowerPoint 97 screen, the Help feature, working in Windows, toolbars, menus, and other necessary preliminary information.

Data and Solution Files

The exercise data files are provided on the accompanying CD-ROM. Please read the installation directions on page v to learn how to access these files. Solutions disks may be purchased separately from DDC Publishing. You may use the data files to complete an exercise without typing lengthy text or data. However, exercise directions are provided for both data disk and non-data disk users.

Exercise directions will include a keyboard icon ⌨ to direct non-data disk users to open documents created in a previous exercise and a diskette icon 💾 to direct data disk users to open the document available on the CD. For example, a typical direction might read: Open ⌨**INVEST**, or open 💾**03INVEST**.

The Solution disk may be used for you to compare your work with the final version or solution on disk. Each solution filename begins with the letter "S" and is followed by the exercise number and a descriptive filename. For example, **S03INVEST** would contain the final solution to the exercise directions in Exercise three.

A directory of data disk and solutions disk filenames are provided in the Log of Exercises section of this book.

✔ *Saving files to a network will automatically truncate all filenames to a maximum of eight characters. Therefore, though Windows 95 allows for longer filenames, a maximum of only eight characters can be saved to a network drive.*

The Teacher's Manual

While this book can be used as a self-paced learning book, a comprehensive Teacher's Manual is also available. The Teacher's Manual contains the following:

- Lesson objectives
- Exercise objectives
- Related vocabulary
- Points to emphasize
- Exercise settings

- A Log of Exercises, which lists filenames in exercise number order
- A Directory of Documents, which lists filenames alphabetically along with the corresponding exercise numbers
- Solution illustrations

The enclosed CD-ROM includes . . .

A Companion Internet Simulation

The CD-ROM that accompanies this book contains a simulation of Internet sites to be used in Lesson Six. This means that you can complete the exercises without an Internet connection, avoiding modems, connection time and fees, wandering to unrelated sites, and long waits for Web sites to load. It's like being live on the Internet with none of the inconvenience.

For example, in Exercise 39, you will do a multi-level search on a site that gives information on ski resorts in Europe. Launch the simulation following the detailed directions and follow the prompts at the bottom of your screen to find the information that you need. You will then copy the results of your search into a PowerPoint presentation. Even if you have never been on the Internet before, you will be able to do the exercises. The result is that you learn how to integrate the power of PowerPoint 97 with the power of the Internet. (*See installation instructions on the right.*)

Multimedia Internet Browser Tutorial

For the new user of the Internet, the CD-ROM includes basic computer based training on how to navigate the Internet using a browser. A browser is a program that helps manage the process of locating information on the Word Wide Web. The tutorial introduces the concepts and then shows you how to apply them. (*See installation instructions at the right.*)

Demo of DDC's Office 97 Multimedia Tutorial

In this excerpt of DDC's Office 97 CBT (Computer Based Training), you will receive a sample of step-by-step directions, illustrations, simulations of desired keystroke or mouse actions, and application problems. (*See installation procedures on the right.*)

Installation Instructions

A separate installation is required for each program. At the designated prompt, indicate which program you wish to install. When installation of one program is complete, you may begin again from step one to install another.

System Requirements

Software	Windows 95 or Windows NT 3.51 (or higher)
Hardware	80486DX or higher, 16 MB RAM, 256 Color Monitor, and CD-ROM Drive
Disk Space	40 MB available hard disk space

To install the programs, place the CD in your CD-ROM drive and follow the listed steps below:

✓ **IMPORTANT:** *If at any time during the installation of the enclosed CD, you see a message similar to the one below, click **No To All** to proceed with the installation. Do not replace any files ending in .dll. If you have any questions, call Customer Service at 800 528-3897.*

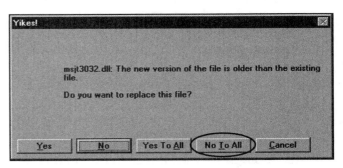

When you install this software, you agree to the following: This software is recorded to be free from defects in materials and faulty workmanship under normal use. Your sole and exclusive remedy in the event of a defect is expressly limited to replacement of the disc. PUBLISHERS WILL NOT BE LIABLE FOR INDIRECT, SPECIAL, OR CONSEQUENTAL DAMAGES RESULTING FROM THE USE OF THIS PRODUCT.

1. **To install from Windows 95:**
   Click Start on the desktop and click Run.
   OR
   To install from Windows NT:
   Go to Program Manager in Main, click File.

2. In the Run window, begin a program installation by typing one of the following:
   - *CD-ROM drive letter*:\PPT97INT\SETUP to install the Internet Simulation.
   - *CD-ROM drive letter*:\OFFICE97\SETUP to install the Office 97 CBT.
   ✓ • *CD-ROM drive letter*:\NETSIM\SETUP to install the Browser tutorial.
3. Click NEXT at the Setup Wizard screen.
4. At the following screen, click NEXT to create a DDCPUB directory for storing program files. Then click YES to confirm the directory choice.
5. At the following screen, allow the default folder to be named **DDC Publishing**, and click NEXT.
6. At the next screen, choose one of the following options based on your individual system needs:
   *NOTE: A **Typical** installation is standard for most individual installation.*
   - **TYPICAL:** installs a minimum number of files to the hard drive with the majority of files remaining on the CD-ROM.
     NOTE: With this installation, the CD must remain in the CD-ROM drive when running the program.
   - **CUSTOM:** installs only those files that you choose to the hard drive. This is generally only recommended for advanced users of Innovus Multimedia software.
   - **Server:** installs the programs on a network server.
7. Click NEXT to begin copying the necessary files to your system.
8. Click OK at the Set Up status Window and then click YES to restart Windows.

To launch a program, click the Start button on the Windows 95 desktop, select Programs, DDC Publishing, and then select one of the following:
- **PPT97INT (to start the Internet Simulation)**
- **DEMO97 (to start the Office97 CBT)**
- **NETCBT (to start the Browser tutorial)**

Data Files

Since this book is designed to teach you how to use the features of PowerPoint 97, not how to type, you can use the data files to avoid typing long documents that are used in many of the exercises.

A disk icon 🖫 preceding a filename means that there is a data file for the exercise. Follow the exercise directions to open the data file and complete the exercise as indicated.

> ✓ *Saving files to a network will automatically truncate all filenames to a maximum of eight characters. Therefore, though Windows 95 allows for longer filenames, a maximum of only eight characters can be saved to a network drive.*

To copy data files on to a hard drive:
- Open Windows 95 Explorer (Right-click on **Start** button and click **Explore**).

- Be sure that the CD is in your CD-ROM drive. Select the CD-ROM drive letter from the All Folders pane of the Explorer window.

- Click to Select the **PPTdata** folder in the Contents of (CD-ROM Drive letter) pane of the Explorer window.

- Drag the folder onto the letter of your hard drive (usually **C:**) in the All Folders pane of the Explorer Window.

LOG OF EXERCISES

Lesson	Exercise	Filename	Data File	Solution File	Page
1	1	INVEST		S01INVEST	17
1	1	RECRUIT		S01RECRUIT	17
1	2	INVEST	02INVEST	S02INVEST	24
1	2	RECRUIT	02RECRUIT	S02RECRUIT	24
1	3	INVEST	03INVEST	S03INVEST	28
1	3	RECRUIT	03RECRUIT	S03RECRUIT	28
1	4	RECRUIT	04RECRUIT	S04RECRUIT	34
1	5	RECRUIT	05RECRUIT	S05RECRUIT	40
1	5	DENVER		S05DENVER	40
1	6	GYM		S06GYM	46
1	7	MOVIE		S07MOVIE	50
1	8	HORSE		S08HORSE	52
2	9	RECRUIT	09RECRUIT	S09RECRUIT	59
2	10	HORSE	10HORSE	S10HORSE	66
2	11	RECRUIT	11RECRUIT	S11RECRUIT	72
2	12	MOVIE	12MOVIE	S12MOVIE	78
2	13	INVEST	13INVEST	S13INVEST	85
2	14	GYM	14GYM	S14GYM	90
2	15	DENVER	15DENVER	S15DENVER	94
3	16	INVEST	16INVEST	S16INVEST	100
3	17	HORSE	17HORSE	S17HORSE	107
3	18	RECRUIT	18RECRUIT	S18RECRUIT	114
3	19	DENVER	19DENVER	S19DENVER	120
3	19	19DENVER.XLS	19DENVER.XLS		120
3	20	20HOUSE.XLS	20HOUSE.XLS		125
3	20	HOUSE		S20HOUSE	125
3	21	FOOD		S21FOOD	128
4	22	WEDDING		S22WEDDING	136
4	23	HOUSE	23HOUSE	S23HOUSE	142
4	24	GYM	24GYM	S24GYM	148
4	25	SILVER		S25SILVER	155
4	26	LECTURE		S26LECTURE	161
4	27	FINLAND		S27FINLAND	164
4	28	PLAN		S28PLAN	168

Lesson	Exercise	Filename	Data File	Solution File	Page
5	29	FOOD		S29FOOD	175
5	30	HOUSE	30HOUSE	S30HOUSE	181
5	31	SILVER	31SILVER	S31SILVER	187
5	32	WEDDING	32WEDDING	S32WEDDING	194
5	33	LECTURE	33LECTURE	S33LECTURE	198
5	34	GYM	34GYM	S34GYM	200
5	35	COLLEGE		S35COLLEGE	204
6	36				214
6	37				218
6	38	SILVER	38SILVER	S38SILVER	221
6	39	PLAN		S39PLAN	226
6	39	WEDDING	39WEDDING	S39WEDDING	226
6	40	SPACE		S40SPACE, S40SPACE.html	235
6	41	SPACE	41SPACE.html		241
6	42	FOOTBALL		S42FOOTBALL	242
6	43	TV		S43TV	248
6	44	UKRAINE		S44UKRAINE	254
6	45	ME		S45ME	260

DIRECTORY OF DOCUMENTS

Filename	Exercise
19DENVER.XLS	19
20HOUSE.XLS	20
COLLEGE	35
DENVER	5
DENVER	15
DENVER	19
FINLAND	27
FOOD	21
FOOD	29
FOOTBALL	42
GYM	6
GYM	14
GYM	24
GYM	34
HORSE	8
HORSE	10
HORSE	17
HOUSE	20
HOUSE	23
HOUSE	30
INVEST	1
INVEST	2
INVEST	3
INVEST	13
INVEST	16
LECTURE	26
LECTURE	33
ME	45
MOVIE	7
MOVIE	12
PLAN	28
PLAN	39
RECRUIT	1
RECRUIT	2
RECRUIT	3
RECRUIT	4
RECRUIT	5
RECRUIT	9
RECRUIT	11
RECRUIT	18

Filename	Exercise
SILVER	25
SILVER	31
SILVER	38
SPACE	40
SPACE	41
TV	43
UKRAINE	44
WEDDING	22
WEDDING	32
WEDDING	39

Lesson 1
Create, Save,
and Print a Presentation

Basics
- About PowerPoint 97
- Using the Mouse
- Microsoft Office Shortcut Bar
- Start PowerPoint 97
- The PowerPoint Screen
- The Zoom Option
- Menus, Toolbars and Commands
- Dialog Box Options
- Slide Rulers and Guides
- Shortcut Menus
- Mouse and Keystroke Procedures
- Help Features
- Office Assistant

Exercise 1
- Create a New Presentation Using the Blank Presentation Option
- Create a New Presentation Using the Template Option
- Select an AutoLayout from the New Slide Dialog Box
- Add Text to Placeholders
- Add Slides to a Presentation
- Save a Presentation
- Properties
- Close a Presentation
- Exit PowerPoint

Exercise 2
- Open a Presentation
- Slide Views
- Move from Slide to Slide
- Spell Checking
- Page Setup
- Print a Presentation

Exercise 3
- Work with Object Placeholders
- Insert Clip Art
- AutoClipArt
- Use Undo

Exercise 4
- Move, Copy, Duplicate, and Delete Slides

Exercise 5
- Change a Presentation's Template
- Change a Slide's Layout

Exercise 6
- Outline View
- Add Slides in Outline View
- Print an Outline

Exercise 7
- Summary

Exercise 8
- Summary

Basics	■ About PowerPoint 97 ■ Using the Mouse ■ Microsoft Office Shortcut Bar ■ Start PowerPoint 97 ■ The PowerPoint Screen ■ The Zoom Option ■ Menus, Toolbars and Commands ■ Dialog Box Options ■ Slide Rulers and Guides ■ Shortcut Menus ■ Mouse and Keystroke Procedures ■ Help Features ■ Office Assistant

NOTES

About PowerPoint 97

■ PowerPoint is the presentation graphics component of Microsoft Office that lets you create and save presentations.

■ A presentation is a collection of slides that you can show while giving an oral report to summarize data and emphasize highlights. From presentation slides, you can prepare audience handouts, speaker notes, an outline, table of contents or overhead transparencies. You can also create 35mm slides of your presentation.

■ PowerPoint slides may include text, drawings, charts, graphics, video, and/or audio clips.

Using the Mouse

■ You must use the mouse to access many features in PowerPoint. Therefore, you must become familiar with its operation.

■ When the mouse is moved on the tabletop, a corresponding movement of the mouse pointer occurs on the screen. The mouse pointer changes shape depending on the object it is pointing to and the action it will be performing. The mouse pointer will not move if the mouse is lifted up and placed back on the tabletop.

■ Specific mouse pointer shapes will be discussed within each exercise as they are activated.

■ All references to the use of mouse buttons in this book refer to the *left* mouse button unless otherwise indicated.

■ The mouse terminology and corresponding actions described below will be used throughout the book:

- **Point to:** move the mouse (on the tabletop) so the pointer touches a specific item.

- **Click:** point to an item and quickly press and release the *left* mouse button.

- **Right-click:** point to an item and press and release the *right* mouse button.

- **Double-click:** point to an item and press the left mouse button twice in rapid succession.

- **Drag:** point to an item and press the left mouse button while moving the mouse.

- **Slide:** move the mouse on the tabletop so that a menu is highlighted.

✓Note: *You must be using an IntelliMouse to use the following mouse actions.*

- **Scroll:** rotate the center wheel of an IntelliMouse forward or backward to move through a presentation.

- **Pan:** Press the center wheel of an IntelliMouse and drag the pointer above/below where you first clicked. The farther you drag, the faster the presentation will move.

- **AutoScroll:** click the center wheel of an IntelliMouse to automatically scroll down in a presentation. Scroll up by moving the pointer above the point of the first click.

- **Zoom:** hold down the Ctrl key while you rotate the center wheel of an IntelliMouse to zoom in or out by 10% increments.

Microsoft Office Shortcut Bar

- After Microsoft Office 97 is installed, the Microsoft Office Shortcut bar appears on your window display and is displayed at all times so that you can access Office features from within Windows or from any Office application.

- The Shortcut bar contains buttons for Office components installed on your system. Only the shortcut bar buttons noted below will be covered in this text.

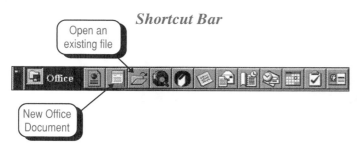

Shortcut Bar

- When you point to a Shortcut bar button, a **ScreenTip** displays with an explanation of that button's function.

  ✓Note: If the Shortcut bar does not appear after installation, click Start, Program, Start Up. Then, select Microsoft Office Shortcut bar.

Start PowerPoint 97

- PowerPoint may be started using any one of the following procedures:

  - **Using the Windows 95 Taskbar:** Click Start, highlight *Programs*, highlight and select Microsoft PowerPoint

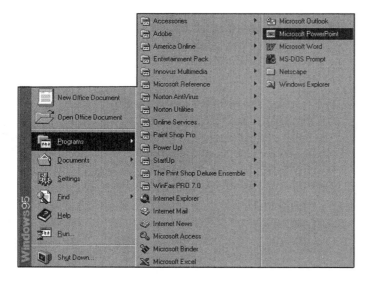

- **Using the Windows 95 Taskbar:** Click Start, highlight and select New Office Document. Click Blank Presentation, or click the Presentation Designs tab, select a presentation design and click OK.

- **Using the Office Shorcut Bar:** Click the New Office Document button. Click presentation type option and click OK.

- If you launch PowerPoint using the first method, the following PowerPoint dialog box appears, which presents options for creating a new presentation or to Open an existing presentation. *(See Exercise 1 to create a new presentation, and Exercise 2 to open an existing presentation.)*

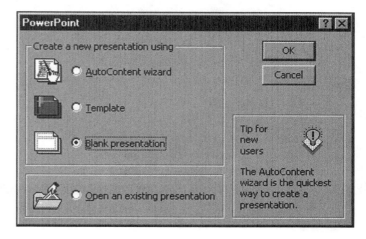

- If you launch PowerPoint using the second or third methods, you will have the option of creating a blank presentation or using a template design. Select the appropriate tab and option in the New Office Document dialog box. *(See Exercise 1 to create a new presentation.)*

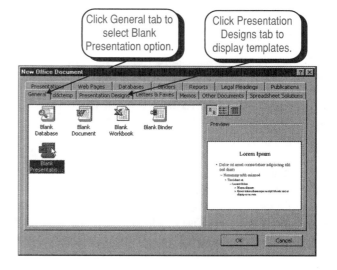

The PowerPoint Screen

- Once a presentation is created or opened, the following PowerPoint screen appears. The following numbered key explains each window element in PowerPoint.

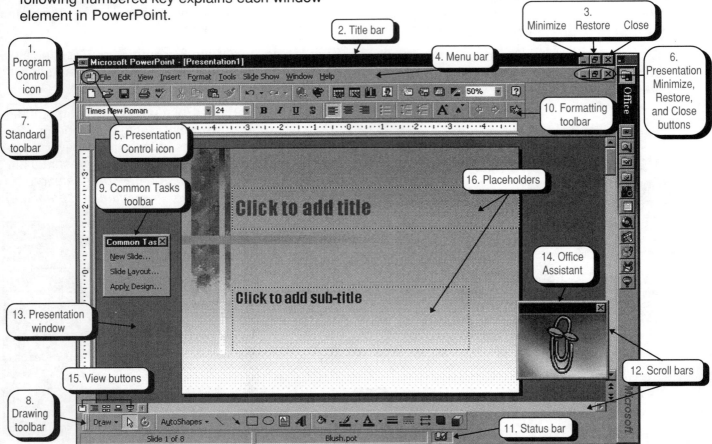

1. The **Program Control icon**, located left of the program window title bar, accesses a drop-down menu from which you can choose commands that control the program window.

2. The **program window Title bar**, located at the top of the application window, displays the program name (Microsoft PowerPoint) and may also display the name of an opened file if the presentation window is maximized.

3. The **program window Minimize**, **Restore**, and **Close buttons** are located right of the program title bar. Clicking the Minimize button shrinks the window to an icon on the Taskbar. Clicking the Restore button creates a small program window and changes the Restore button to a Maximize button. Clicking the Maximize button enlarges the program window to fill the screen. Clicking the Close button closes PowerPoint.

4. The **Menu bar**, located below the title bar, displays menu names from which drop-down menus may be accessed. When you click on a menu, a drop-down menu appears.

5. The **Presentation Control icon**, located left of the Menu bar, accesses a drop-down menu from which you can choose commands to control the presentation window.

6. The **presentation window Minimize**, **Restore**, and **Close** buttons are located right of the Menu bar. When the presentation window is maximized, clicking the Minimize button shrinks the window to an icon that displays at the bottom of the screen. Clicking the Restore button creates a small presentation window (below the toolbars) including a presentation title bar. The Presentation title bar then contains the Presentation Control button and the Minimize,

Maximize, and Close buttons. Clicking the Maximize button ▣ on the presentation title bar returns the window to the size of the opening screen. Clicking the Close button ☒ closes the presentation.

7. The **Standard toolbar** contains many buttons that appear in the other applications, but it also includes buttons unique to PowerPoint. Each button will be presented when it is relevant to an exercise.

8. The **Drawing toolbar**, located above the Status bar at the bottom of the screen, contains some of the most common tools used to add and edit drawings to slides.

9. The **Common Tasks toolbar** is displayed when you open a new presentation. Several of the most common functions are available on this toolbar. You can close this bar if it gets in your way.

10. The **Formatting toolbar**, located below the Standard toolbar in the program window, contains buttons that allow you to quickly change the appearance of text on a slide.

■ Pointing to and resting the pointer on a toolbar button displays a **ScreenTip**, which names the button.

11. The **Status bar**, located at the bottom of the window, displays the following information:

• **Slide number:**	identifies the slide currently displayed.
• **Template Name:**	identifies the template design name.
• **Spell Check icon:**	indicates if Automatic Spell Check is on or off.

12. The **Horizontal** and **Vertical Scroll bars** are used to move the screen view horizontally or vertically. Drag the **Scroll box** on the vertical scroll bar up or down to move more quickly toward the beginning or end of a presentation.

13. The **Presentation Window** is the area where you will work on and view the presentation.

14. The **Office Assistant** appears when you first open a PowerPoint presentation. *(See page 9 for more on the Office Assistant.)*

15. **View buttons**, located at the bottom left of the presentation window, control the number of slides PowerPoint displays and the display layout. *(Views will be covered in Exercise 2.)*

16. **Placeholders** are empty boxes in which you can enter text or an object.

The Zoom Option

■ The <u>V</u>iew menu contains a <u>Z</u>oom option that allows you to set the magnification of the data on the screen. When <u>Z</u>oom is selected, the following dialog box appears:

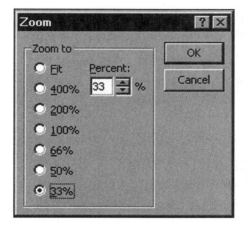

■ By clicking an option button, you can display the text at **<u>400</u>%**, **<u>200</u>%**, **<u>100</u>%, <u>66</u>%**, etc. However, the Zoom Control box 33% , located on the Standard toolbar, lets you easily set text magnification without opening the menu or dialog box.

✓ *Note:* *If you are using the IntelliMouse, you can hold down the Ctrl button and roll the wheel on the IntelliMouse to adjust the view by 10% increments (from 10% to 500%).*

Menus, Toolbars, and Commands

■ The Menu bar and toolbars may be used to access commands. PowerPoint opens with two default toolbars. The **Standard toolbar**, located below the Menu bar, contains buttons that accomplish many common tasks easily, like saving and printing a file.

Standard Toolbar

■ The **Formatting toolbar**, located below the Standard toolbar, contains buttons that easily change the appearance of data.

Formatting Toolbar

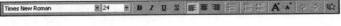

✓ *Note:* *To work through the exercises in this text, the Standard and Formatting toolbars must be displayed on your screen. To display or hide these items, see the keystrokes on page 11.*

■ **To select a command from a toolbar:**

• Use the mouse to point to a toolbar button and click once.

■ **To access Menu bar items:**

• Use the mouse to point to a menu item on the menu bar and click once.

OR

• Press Alt + *underlined letter* in the menu name.

■ **To select a command from a drop-down menu:**

• Use the mouse to point to the command on the drop-down menu and click once, or

• Press the underlined letter in the command name, or

• Use the up or down arrow key to highlight the command, then press Enter.

■ Some menu options are dimmed, while others appear black. Dimmed options are not available for selection at this time, while black options are.

✓ *Note:* *Notice the drop-down menu that appears when Insert is selected.*

■ A check mark next to a drop-down menu item means the option is currently selected.

■ A menu item followed by an arrow ▶ opens a **submenu** with additional choices.

■ A menu item followed by an **ellipsis** (...) indicates that a dialog box (which requires you to provide additional information to complete a task) is forthcoming.

✓ *Note:* *Icons that appear next to menu items are available on the Standard or Formatting toolbars.*

■ Note the Page Setup dialog box below, which appears after you select Page Setup from the File menu; the Font dialog box, which appears after you select Font from the Format menu; and the Color Scheme dialog box, which appears after you select Slide Color Scheme from the Format menu.

Page Setup Dialog Box

Font Dialog Box

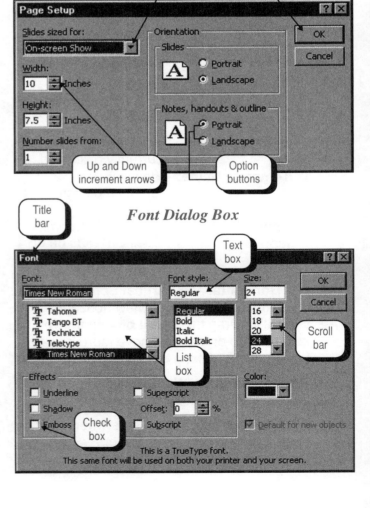

Color Scheme Dialog Box

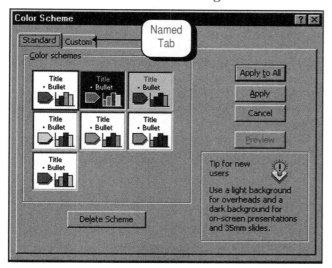

Dialog Box Options

- A **dialog box** contains different ways for you to enter information. A description of dialog box parts appears below:

  ✓ Note: Note the labeled parts in the dialog boxes above and on the previous page.

  - The **Title bar** identifies the title of the dialog box.

  - A **text box** is a location where you type information.

  - **Command buttons** carry out actions described on the button.

  - A **drop-down list** is marked with a down arrow. Clicking the drop-down list box accesses a short list of options.

  - An **increment box** provides a space for typing a value. An up or down arrow (usually to the right of the box) gives you a way to select a value with the mouse.

  - A **named tab** is used to display options related to the tab's name in the same dialog box.

  - **Option buttons** are small circular buttons marking options in a set. You may choose only one option from the set. A selected option button contains a dark circle.

  - A **check box** is a small square box where an option may be selected or deselected. A "✔" in the box indicates the option is selected. If several check boxes are offered, you may select more than one.

- A **list box** displays a list of items from which selections can be made. A list box may have a scroll bar that can be used to show hidden items in the list.

- A **scroll bar** is a horizontal or vertical bar providing scroll arrows and a scroll box that can be dragged up or down to move more quickly through the file.

Slide Rulers

- Horizontal and vertical Rulers can be displayed to allow objects and text to be placed on the slide more accurately. Rulers may be displayed by selecting Ruler from the View menu.

- Ruler measurements display differently depending on what is selected on the slide. If an object is selected, the zero point is at the center of each Ruler. If text is selected, the horizontal Ruler displays with indent markers and tabs, and both the horizontal and vertical Rulers highlight the measurement of the text placeholder.

Rulers with Object Selected

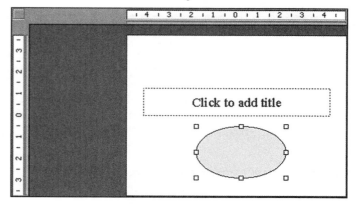

Rulers with Text Selected

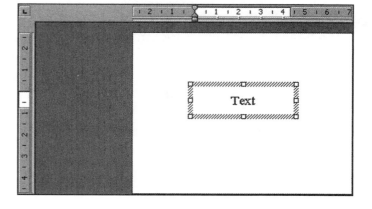

- A slide measures 10 inches wide by 7.5 inches tall.

- As you move your mouse on the slide, a corresponding indicator displays on the Rulers, showing you the horizontal and vertical position of your mouse pointer on the slide.

Guides

- **Guides** may also be displayed by selecting Guides from the View menu. Guides assist you in aligning objects or text on a slide.

Slide with Guides Displayed

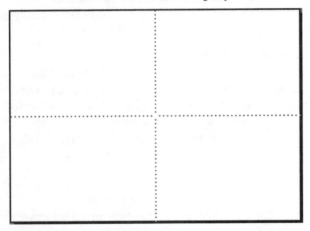

Shortcut Menus

- Shortcut menus appear when the *right* mouse button is pressed. The menu items that appear vary depending on the task being performed and the position of the mouse pointer on the screen.

Mouse and Keystroke Procedures

- Procedures for completing a task will be illustrated throughout this book as shown below. Mouse actions are illustrated on the left, while keystroke procedures are illustrated to the right, and keyboard shortcut keys are illustrated below the heading. Use whichever method you find most convenient.

Help Features

- Help is available from a variety of sources in PowerPoint. Below is an illustration of the help features available on the PowerPoint Help menu.

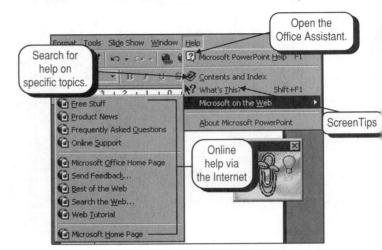

Contents, Index, and Find

- If you select Contents and Index on the Help menu, you will be able to use the Contents, Index and/or the Find options to look for help.

Contents

- The **Contents** tab displays a page listing the help contents by topic in PowerPoint. Double-clicking on a topic presents a list of subtopics and/or display screens. Note the PowerPoint Contents page below.

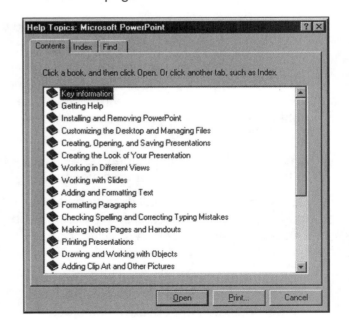

Index

- The **Index** tab allows you to enter the first few letters of your topic, then brings you to the index entry. Double-click the entry or select the entry and click <u>D</u>isplay. The help screen related to your topic is then displayed.

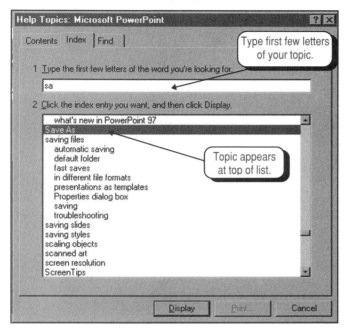

Find

- The **Find** tab accesses the Help database feature. It allows you to search the Help database for the occurrence of any word or phrase in a help topic. The Index and Find features are similar; however, Find offers more options to search for a topic.

ScreenTips

- You can find out information about screen elements by selecting the What's <u>T</u>his? feature on the <u>H</u>elp menu, then pointing to the element you want information about, and clicking the mouse.

- Or you may click the question mark icon in the upper right corner of a dialog box, and click on the option on which you want information.

Office Assistant

- By default, the Office Assistant appears on screen when you open PowerPoint. The Office Assistant will answer questions, offer suggestions, and provide help unique to PowerPoint.

- When you click on the Assistant, type your question and click <u>S</u>earch. The suggested procedures display.

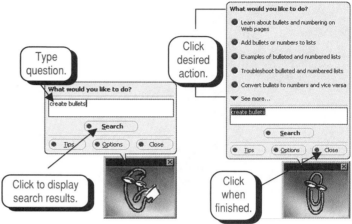

Office Assistant Options

- You can control the way the Office Assistant appears on screen as well as the kind of information that it presents. You can also turn the Assistant off. If you turn the Assistant off, you can easily turn it on again by clicking the Assistant button 🔲 on the Standard toolbar.

- To change the Assistant options:

  - Click the Office Assistant (if it is on screen) or click the Office Assistant button on the Standard toolbar and click <u>O</u>ptions. Click the <u>O</u>ptions tab and select the desired options.

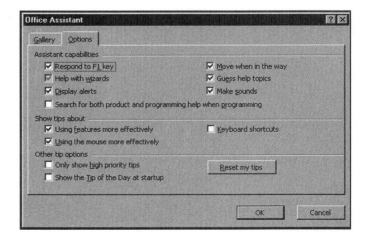

Select a Different Office Assistant

■ The Gallery tab in the Office Assistant dialog box offers several different Assistant characters. Click the Gallery tab on the Office Assistant dialog box and click Next to view the different Assistants. Click OK to select the assistant displayed.

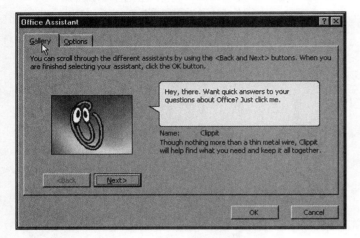

Exit Help

• Click Cancel or Close or press Escape to exit.

KEYSTROKES

START POWERPOINT

Using the Taskbar:

1. Click **Start** .... `Ctrl`+`Esc`
2. Highlight **Programs** .... `P`
3. Select **Microsoft PowerPoint** .... `⊞`

OR

1. Click **Start** .... `Ctrl`+`Esc`
2. Click **New Office Document** .... `⊞`
3. Double-click **Blank** .... `⊞`
   Presentation to create a blank presentation.

   OR

   a. Click **Presentation** .... `Presentation Designs`
      Designs tab.
   b. Select a Template design to create a designed presentation.
   c. Click **OK** .... `Enter`

Using the Office Shortcut Bar:

1. Click **Start a New Office** .... `⊞`
   Document button on Office Shortcut Bar.
2. Double-click **Blank Presentation** .... `⊞`
   to create a blank presentation.

   OR

   a. Click **Presentation** .... `Presentation Designs`
      Designs tab.
   b. Select a Template design to create a designed presentation.
   c. Click **OK** .... `Enter`

HIDE/DISPLAY TOOLBARS

1. Click **View** .... `Alt`+`V`
2. Click **Toolbars** .... `T`
3. Select desired toolbar.
4. Repeat steps 1-3 for each additional toolbar you want to appear.

ZOOM

To specify a custom zoom:

1. Click on **Zoom Control** box on the Standard toolbar.
2. Type (10-500) zoom percentage number
3. Press **Enter** .... `Enter`

To select a zoom:

4. Click drop-down arrow in **Zoom Control** box on Standard toolbar.
5. Select zoom percentages.

To change zoom with IntelliMouse:

6. Hold down **Ctrl** and roll the wheel to zoom in or out by 10% increments.

DISPLAY RULER AND GUIDES

1. Click **View** .... `Alt`+`V`
2. Click **Ruler** .... `R`
   AND/OR
   Click **Guides** .... `G`

START OFFICE ASSISTANT

✓ By default, the Office Assistant will appear when you open PowerPoint. If the Assistant is not on screen, use these steps to activate the Assistant.

Click **Office Assistant** button `②` on the Standard toolbar.

OR

Press **F1** .... `F1`

✓ If the Contents, Index and Find window opens instead of the Office Assistant, the F1 key option has been disabled in the Office Assistant Options dialog box. See below on how to change Office Assistant options.

CLOSE OFFICE ASSISTANT

Click the **Close** button on Office Assistant.

USE OFFICE ASSISTANT

1. Click **Office Assistant** `②` .... `F1`
   button on the Standard toolbar.
2. Type question in Assistant text box.
3. Click **Search** .... `Alt`+`S`
4. Select from list of procedures to view more information.
5. Press **Escape** .... `Esc`
   to close Help window.

CHANGE OFFICE ASSISTANT OPTIONS

1. Click **Office Assistant** `②` .... `F1`
   button on the Standard toolbar.
2. Click **Options** .... `Alt`+`O`
3. Click **Options** tab .... `Alt`+`O`
4. Select desired options.
5. Click **OK** .... `Enter`

USE CONTENTS AND INDEX

1. Click **Help** .... `Alt`+`H`
2. Click **Contents and Index** .... `C`
3. Click the **Contents** tab.
   a. Double-click a book or topic.
   b. Double-click a submenu item or a display item.

   OR

   Click the **Index** tab.
   a. Type first letters of topic word in **Step 1** text box.
   b. Double-click topic in **Step 2** box.

   OR

   a. Select topic.
   b. Click **Display** .... `Alt`+`D`

   OR

   Click the **Find** tab.
   a. Type and enter a search word or phrase in **Step 1** text box.
   b. Select matching words in **Step 2** box, if presented.
   c. Double-click topic in **Step 3** box.

   OR

   a. Select topic.
   b. Click **Display** .... `D`

EXIT HELP

Click **Cancel** .... `Esc`
OR
Click **Close** button .... `✕`

Exercise 1

- Create a New Presentation Using the Blank Presentation Option
- Create a New Presentation Using the Template Option
- Select an AutoLayout from the New Slide Dialog Box
- Add Text to Placeholders ■ Add Slides to a Presentation
- Save a Presentation ■ Properties ■ Close a Presentation
- Exit PowerPoint

Standard Toolbar

Save

Insert New Slide

NOTES

Create a New Presentation Using the Blank Presentation Option

- You can create a PowerPoint presentation using either blank presentation slides or predesigned template slides.

- The **Blank Presentation** option lets you build your own unique presentation from blank slides that contain standard default formats and layouts.

- The way you access the blank presentation option depends on how you started PowerPoint. If you started PowerPoint using the Taskbar (Start, Programs, PowerPoint), the following dialog box appears:

Select to open the New Presentation dialog box and choose a predesigned presentation format.

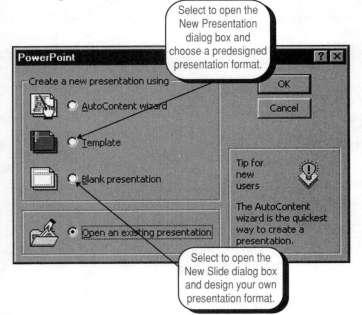

Select to open the New Slide dialog box and design your own presentation format.

- Select the Blank presentation option and click OK. The New slide dialog appears. *(See Select an AutoLayout from the New Slide Dialog Box on page 14.)*

- If you started PowerPoint by selecting the New Office Document option on the Office Shortcut bar or on the Taskbar, the following New Office Document dialog box appears:

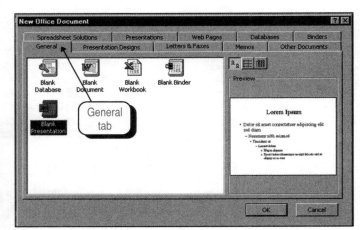

General tab

- Click the General tab, select Blank Presentation, and click OK. The New Slide dialog box appears. *(See Select an AutoLayout from the New Slide Dialog Box on page 14.)*

Create a New Presentation
Using the Template Option

- The **Template** option lets you create slides with a predesigned format. PowerPoint provides over 100 professionally designed formats with colorful backgrounds and text from which you can choose.

- As with the Blank Presentation option, the way you access the Template option depends on how you started PowerPoint. If you started PowerPoint using the Taskbar (Start, Programs, PowerPoint), the PowerPoint dialog box appears:

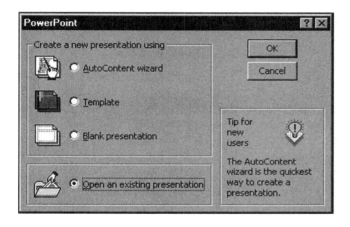

- Select Template and click OK. The New Presentation dialog box appears:

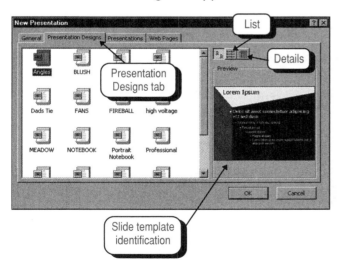

- To select a template design, click the Presentation Designs tab and select a template design. A large icon displays each template. (You can also display templates in List or Details view by clicking the appropriate icon.)

- The New Slide dialog box appears. (See Select an AutoLayout from the New Slide Dialog Box, on the following page.)

- If you started PowerPoint by selecting the New Office Document option on the Office Shortcut bar or from the Taskbar, the New Office Document dialog box appears.

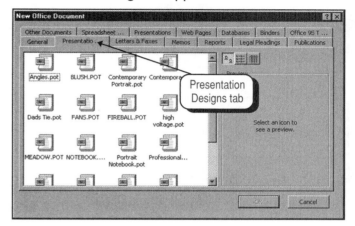

- Select the Presentation Designs tab, select a template design and click OK. The New Slide dialog box appears. (See Select an AutoLayout from the New Slide Dialog Box, on the following page.)

- **To start a new presentation from within PowerPoint,** select New from the File menu. The New Presentation dialog box appears.

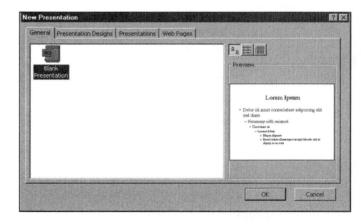

- Select the General tab and choose Blank Presentation or select the Presentation Designs tab and select a Template design. After clicking OK, the New Slide dialog box displays. (See Select an AutoLayout from the New Slide Dialog Box, on the following page.)

Select an AutoLayout from the New Slide Dialog Box

- The **New Slide dialog box** includes a set of 24 different AutoLayout formats that arrange various types of objects on slides. Objects include such things as titles, charts, graphics, or bulleted lists—standard objects that you might want to place on a slide.

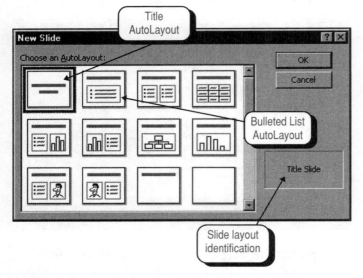

- AutoLayout formats follow the natural progression of a presentation. Starting with a Title Slide format they move to more complex layouts.

- Each layout is identified in the box in the lower right corner of the New Slide dialog box. Select a slide layout that is appropriate to the data you are presenting. The Title Slide is the default setting for the first slide in every presentation.

- After you select the Title Slide layout and click OK, the PowerPoint screen appears, ready for you to enter text into the Title Slide.

Add Text to Placeholders

- PowerPoint slides contain **placeholders** (empty boxes), which identify the placement of objects on the slide. Each placeholder contains directions to help you complete the slide.

- Whether you create your presentation using the Blank Presentation option or the Template option, all **title placeholders** contain the formatting for title text, while all **body text placeholders** include formatting for sub-titles or bulleted lists.

- To type text into a placeholder, click inside the placeholder and note the handles that appear. Enter the text as prompted.

  - ✓ *Note:* *You must be in Slide view to add text to a placeholder. (Slide views will be covered in Exercise 2.)*

- If you start typing without selecting the text placeholder, PowerPoint automatically places the text in the first text placeholder.

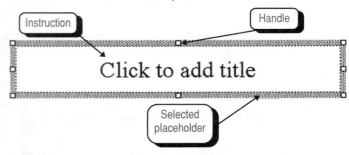

Add Slides to a Presentation

- There are four methods that can be used to add a new slide to a presentation:

  - Click the Insert New Slide button ![icon] on the Standard toolbar.

  - Click New Slide on the Common Tasks toolbar.

  - Press Ctrl + M.

  - Select New Slide from the Insert menu.

- When the New Slide dialog box appears, select a layout for the new slide.

- The Bulleted List slide is the default setting for the second slide in every presentation.

- Five different bulleted sublevels are available. Pressing the Tab key indents text and produces sublevels of bulleted items. Different bullet shapes identify each tab level, and the text size decreases with each sublevel. Pressing Shift + Tab returns you to the previous bullet level.

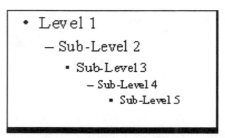

- PowerPoint places the new slide immediately after the slide that is displayed or selected at the time you create the new slide.

Save a Presentation

- Presentations must be given a name for identification. A presentation filename may contain a maximum of 255 characters, can include spaces, and is automatically assigned a .PPT extension to identify it as a PowerPoint file.

- Filenames are displayed in the case in which you type them.

- When saving a file, you must indicate the location where you wish to save it. Presentations may be saved on a removable disk or on an internal hard drive. If you save a file to a removable disk, you must indicate that you are saving to the A drive. The hard drive is usually designated as the C drive.

- If you save to the hard drive, PowerPoint provides folders that you may use to save your work. To save a file for the first time, select Save from the File menu or click the Save button 🖫 on the Standard toolbar. The following Save dialog box appears.

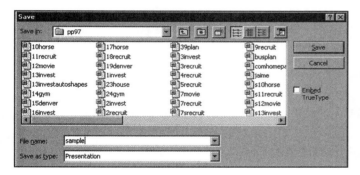

- Note the Save in drop-down list box, where PowerPoint displays the current default storage location, or folder, where you can save your file. You can select a storage location other than the default by clicking the drop-down arrow next to the Save in box and selecting the desired drive in which to save the presentation. The area below the Save in box displays the contents of the current drive. Double-click on the folder in which to save the presentation. The large area below the Save in box displays the contents of the current folder.

- Enter a desired filename or use the one that PowerPoint assigns for you in the File name text box, and click Save to save your presentation. Once your presentation is named, the filename appears in the title bar.

- After saving your presentation for the first time, you can save it again and continue working (updating it) by selecting Save from the File menu or by clicking the Save button 🖫 on the Standard toolbar. The Save dialog box does not reappear; PowerPoint simply saves any changes you have made to your file. Save often to prevent losing data.

- You can also save a presentation by selecting Save As from the File menu. Use this command when you want to save a copy of your presentation under a different filename or in a different drive and/or folder.

Properties

- The Properties feature allows you to save summary information with each presentation, making it easier to locate. The information includes a presentation title, subject, author, keywords and comments.

- You can create, display, and edit summary information at any time by selecting Properties from the File menu, then selecting the Summary tab.

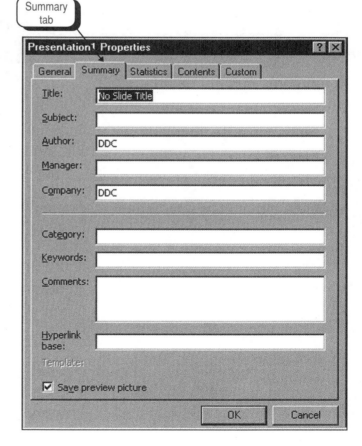

- To see a statistical summary of your presentation, click the Statistics tab. It lists the number of slides, paragraphs, words, notes, bytes and hidden slides in your presentation.

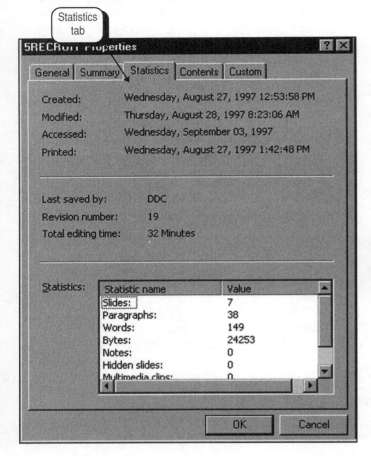

Close a Presentation

- When a presentation has been saved, it remains on your screen. If you wish to clear the screen, you may close the document window by selecting Close from the File menu or double-clicking the Presentation Control button.

- If you attempt to close a presentation before saving it, PowerPoint will prompt you to save it before exiting. You may respond Y for Yes or N for No.

Exit PowerPoin

- To exit PowerPoint, select Exit from the File menu or double-click the Program Control button.

In Part I of this exercise, you will create a title slide and a bulleted list slide using the Blank Presentation option. In Part II of the exercise, you will create a title slide and a bulleted list slide using the Template option. You will save each as a presentation.

EXERCISE DIRECTIONS

Part I

1. Start PowerPoint using the Windows Taskbar (highlight Programs) and create a new Blank Presentation.

2. Accept the default Title Slide layout for the first slide.

3. Type the title and sub-title as shown in Illustration A.

4. Select New Slide and accept the default Bulleted List layout for the second slide.

5. Type the bulleted list title and list items, as shown in Illustration A.

6. Save the presentation; name it **RECRUIT**. Fill in the summary information as follows:

Title:	(Accept the default)
Subject:	Sales Presentation
Author:	Your name
Manager:	Your supervisor or teacher's name
Company:	Your company or school name
Category:	Sales
Keywords:	Client, product

7. Close the presentation window.

Part II

1. Create a new Template presentation using the Fireball design.

2. Accept the default Title Slide layout for the first slide and the Bulleted List layout for the second slide.

3. Type the title and bulleted list slides shown in Illustration B on the following page.

4. Save the presentation; name it **INVEST**. Fill in the summary information as follows:

Title:	(Accept the default)
Subject:	Company Introduction
Author:	Your name
Manager:	Your supervisor or teacher's name
Company:	Your company or school name
Category:	Sales
Keywords:	North Fork

5. Close the presentation window.

Illustration A

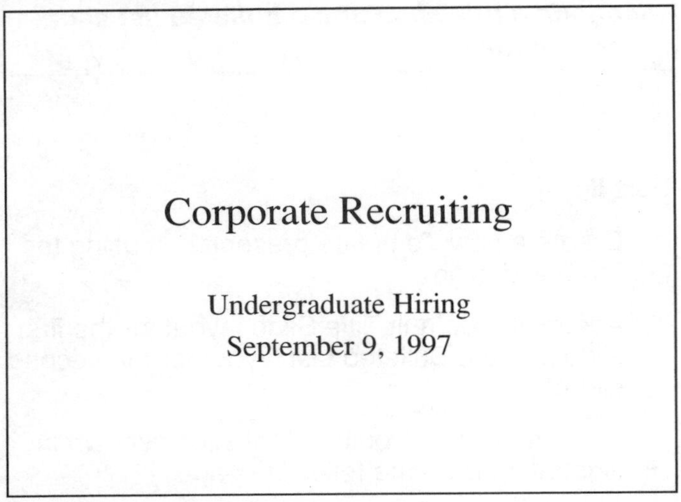

Corporate Recruiting

Undergraduate Hiring
September 9, 1997

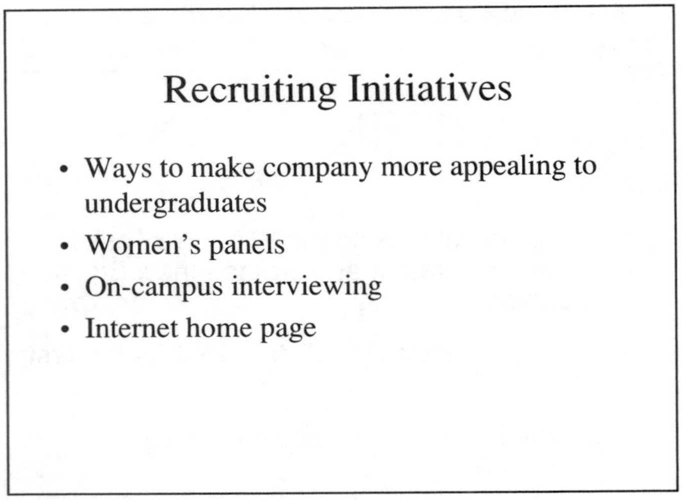

Recruiting Initiatives

- Ways to make company more appealing to undergraduates
- Women's panels
- On-campus interviewing
- Internet home page

Illustration B

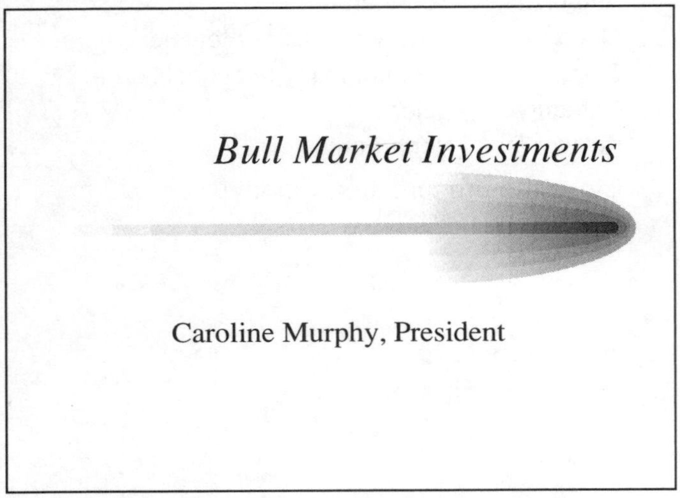

Bull Market Investments

Caroline Murphy, President

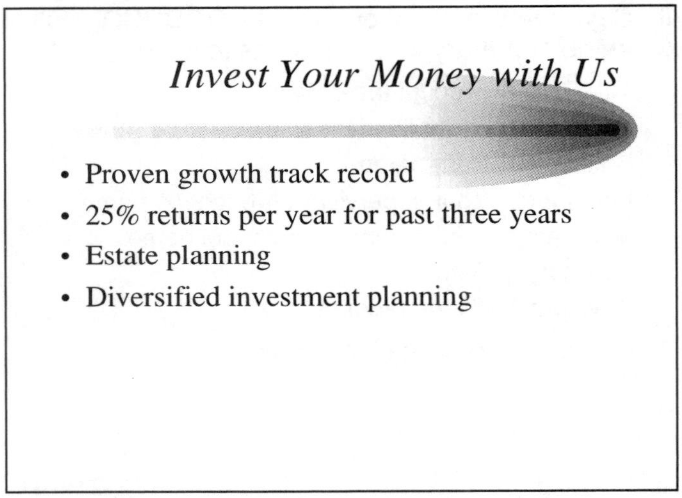

Invest Your Money with Us

- Proven growth track record
- 25% returns per year for past three years
- Estate planning
- Diversified investment planning

KEYSTROKES

CREATE A NEW PRESENTATION USING THE BLANK PRESENTATION OPTION

Using the Taskbar:
1. Click **Start** .... `Ctrl`+`Esc`
2. Highlight **Programs** .... `P`
3. Select **Microsoft PowerPoint** .... 🖳
4. Select **Blank Presentation** ..... `Alt`+`B`
5. Click **OK** .... `Enter`

OR

1. Click **Start** .... `Ctrl`+`Esc`
2. Click **New Office Document** .... 📄
3. Double-click **Blank** .... 🖳
   Presentation icon to create a blank presentation.

Using the Office Shortcut Bar:

1. Click **Start a New Office** .... 📄
   Document button.
2. Double-click **Blank Presentation** .... 🖳
   to create a blank presentation.

CREATE A NEW PRESENTATION USING THE TEMPLATE OPTION

Using the Taskbar:
1. Click **Start** .... `Ctrl`+`Esc`
2. Highlight **Programs** .... `P`
3. Select **Microsoft PowerPoint** .... 🖳
4. Select **Template** .... `Alt`+`T`
5. Click **OK** .... `Enter`
6. Select a Template design to create a predesigned presentation.
7. Click **OK** .... `Enter`

OR

1. Click **Start** .... `Ctrl`+`Esc`
2. Click **New Office Document** .... 📄
3. Click **Presentation** ...... `Presentation Designs`
   Designs tab.
4. Select a Template design to create a predesigned presentation.
5. Click **OK** .... `Enter`

Using the Office Shortcut Bar:

1. Click **New Office Document** .... 📄
2. Click **Presentation** ...... `Presentation Designs`
   Designs tab.
3. Select a Template design to create a predesigned presentation.
4. Click **OK** .... `Enter`

SAVE A PRESENTATION

1. Click **Save** button .... 💾
   on the Standard toolbar.
   OR
   a. Click **File** .... `Alt`+`F`
   b. Click **Save** .... `S`
2. Click **Save in** drop-down .... `Alt`+`I`
   list box to select drive and/or folder.
3. Select desired .... `↓`,`Enter`
   drive and/or folder.
   To select subfolder, if necessary:
   Double-click folder .... `Tab`,`↓`,`Enter`
4. Click **File name** .... `Alt`+`N`
   text box.
5. Type presentation name .... *filename*
6. Click **Save** .... `Enter`

   ✓ *Saved presentation files will be assigned the extension .PPT*

ADD SLIDES TO A PRESENTATION

CTRL + M

1. Click **Insert** .... `Alt`+`I`
2. Click **New Slide** .... `N`

   OR

   Click the **Insert New Slide** button ... 🖳
   on the Standard toolbar.

   OR

   Click **New Slide** on the Common Tasks toolbar.
3. Select a slide AutoLayout from the New Slide dialog box.
4. Click **OK** .... `Enter`

CLOSE A PRESENTATION

1. Double-click the **Presentation** .... 🖳
   Control icon.
2. Click **Yes** .... `Y`
   to save changes.
   OR
   Click **No** .... `N`
   to abandon changes.

OR

1. Click **File**, **Close** .... `Alt`+`F`,`C`
2. Click **Yes** .... `Y`
   to save changes.
   OR
   Click **No** .... `N`
   to abandon changes.

EXIT POWERPOINT

1. Double-click **Program Control** icon .... 🖳
2. Click **Yes** .... `Y`
   to save changes.
   OR
   Click **No** .... `N`
   to abandon changes.

OR

1. Click **File** .... `Alt`+`F`
2. Click **Exit** .... `X`
3. Click **Yes** .... `Y`
   to save changes.
   OR
   Click **No** .... `N`
   to abandon changes.

Exercise 2

■ **Open a Presentation** ■ **Slide Views** ■ **Move from Slide to Slide**
■ **Spell Checking** ■ **Page Setup** ■ **Print a Presentation**

Standard Toolbar

Open a Presentation   Print   Spell Check

NOTES

Open a Presentation

■ Presentations may be opened by selecting <u>O</u>pen an Existing Presentation from the PowerPoint dialog box, by clicking the Open button 🖼 on the Standard toolbar or by selecting <u>O</u>pen from the <u>F</u>ile menu.

Slide Views

■ PowerPoint lets you view your presentation in five different ways. They are Slide view, Outline view, Slide Sorter view, Notes Page view, and Slide Show view.

- **Slide view**, the default, allows you to see a single slide on screen. Use this view to edit or modify a slide.

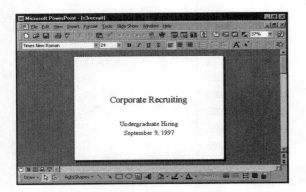

- **Outline view** displays slide text in a notebook page layout. Use this view to organize a presentation. *(This view will be detailed in Exercise 6.)*

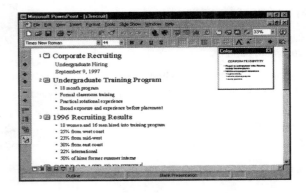

- **Slide Sorter view** displays miniature copies of slides on screen so that you can see the flow of the presentation. Use this view to move, copy, and delete slides. *(Moving, copying, and deleting slides will be detailed in Exercise 4.)*

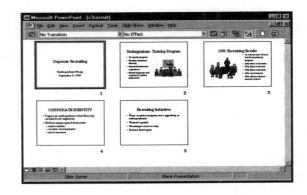

- **Notes Page view** lets you display speaker's notes pages for each slide. *(This view will be detailed in Exercise 31.)*

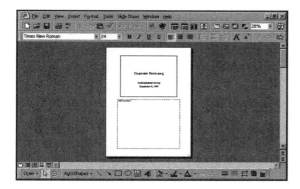

- **Slide Show view** lets you see your slides as an on-screen presentation. *(This view will be detailed in Exercise 29.)*

- Views may be changed by clicking the appropriate view button on the bottom left of the presentation window or by selecting the desired view from the <u>V</u>iew menu.

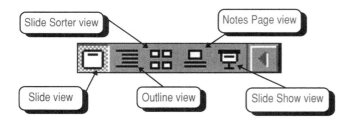

Move from Slide to Slide

- When there are a number of slides included in a presentation, you will find it necessary to move from slide to slide in Slide view to edit, enhance, or view the slide information. PowerPoint offers a variety of ways to select and display slides in Slide View:

  - Press the PgDn key to display the next slide or the PgUp key to display the previous slide.

  - Click the **Next Slide** or **Previous Slide** button on the vertical scroll bar.

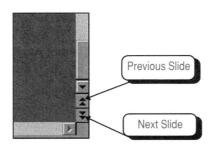

- Drag the vertical scroll box up or down until the desired slide number is displayed.

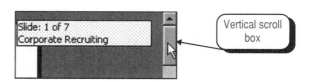

Spell Checking

- If automatic spell checking is activated, wavy red lines will appear under words that PowerPoint recognizes as possible errors. To disable automatic spell checking:

  - Click <u>O</u>ptions on the <u>T</u>ools menu.
  - Select the Spelling tab.
  - Deselect S<u>p</u>elling.
    OR
  - Click Hide <u>s</u>pelling errors.

  ✓ *Note:* *When you finish your presentation, you can deselect Hide <u>s</u>pelling errors and check the words that have been identified as errors.*

- After creating your presentation, you can run a spell check by clicking the Spelling button [icon] on the Standard toolbar or by selecting <u>S</u>pelling from the <u>T</u>ools menu.

- In the Spelling dialog box that follows, PowerPoint displays any possible misspellings in the Not in dictionar<u>y</u> box. The most likely replacement appears in the Change <u>t</u>o box. Other suggestions appear in the Suggestio<u>n</u>s list box.

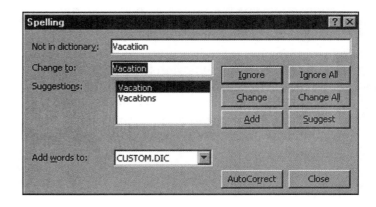

- Click Ignore if the word is spelled correctly, and you want to skip to the next misspelling, or click Ignore All to skip every occurrence of the current misspelling in the presentation.

- Click Change to replace the misspelling with the word listed in the Change to box. Or, you can select a different spelling from the Suggestions list, or type your own spelling in the Change to box, and then click Change. Click Change All to replace every occurrence of the misspelling with the selected replacement.

Page Setup

- Slides in your presentation may be printed in Portrait or Landscape orientation and sized as needed for different presentation viewing formats, including an on-screen show, an outline, transparencies, 35mm slides, notes pages, or handouts.

- You must specify these settings by selecting Page Setup from the File menu, and selecting the desired options in the Page Setup dialog box that follows.

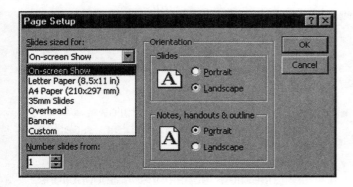

- To change slide orientation, choose Portrait or Landscape. To change notes, handouts and outline orientation, select Portrait or Landscape.

- Click the Slides sized for drop-down list box and select a presentation viewing format (on-screen show, handouts, etc.). To set slides to a custom size, select Custom from the list and type the dimensions in the Width and Height boxes.

Print a Presentation

- To print PowerPoint slides, select Print from the File menu, or press Ctrl+P. In the Print dialog box that follows, you may print the Current slide, a highlighted Selection of the presentation, selected Slides, or All slides in a presentation. When you print all slides of a presentation, each slide prints on a separate page.

- The Print what feature lets you indicate whether you want your presentation printed as Slides, Notes pages, Handouts with 2, 3, or 6 slides per page, or as an Outline. *(Notes pages and handouts will be detailed in Exercise 31. Outlines will be covered in Exercise 6.)*

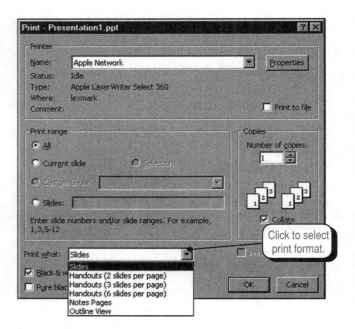

- You can also click the Print button 🖨 on the Standard toolbar. When you use this technique, you bypass the Print dialog box and send the print command directly to the printer. PowerPoint automatically prints information using the settings last selected in the Print dialog box.

■ The default selection in the Print dialog box prints <u>A</u>ll slides. Other options include:

Option	Description
<u>P</u>roperties	Changes elements specific to the printer, such as paper size, paper orientation, graphics, fonts, and so on.
Print to fi<u>l</u>e	Prints the presentation to a disk file so that it may be sent to a service bureau for printing in an alternate format such as 35mm slides.
Print <u>h</u>idden slides	Prints slides that have been hidden.
<u>B</u>lack & white	Turns all color fills to white and adds a thin black frame to all unbordered objects without text. Use this option if you plan to use your slides as overhead transparencies or if you have a printer that only prints black and white.
Colla<u>t</u>e	Prints multiple copies as collated sets.
Scale to <u>f</u>it paper	Scales presentation slides to fit a custom or different sized paper.
Fra<u>m</u>e slides	Adds a frame to Slides when printed.
P<u>u</u>re black & white	Prints in black and white without gray scale.

In this exercise, you will add new slides to a previously created presentation. You will then use different slide views to see the flow of your presentation.

EXERCISE DIRECTIONS

Part I

1. Start PowerPoint using the Windows Taskbar (click Programs) and select Open an Existing Presentation from the PowerPoint dialog box.

   ✓ *If PowerPoint is already running, select File, Open to open a presentation.*

2. Open ⌨ **INVEST**, or open 💾 **02INVEST**.

3. Change slide orientation to portrait.

4. Display Slide 2 by clicking the Next Slide button.

5. Display Slide 1 by dragging the vertical scroll box.

6. Create a new bulleted list slide using the following information:

   ✓ *The slide will be inserted after Slide 1. You will move it into desired order in a later exercise.*

SERVICES INCLUDE
• Private financial evaluation
• Various mutual fund investments
• Retirement savings planning
• Tax-deferred investment options

7. Switch to Slide Sorter view.

8. Switch back to Slide view.

9. Correct all spelling errors.

10. In the Print dialog box, select Handouts (3 slides per page) as the Print what option. Print one copy in Black and White.

11. Close the file; save the changes.

Part II

1. Open ⌨ **RECRUIT**, or open 💾 **02RECRUIT**.

2. Display Slide 2 using the PgDn key.

3. Display Slide 1 using the PgUp key.

4. Create a new bulleted list slide using the following information:

CORPORATE IDENTITY
• Prepare an undergraduate video featuring recently hired employees
• Hold campus panel discussions
– explain industry
– introduce training program
– answer questions

5. Switch to Slide Sorter view.

6. Switch to Slide view.

7. Correct all spelling errors.

8. View your presentation in portrait orientation.

9. Switch slide orientation back to landscape.

10. In the Print dialog box, select Handouts (3 slides per page) as the Print what option. Print one copy in Black and White.

11. Close the file; save the changes.

KEYSTROKES

OPEN A PRESENTATION

CTRL + O

1. Click 📂 .... [Alt]+[F],[O]
2. Click the **Look in** box .... [Alt]+[I]
   and select drive and/or folder
   containing file to open.
3. Type presentation name..... [Alt]+[N],*name*
   in **File name** text box, or
   select presentation in list.
4. Click **Open** .... [Enter]

SWITCH SLIDE VIEWS

Select desired view button:

- 🔲 **Slide** .... [Alt]+[V],[S]
- 📄 **Outline** .... [Alt]+[V],[O]
- 🖥 **Notes Page** .... [Alt]+[V],[N]
- 🔳 **Slide Sorter** .... [Alt]+[V],[D]
- 📺 **Slide Show** .... [Alt]+[V],[W]

MOVE FROM SLIDE TO SLIDE

Press **PgUp** .... [Page Up]
to display previous slide.

OR

Press **PgDn** .... [Page Down]
to display next slide.

OR

Click **Next Slide** ▼ or **Previous Slide** ▲
button on scroll bar.

OR

Drag vertical scroll box until desired slide
is displayed.

SPELL CHECK

F7

1. Click **Spelling** button .... [ABC✓]
   on Standard toolbar.

   OR

   a. Click **Tools** .... [Alt]+[T]
   b. Click **Spelling** .... [S]

   ✓ *If Automatic Spell Check is activated,*
   red wavy lines will appear under
   misspelled words. To correct the
   word(s), right-click on the word(s)
   and select the desired choice.

2. Click **Ignore** .... [Alt]+[I]
   to skip the current misspelling
   and go to the next one.

   OR

   Click **Ignore All** .... [Alt]+[G]
   to skip every occurrence of the current
   misspelling in the presentation.

   OR

   Click **Change** .... [Alt]+[C]
   to replace the misspelling with the
   word listed in the **Change to** box.

   OR

   a. Click in **Suggestions** box... [Alt]+[N]
      and select a different replacement
      spelling from the list.
   b. Click **Change** .... [Alt]+[C]

   OR

   Click **Change All** .... [Alt]+[L]
   to replace every occurrence of the
   word with the selected replacement.

PAGE SETUP

1. Click **File** .... [Alt]+[F]
2. Click **Page Setup** .... [U]
3. Make desired changes.
4. Click **OK**.

PRINT A PRESENTATION

CTRL + P

1. Click **File** .... [Alt]+[F]
2. Click **Print** .... [P]
3. Select desired options.
4. Click **OK** .... [Enter]

   OR

   Click 🖨 to print presentation using
   settings last selected in Print dialog
   box.

<table>
<tr><td>

Exercise
3

</td><td>

■ **Work with Object Placeholders** ■ **Insert Clip Art**
■ **AutoClipArt** ■ **Use Undo**

</td></tr>
</table>

Standard Toolbar Insert Clip Art

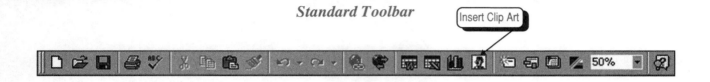

NOTES

Work with Object Placeholders

■ In Exercise 1, you learned that a placeholder is an empty box that identifies the placement of text or objects on a slide. You entered text into placeholders for a title and a bulleted list. There are also placeholders for objects, such as clip art, a graph, or a chart. Although object placeholders are labeled to hold a particular type of object, each one can hold any type of object—clip art, a chart, graph, or media clip.

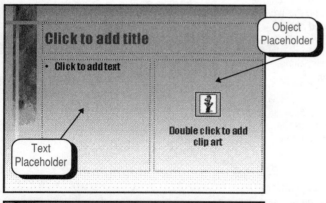

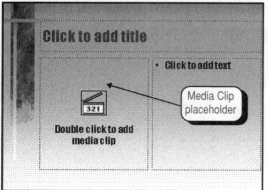

■ When you select a slide layout containing an object placeholder, double-click within the placeholder to add the object. You must be in Slide or Slide Master view to add an object to a slide. *(For specific information on inserting clip art, see Insert Clip Art below. Inserting a graph or chart into placeholders will be covered in later exercises.)*

Insert Clip Art

■ Like other objects, clip art can be inserted into an object placeholder or directly into a slide without a placeholder.

■ **To add a clip art image to a clip art placeholder,** double-click the clip art icon in the placeholder. The Microsoft Clip Gallery opens. Select the desired clip art image and click Insert.

- **To insert clip art without using an object placeholder**, click Insert, Picture, Clip Art, or click on the Insert Clip Art button 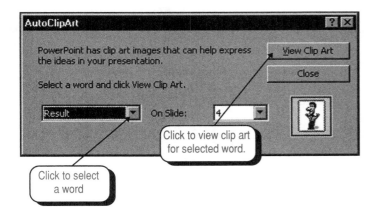 on the Standard toolbar, select the desired image from the Clip Gallery and click Insert. You can then resize and move the image as desired. *(See Exercise 12 to move, size, or delete pictures and other objects.)*

AutoClipArt

- The AutoClipArt feature suggests relevant clip art based on the text you type on your slides. To use AutoClipArt, switch to Slide view, display the slide you want clip art for, and select AutoClipArt from the Tools menu.

- In the AutoClipArt dialog box that follows, select the first list arrow to display words in your presentation for which PowerPoint has found relevant pictures. Select a word from the list and click the View Clip Art button to see the pictures that relate to that word. The On Slide text box displays the number of the slide where the word appears.

Click to select a word

Click to view clip art for selected word.

- You may find, however, that the picture(s) selected by PowerPoint is not one you desire. Remember, it is only a suggestion.

Use Undo

- Clicking the Undo button on the Standard toolbar allows you to undo the most recent action.

- Clicking the list arrow next to the Undo button provides a history of previous actions. Clicking one of the actions in the list will undo the action and all previous actions listed.

- The Redo feature allows you to reverse an undone action. Clicking the Redo button on the Standard toolbar allows you to redo the most recently undone action.

- Clicking the list arrow next to the Redo button provides a history of previous undone actions. Clicking one of the actions in the list will redo the action and all previous actions listed.

In this exercise, you will add a slide to each of the presentations you created in previous exercises.

EXERCISE DIRECTIONS

Part I

1. Open 🖮 **INVEST**, or open 💾 **03INVEST**.

2. Switch slide orientation to landscape.

3. Create a new slide using the Text & Clip Art layout.

   ✓ *This slide will be inserted after slide one.*

4. Enter the title and bulleted information shown in Illustration A on the following page. Insert any relevant clip art.

5. Create another new slide using the Clip Art & Text layout.

6. Enter the title and bulleted information shown in Illustration B on the following page. Use the AutoClipArt feature to insert relevant clip art.

   ✓ *(Hint: After inserting the image, click on it, hold down the mouse button, and drag it into the clip art placeholder. The image will then resize to fit the placeholder automatically.)*

7. Switch to Slide Sorter view.

8. Switch back to Slide view.

9. Correct all spelling errors.

10. In the Print dialog box, select Handouts (6 slides per page) as the Print what option.

11. Print one copy in Black and White.

12. Close the file; save the changes.

Part II

1. Open 🖮 **RECRUIT**, or open 💾 **03RECRUIT**.

2. Create a new slide using the Text & Clip Art layout.

   ✓ *This slide will be inserted after slide one. You will move the slides into desired order in the next exercise.*

3. Enter the title and bulleted information shown in Illustration C on the following page. Insert any relevant clip art.

4. Create another new slide using the Clip Art & Text layout.

5. Enter the title and bulleted information shown in Illustration D on the following page; use the AutoClipArt feature to insert relevant clip art.

   ✓ *(Hint: After inserting the image, click on it, hold down the mouse button, and drag it into the clip art placeholder. The image will then resize to fit the placeholder automatically.)*

6. Switch to Slide Sorter view.

7. Switch back to Slide view.

8. In the Print dialog box, select Handouts (6 slides per page) as the Print what option.

9. Print one copy.

10. Close the file; save the changes.

Part I

Illustration A

INVESTMENT TYPES

- Fixed Income
- Equities
- Mutual Funds
- Commodity Funds
- Emerging Market Funds

Illustration B

PORTFOLIO MANAGEMENT

- Minimum of $250,000 invested
- Personal risk analysis
- Diversified portfolio strategy
- Quarterly account statements

Part II

Illustration C

Undergraduate Training Program

- 18 month program
- Formal classroom training
- Practical rotational experience
- Broad exposure and experience before placement

Illustration D

1996 Recruiting Results

- 18 women and 16 men hired into training program
- 25% from West Coast
- 23% from Midwest
- 30% from East Coast
- 22% international
- 50% of hires former summer interns

KEYSTROKES

UNDO

CTRL + Z

Click 🔙 .... Alt + E , U
to undo your most recent action.

OR

Click the Undo list arrow 🔙▾ and select
a series of consecutive actions, starting
with your most recent.

REDO

CTRL + Y

Click 🔜 .... Alt + E , R
to redo most recently undone action.

OR

Click the Redo list arrow 🔜▾ and select
a series of consecutive actions, starting
with the most recent.

USE CLIP ART PLACEHOLDER TO INSERT CLIP ART

1. Select an AutoLayout that contains a clip art object placeholder.
2. Double-click clip art icon in placeholder.
3. Click desired clip art graphic.
4. Click **Insert** .... Enter

INSERT CLIP ART WITHOUT A PLACEHOLDER

1. Click **Insert Clip Art** button............. 🖼
   on the Standard toolbar.
   OR
   a. Click **Insert** .... Alt + I
   b. Click **Picture** .... P
   c. Select **Clip Art** C
2. Click desired clip art graphic.
3. Click **Insert** .... Enter

AUTOCLIPART

1. Click **Tools** .... Alt + T
2. Click **AutoClipArt** .... U
3. Click first list arrow to display words in presentation for which PowerPoint has located a relevant picture.
4. Select word from list.
5. Click **View Clip Art** .... Alt + V
6. Select relevant picture from those displayed.
7. Click **Insert** .... Enter
8. Repeat to insert additional clip art images.
   OR
   Click **Close**.

NEXT EXERCISE

Exercise 4

■ Move, Copy, Duplicate, and Delete Slides

Standard Toolbar

NOTES

Move, Copy Duplicate, and Delete Slides

■ Each slide in a presentation is part of the entire presentation. Slides may be moved, copied, duplicated, or deleted within the presentation. You can also move and copy slides from one presentation to another.

■ You should save a presentation before moving, copying, duplicating, or deleting slides to prevent loss of data. If you move, copy, or delete a slide and change your mind, use the Undo feature to reverse the action.

■ The **Duplicate** slide command lets you create a copy of a slide in Slide view. (The Copy command is not available in Slide view.) If you have created a custom slide that contains effects that you want to repeat on subsequent slides, you can duplicate the slide. You can also use the Duplicate slide command in Outline and Slide Sorter views. To duplicate a slide, select the slide and then select Duplicate Slide from the Insert menu. The duplicate slide will be inserted immediately following the original slide.

■ You can move, copy, or delete slides using menu commands or cut/copy and paste procedures in Slide Sorter or Outline view. However, it is easiest and most efficient to perform these tasks using drag and drop in Slide Sorter view, since all slides are displayed in miniature, and you can easily see the flow of the presentation in this view.

Slide Sorter View

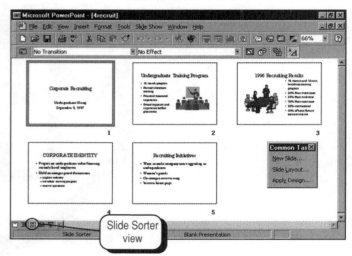

■ To move, copy, or delete a slide in Slide Sorter view, first click the Slide Sorter view button ⊞ or select Sli**d**e Sorter from the **V**iew menu.

■ Select the slide to be moved, copied, or deleted. (Selected slides are outlined by a darker border.) You can select slides using a number of different techniques:

• Click the desired slide.

• Press the insertion point arrow keys until a dark border outlines the desired slide.

• Press Shift and click each slide when you want to select multiple slides. Selecting multiple slides allows you to move, copy, duplicate, or delete them as a group.

- Drag the selected slide to a new location. When the slide is being moved, the mouse pointer becomes a slide icon, and a vertical bar identifies the new position of the slide. When the bar appears in the position where you want to place the slide, release the mouse button.

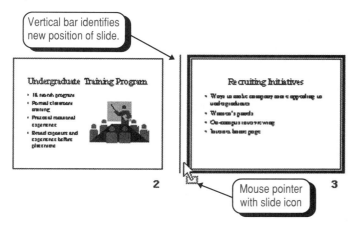

Vertical bar identifies new position of slide.

Mouse pointer with slide icon

- You can also move a slide by selecting the slide, clicking the Cut button [✂] on the Standard toolbar, clicking in the new location, then clicking the Paste button [📋] on the toolbar.

- To copy a slide, press Ctrl and drag the slide you want to copy to a new location. The mouse pointer becomes a slide icon carrying a + sign.

- You can also copy a slide by selecting the slide, clicking the Copy button [📋] on the Standard toolbar, clicking in the new location, then clicking the Paste button [📋] on the Standard toolbar.

- To delete a slide, select the slide and press the Delete key.

- Since you cannot edit slide contents in Slide Sorter view, you will need to return to Slide view to make changes and adjust text. You can return to Slide view using one of the following techniques:

  • Double-click a slide.

  • Select the slide and click the Slide view button [□] on the Status bar.

  • Select the desired slide and select Slide from the View menu.

In this exercise, you will insert several slides into an existing presentation.

EXERCISE DIRECTIONS

1. Open 🖫 **RECRUIT**, or open 🖫 **04RECRUIT**.

2. Create a new slide using the Bulleted List layout.

3. Enter the information shown in Illustration A.

4. Create a new slide using the 2 Column Text layout.

5. Enter the text in each column as shown in Illustration B.

6. Create a new slide using the Text & Clip Art layout.

7. Enter the information shown in Illustration C. Insert a relevant clip art image.

8. Switch to Slide Sorter view.

9. Delete the slide entitled CORPORATE IDENTITY.

10. Move the slides into the order shown in Illustration D on pages 36 and 37.

11. Switch to Slide view.

12. Correct all spelling errors.

13. Print one copy of the presentation as Handouts (6 slides per page) in Black and White.

14. Close the file; save the changes.

1997 Recruiting Season

- Received 2578 resumes
- Interviewed 68 candidates
- Extended 2 offers
- 1997 target of 25 new hires

Illustration B

Internal Recruiting Initiatives

- Conduct interviewing skills workshops for group leaders who interview candidates
- Set up "round robin" interview format

- Create BA video to be shown on campuses
- Create network of mentors for new hires

Illustration C

Corporate Recruiters

- Amy Williams, Managing Director
- MBA Recruiting
  - Roberta Salto, VP
- BA Recruiting
  - Carmen Vasquez, VP
- Corporate Home Page
  - http://www.recruit.com

Illustration D

Corporate Recruiting

Undergraduate Hiring
September 9, 1997

1

Undergraduate Training Program

- 18 month program
- Formal classroom training
- Practical rotational experience
- Broad exposure and experience before placement

2

Recruiting Initiatives

- Ways to make company more appealing to undergraduates
- Women's panels
- On-campus interviewing
- Internet home page

3

1996 Recruiting Results

- 18 women and 16 men hired into training program
- 25% from West Coast
- 23% from Midwest
- 30% from East Coast
- 22% international
- 50% of hires former summer interns

4

1997 Recruiting Season

- Received 2578 resumes
- Interviewed 68 candidates
- Extended 2 offers
- 1997 target of 25 new hires

5

Internal Recruiting Initiatives

- Conduct interviewing skills workshops for group leaders who interview candidates
- Set up "round robin" interview format
- Create BA video to be shown on campuses
- Create network of mentors for new hires

6

Corporate Recruiters

- Amy Williams, Managing Director
- MBA Recruiting
  - Roberta Salto, VP
- BA Recruiting
  - Carmen Vasquez, VP
- Corporate Home Page
  - http://www.recruit.com

7

KEYSTROKES

MOVE SLIDES

–SLIDE SORTER VIEW–

1. Select slide to move.
2. Drag slide to new location.

COPY SLIDES

–SLIDE SORTER VIEW–

1. Select slide to copy.
2. Press **Ctrl** and drag slide to new location.

DUPLICATE SLIDES

–SLIDE SORTER VIEW–

1. Select slide to duplicate.
2. Click **Insert**..............................Alt+I
3. Click **Duplicate Slide** ....D

DELETE SLIDES

–SLIDE SORTER VIEW–

1. Select slide to delete.
2. Press **Del** ....Delete

Exercise 5

- **Change a Presentation's Template**
- **Change a Slide's Layout**

Standard Toolbar

NOTES

Change a Presentation's Template

- Templates are organized by type and saved in the Presentation Designs subdirectory (folder) within the template subdirectory of the MSOffice directory.

- To change the template design of the current presentation, double-click the template name button on the Status bar or select Apply Design from the Format menu or click the Apply Design button on the Standard toolbar.

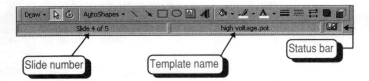

- The Apply Design dialog box appears, letting you make another template selection.

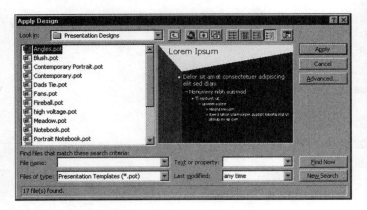

- When you select a template from the file list, an example of the template design appears in the right side of the window. Click Apply to apply the selected template to the current presentation.

- Sometimes it is distracting to see the color and design of the template while creating slide information. To display the slide in black and white, click the Black and White view button on the Standard toolbar or select Black and White from the View menu. If Slide Miniature is selected in the View menu, a miniature slide appears on the screen, displaying the slide in its original colors:

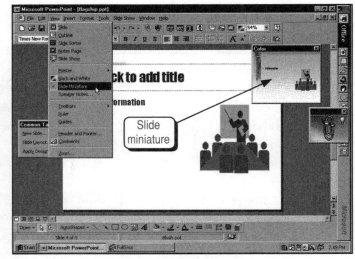

Change a Slide's Layout

- The layout of a slide may be changed at any time. If you have objects on the slide when changing the layout, they will not be lost; they will be rearranged.

- Use Slide view when changing a slide's layout.

- To change the layout, click the Slide Layout button on the Common Tasks toolbar or select Slide Layout from the Format menu. The Slide Layout dialog box appears, letting you make another layout selection.

In Part I of this exercise, you will change the template in a previously created presentation. In Part II of this exercise, you will create a new presentation. After doing so, you will change the presentation's template and change the layout of various slides.

EXERCISE DIRECTIONS

Part I

1. Open 📠 **RECRUIT**, or open 💾 **05RECRUIT**.

2. Apply the Contemporary template to the presentation.

3. View the presentation in Black and White view.

4. Print one copy as handouts (6 slides per page) in Black and White.

5. Close the file; save the changes.

Part II

1. Create a new Presentation using the Professional template.

2. Accept the default Title layout for Slide 1 and the Bulleted List layout for Slides 2 and 3. Enter the text as shown in Illustration A.

3. Create Slides 4 and 5 using the Text & Clip Art layout. Enter the titles and bulleted information as shown in Illustration B and insert relevant clip art.

4. Change the layout of Slide 2 to Clip Art & Text.

5. Insert relevant clip art.

6. Switch to Slide Sorter view.

7. Change the presentation template to Meadow.

8. Switch to Black and White view.

9. Spell check.

10. Compare your presentation to the Desired Result on page 42. Make any necessary adjustments to the slide order, if necessary.

11. Print one copy as Handouts (6 slides per page) in Black and White.

12. Save the presentation; name it **DENVER**.

13. Close the presentation.

ILLUSTRATION A

Visit Us Out West!

Denver, Colorado
Denver Tourism Bureau

1

Denver…Colorado's Capitol

- Distinct architecture
- Various museums
- Ethnic neighborhoods
- Shopping
- Art galleries

2

Museums

- Denver Art Museum
- Colorado History Museum
- Museum of Western Art

3

ILLUSTRATION B

Denver's Architecture

- Colorado State Capitol was built in Federal Revival style
- Denver City and County Building was built in 1932 in Neoclassical style
- 90% of the structures in the LoDo region of Denver are historic

4

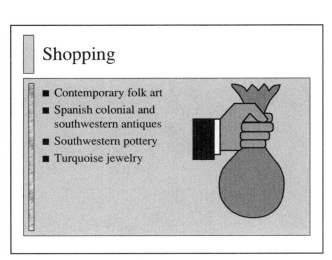

Shopping

- Contemporary folk art
- Spanish colonial and southwestern antiques
- Southwestern pottery
- Turquoise jewelry

5

DESIRED RESULT

Visit Us Out West!

Denver, Colorado
Denver Tourism Bureau

1

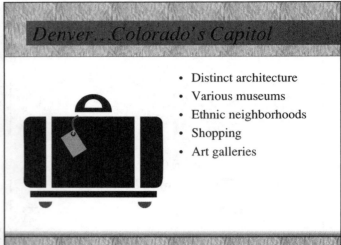

Denver...Colorado's Capitol

- Distinct architecture
- Various museums
- Ethnic neighborhoods
- Shopping
- Art galleries

2

Museums

- Denver Art Museum
- Colorado History Museum
- Museum of Western Art

3

Denver's Architecture

- Colorado State Capitol was built in Federal Revival style
- Denver City and County Building was built in 1932 in Neoclassical style
- 90% of the structures in the LoDo region of Denver are historic

4

Shopping

- Contemporary folk art
- Spanish colonial and southwestern antiques
- Southwestern pottery
- Turquoise jewelry

5

KEYSTROKES

CHANGE PRESENTATION TEMPLATE

1. Click **Apply Design** button .... [icon]
   on Standard toolbar.

   OR

   Double-click template name on Status
   bar (Angles, Blush, etc.).

   OR

   a. Click **Format**..................... Alt + O
   b. Click **Apply Design**.................... Y

2. Select a template design.

3. Click **Apply**............................ Alt + P

CHANGE SLIDE LAYOUT

Display Slide view:

1. Click **Slide Layout** button .... [icon]
   on Standard toolbar.

   OR

   Click **Slide Layout**................. Alt + L
   on the Common Tasks toolbar.

   OR

   a. Click **Format**..................... Alt + O
   b. Click **Slide Layout**...................... L

2. Select a desired layout.

3. Click **Apply**.................... Alt + A
   to apply new layout.

   OR

   Click **Reapply**...................... Alt + A
   to keep original layout.

Exercise 6

- ■ **Outline View** ■ **Add Slides in Outline View**
- ■ **Print an Outline**

NOTES

Outline View

- ■ **Outline** view displays slide text as titles and subtitles in an outline format to give an overview of the content of a presentation. This view is used to organize a presentation.

- ■ To display Outline view, click the Outline View button ■ on the bottom left of the presentation window or select Outline from the View menu.

- ■ Outline view can be used before creating text on slides to organize your thoughts in an outline format. To do so, enter your presentation text, pressing the Tab key to create sublevels and pressing Shift + Tab to return to previous levels.

- ■ Or, you may create your presentation in Slide view first, then switch to Outline view to see the flow of your presentation in an outline format. Outline view can also serve as a Table of Contents to distribute to your audience.

- ■ Note the illustration below of the KIT presentation displayed in Outline view. Slides are numbered down the left side of the screen, and slide icons identify the start of each new slide. A miniature of the selected slide appears in the window. If the miniature is not on screen, select Slide Miniature from the View menu.

- ■ If Slide Miniature is turned off, you will not see graphics and objects in Outline view. However, a slide that contains such items will be identified by shapes in the miniature slide icon ■ that appears to the right of the slide numbers.

- ■ The Outlining toolbar replaces the Drawing toolbar in the presentation window in Outline view. The Outlining toolbar contains tools for making some of the more common tasks associated with outlines more efficient. Many of these tasks are not available on the menus.

Outline View

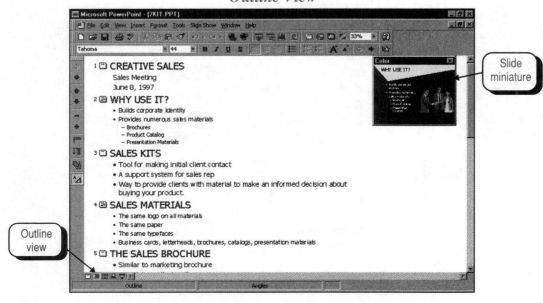

Outlining Toolbar

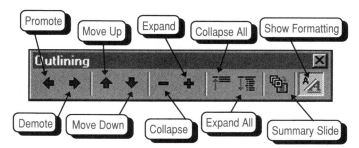

- **Promote/Demote** buttons ◄ ► let you quickly reformat bulleted text to title text (promote) and title text to subitem text (demote).

- **Move up/Move down** buttons ▲ ▼ let you select text from one slide and move it to a new location. This procedure can be used effectively to move or rearrange individual text items or complete slides.

- **Expand Selection** button ➕ lets you display all title text as well as subitem text for selected slides and/or items containing multiple levels and subitems.

- **Collapse Selection** button ➖ lets you remove subitems from display for individual items or for groups of selected items.

- **Collapse All** button lets you display only the title text for all slides in a presentation.

- **Expand All** button lets you display all levels of text for every slide in a presentation.

- **Summary Slide** button creates a new slide from the titles of slides you select in Slide Sorter or Outline views and creates a bulleted list of the titles.

- **Show Formatting** button lets you display text formats and enhancements, as they appear on the slide. When this feature is inactive, text for all slides appears as plain text in the default font.

Add Slides in Outline View

- The same four methods can be used to add slides in Outline view that were used to add slides to a presentation in Slide view:

  - Click Insert New Slide button 🖼 on the Standard toolbar.

  - Click New Slide on the Common Tasks toolbar.

  - Press Ctrl+M.

  - Select New Slide from the Insert menu.

Print an Outline

- You can print an outline using the same procedures that were used to print copies of your slides. You must, however, select Outline View from the Print what drop-down list in the Print dialog box.

> *In this exercise, you will create a presentation in Outline view. After creating the presentation, you will move slides, and print the presentation.*

EXERCISE DIRECTIONS

1. Create a new Blank Presentation and accept the default Title Slide layout as the first slide.

2. Switch to Outline view.

3. Enter the following titles and subtitles to create your outline:

   1. New World Gym
      - "A New Way of Life"
   2. New World Gym Features:
      - Fitness evaluation tests
      - 100 aerobics classes each week
      - Yoga
      - Personal trainers
      - Boxing program
   3. What Makes Us Different…
      - Open 24 hours each day
      - Spa café with nutritional clinics
   4. New World Gym Membership Includes…
      - 7 guest passes
      - 2 free personal training sessions
      - 1 free massage
      - Fitness evaluation test
      - Permanent locker
      - New World Gym T-shirt

   ✓ *If the slide miniature of Slide 4 is not on screen, display it.*

4. Switch to Slide view.

5. Display Slide 1.

   ✓ *PowerPoint selected the slide layouts for you. You may, however, change them.*

6. Switch to Slide Sorter view.

7. Move slide 4 to become Slide 3.

8. Switch to Slide view and display Slide 2 (New World Gym Features).

9. Change the layout to Text & Clip Art. Insert a relevant graphic.

10. Apply the High Voltage template design.

11. Insert a new bulleted list slide after Slide 3 that reads:

    > Various Locations
    > - New York
    > - Los Angeles
    > - Miami
    > - Chicago

12. Change the layout to Text & Clip Art. Insert a relevant graphic.

13. Switch to Slide Sorter view.

14. Correct spelling errors.

15. Compare your presentation to the Desired Result on page 47. Change the order of your slides if necessary.

16. In the Page Setup dialog box, change the orientation for Handouts to Landscape.

17. Print one copy as Handouts (6 slides per page) in Pure Black and White.

18. In the Page Setup dialog box, change the orientation for Handouts to Portrait.

19. Print one copy as Handouts (6 slides per page) in Pure Black and White.

20. Save the file; name it **GYM**. Fill in the appropriate summary information.

21. Close the presentation window.

Desired Result

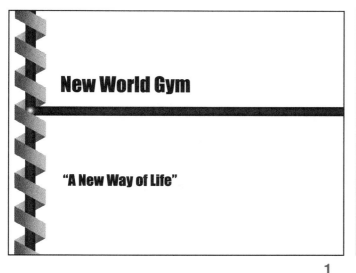

New World Gym

"A New Way of Life"

1

New World Gym Features:

- Fitness evaluation tests
- 100 aerobics classes each week
- Yoga
- Personal trainers
- Boxing program

2

New World Gym Membership Includes...

- 7 guest passes
- 2 free personal training sessions
- 1 free massage
- Fitness evaluation test
- Permanent locker
- New World Gym T-shirt

3

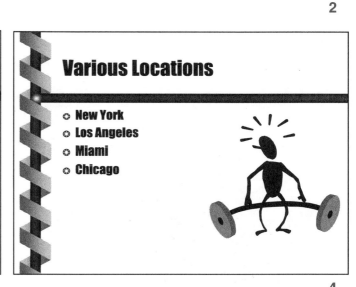

Various Locations

- New York
- Los Angeles
- Miami
- Chicago

4

What Makes Us Different...

- Open 24 hours each day
- Spa café with nutrition clinics

5

KEYSTROKES

SWITCH TO OUTLINE VIEW

Click the **Outline View** button..............▤

OR

1. Click **View** ....Alt+V
2. Select **Outline** ....O

ADD SLIDES IN OUTLINE VIEW

CTRL + M

Click **New Slide** button ....▣
on Standard toolbar.

OR

1. Click **Insert**...........................Alt+I
2. Click **New Slide**.................................N

OR

Click **New Slide** ....Alt+N
on the Common Tasks toolbar.

ADD TEXT IN OUTLINE VIEW

Click ➡ to indent.............................Tab
or add subitems.

✓ *To add a bulleted item under the Title line, press Enter and then press Tab.*

OR

Click ⬅ ....Shift+Tab
to go back one text or subitem level.

NEXT EXERCISE

Exercise

7

■ **Summary**

In this exercise, you will create a presentation in Outline View. You will move the slides, change the layouts of selected slides, change the presentation template, and print the presentation.

EXERCISE DIRECTIONS

1. Create a new Blank Presentation.

2. Accept the default Title slide layout.

3. Switch to Outline view.

4. Enter the outline text shown on the following page. (*Hint: To create the line break in the title of the first slide as illustrated, place the cursor in front of the word SPACE and press Shift + Enter to create a soft line break.*)

5. Switch to Slide Sorter view.

6. Move Slide 3 to become Slide 2.

7. Switch to Slide view.

8. Change the layout of Slides 4 and 7 to Clip Art & Text. Insert relevant graphics.

9. Change the layout of Slides 6 and 8 to Text & Clip Art. Insert relevant graphics.

10. Change the presentation template to Ribbons.

11. Correct spelling errors.

12. Print one copy as Handouts (6 slides per page) in Black and white.

13. Save the file; name it **MOVIE**. Fill in the appropriate summary information.

14. Close the presentation window.

Outline

1. Marketing Strategies for
   SPACE ADVENTURES
   A Science-Fiction Film by J. Warber
   June 15, 1998

2. Trilogy's Vision
   - Widespread name recognition
   - An animated TV series following the release of the film
   - An expanding marketing and franchising department

3. Goals and Objectives
   - International support/recognition for the film
   - Profitable franchising
   - Financial returns

4. Positioning our Product
   - Internet Web site development
   - Release of the soundtrack to the film
   - Toys and stuffed animals
   - Clothing and hats

5. The Space Adventures Web Site
   - http://www.space.com
   - Latest news on the feature film
   - Ability to purchase Space Adventures paraphernalia
   - Profile of a character each month
   - Chat Channel for fans
   - Interactive games with the characters

6. The Soundtrack
   - Targeted to a wider market
   - International availability
   - Use as a promotional item

7. Toys and Dolls
   - Merchandiser will create toys and dolls
   - Distribution
     - large toy stores/chains
     - houseware stores
     - children's apparel stores

8. Clothing and Hats
   - Use as promotional items before release of film
   - Adult and Children's sizes
   - Distribution
     - large toy stores/chains
     - houseware stores
     - apparel stores (that sell similar merchandise)

9. Summary
   - 30 years of marketing experience
   - Past record of successful film marketing
     - The Wave -- grossed $35 million
     - Money Makes Us Move -- grossed $75 million
     - Spaced Out -- grossed $108 million

Exercise 8

■ Summary

In this exercise, you will create a presentation in Outline View. You will apply a template design, move the slides, change the layouts of selected slides, and print the presentation.

EXERCISE DIRECTIONS

1. Create a new Blank Presentation.

2. Accept the default Title Slide layout.

3. Switch to Outline view.

4. Create the outline shown on the following page. Display the Slide Miniature.

5. Print one copy of the outline.

6. Switch to Slide view.

7. Display Slide 1.

8. Apply the Fans template design.

9. Switch to Slide Sorter view.

10. Switch to Slide view.

11. Display Slide 6 (Riding Basics) and change the layout to Title Slide.

12. Display Slide 10 (Conclusion) and change the layout to Text & Clip Art. Insert a relevant graphic.

13. Display Slide 9 (Riding Levels) and change the layout to Clip Art & Text. Insert a relevant graphic.

14. Insert a new slide after Three-day Eventing.

   ✓ *Use a layout that includes a bulleted list and clip art placeholders. Enter the following text and insert any relevant clip art.*

Care of the Horse
• Grooming Tools
• Veterinary Supplies
• Health and Maintenance

15. Correct spelling errors.

16. Switch to Slide Sorter view.

17. Print one copy as Handouts (6 slides per page) in Black and White.

18. Save the file; name it **HORSE**. Fill in the appropriate summary information.

19. Close the presentation window.

1 ▢ **The Equestrian Sport**

A Guide to Horseback Riding

Gallop Riding Academy

2 ▢ **Equestrian Events in the Olympics**

- Equestrian Events in the Olympics for first time in 1912
    - Held in Stockholm, Sweden
    - 88 horses competed from 8 different nations
- Dressage
- Three-day Eventing
- Show Jumping

3 ▢ **Dressage**

- Originates from Ancient Greece
- Tests horse's physique and ability
- Demonstrates high degree of understanding between horse and rider

4 ▢ **Show Jumping**

- Must complete course in designated time
- Rider accumulates "faults" for errors

5 ▢ **Three-day Eventing**

- Dressage phase
- Endurance phase
- Stadium jumping phase

6 ▢ **Riding Basics**

7 ▢ **Riding Attire**

- English riding hard hat
- Hunt boots
- Paddock boots

8 ▢ **Tacking Up**

- Saddle
- Bridle
- Girth

9 ▢ **Riding Levels**

- Walking
- Trotting
- Cantering

10 ▢ **Conclusion**

- Ride at Gallop Riding Academy
    - Expert riding instructors
    - Modern boarding facilities
    - Indoor riding arena

Lesson 2
Enhance Slides;
Work with Text and Objects

Exercise 9
- ◆ Select, Align, and Change the Appearance of Text
- ◆ Change Case
- ◆ Change Slide Color Scheme
- ◆ Change Slide Background

Exercise 10
- ◆ Copy Text Formatting
- ◆ Move and Copy Text
- ◆ Increase/Decrease Paragraph Spacing

Exercise 11
- ◆ Change Paragraph Indent
- ◆ Set Tabs

Exercise 12
- ◆ Create a Text Box
- ◆ Move, Size, Copy, and Delete Placeholders and Other Objects

Exercise 13
- ◆ Use Slide and Title Master
- ◆ Save as Template
- ◆ Insert Slide Numbers, Date and Time, and Other Footer Text
- ◆ Format Bullets

Exercise 14
- ◆ Summary

Exercise 15
- ◆ Summary

Exercise 9

- Select, Align, and Change the Appearance of Text
- Change Case ■ Change Slide Color Scheme
- Change Slide Background

Formatting Toolbar

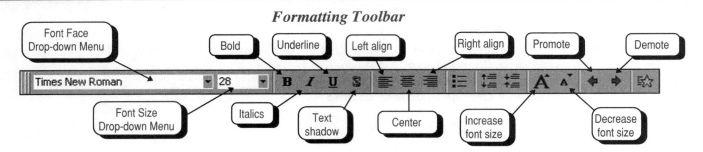

NOTES

Select Text

■ When pointing to text with the mouse, the mouse pointer changes to an I-beam to signify that the text insertion mode is active. Click the text you want to edit, and use the following techniques for selecting blocks of text in PowerPoint:

- Double-click to select a word.

- Triple-click to select a paragraph, complete title, or bulleted item, including all subitems.

- Click and drag across text to highlight it.

■ These techniques can be used to select and edit text in Slide or Outline views. Text may not be edited in Slide Sorter or Notes Page views.

Align Text

■ PowerPoint lets you align text to the left, center, or right in a placeholder or text box. Because the most frequently used alignments in PowerPoint are left, right, and center, buttons for these three alignment options are included on the Formatting toolbar. Justified alignment is available by selecting Alignment, Justify from the Format menu.

■ To change the alignment of title text or text for one bulleted item, position the I-beam in the title or bulleted item and click the desired alignment button.

■ To change the alignment for more than one bulleted item, select text for the bulleted items you want to change before clicking the alignment button or selecting the alignment option from the Format menu.

■ While you can set alignment in either Outline or Slide view, it is better to do so in Slide view, because text formatting is displayed in this view.

■ When you want to change the alignment of title text, all text in the title placeholder for that slide is realigned. To align text on one line of a title differently from text of other lines, remove the lines you want to align differently from the title placeholder and include them in the body placeholder. Each line in the body placeholder can then be aligned separately.

Change the Appearance of Text

■ PowerPoint controls the font face, size, emphasis (bold, italics, shadow, underline), and color of text on each slide layout. However, you can change the font face and other attributes of any text on a PowerPoint slide at any time.

■ Format changes and enhancements affect the word in which the insertion point rests unless you have selected specific text.

- Use the Formatting toolbar to change one text attribute quickly; use the Font dialog box to apply more than one change, or to apply a different font color. See the Keystrokes on page 62 for procedures for applying specific text changes.

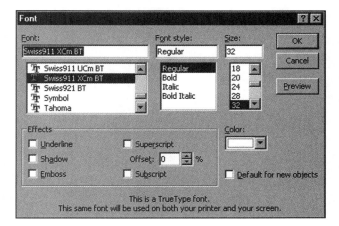

- The Formatting toolbar contains the following commonly used buttons:

  - Use the Bold **B**, Italics *I*, or Underline <u>U</u> buttons to apply these attributes.

  - Use the **Increase/Decrease Font Size** buttons **A A** to increase or decrease the font size incrementally.

  - Use the **Text Shadow** button **S** to apply shadow effects to text.

  - Use the **Promote (Indent less)** and **Demote (Indent more)** buttons ← → to adjust the levels of bulleted items.

  - Use the **Animation Effects** button to apply animation to objects or text. Animation will activate in Slide Show view. (*Animation effects will be covered in Exercise 30.*)

  - Use the **Font Size** drop-down menu 24 to apply a different font size.

  - Use the **Font Face** drop-down menu Times New Roman to apply a different font face.

  ✓ *Note:* *There are three types of font faces: serif, sans serif, and script. A serif font has lines curves, or edges extending from the ends of the letter (T), a sans serif font is straight-edged (T), and a script font imitates handwriting (*7*).*

- You can quickly replace one font face with another font face on all slides in a presentation at once. To do so, select <u>R</u>eplace Fonts from the F<u>o</u>rmat menu.

- In the Replace Font dialog box that follows, select a font to replace from the Re<u>p</u>lace drop-down list box. Then select a font to replace it with from the <u>W</u>ith drop-down list box, and click <u>R</u>eplace.

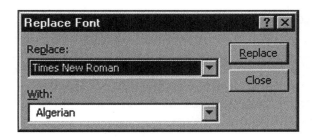

- The Show Formatting button, available on the Outlining toolbar in Outline view and on the Slide Sorter toolbar in Slide Sorter view, is defaulted to display font style, font size, bold, italics, and underline. When you turn off the Show Formatting feature, text appears in the default font with no enhancements.

Change Case

- The change case feature lets you change an existing block of text to sentence case, lowercase, uppercase, title case or toggle case. To change case, highlight the text and select Change Cas<u>e</u> from the F<u>o</u>rmat menu. In the Change Case dialog box that follows, choose the desired case.

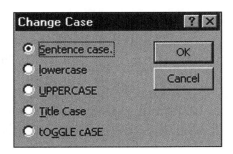

Change Slide Color Scheme

■ Each template design has a predefined color scheme. Specific colors were chosen for the slide background, title text, fills, lines, shadows, and accents. PowerPoint lets you change the entire color scheme of your presentation or change individual parts (for example, line colors and slide background only). You may change the color scheme of one or all slides in your presentation.

■ To change a slide's color scheme, select Slide Color Scheme from the Format menu or right-click the slide and select Color Scheme from the shortcut menu. In the Color Scheme dialog box that follows, you may select one of the predefined options indicated on the Standard tab.

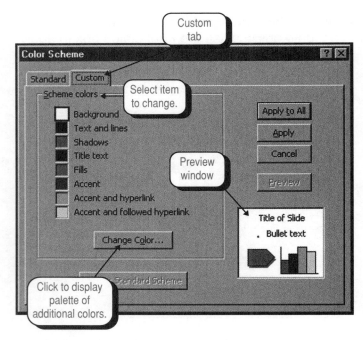

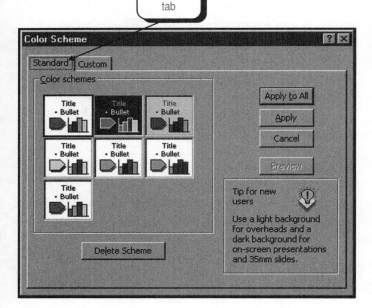

■ To make custom changes to individual slide parts, click the Custom tab. Select the item to change (Background, Text and Lines, Title Text, etc.) from the Scheme Colors list. Then click the Change Color button to select from a palette of additional colors. The preview window displays the results of your choices. Click Apply to All to change all slides or click Apply to change only the current slide.

Change Slide Background

■ To change a slide's background, color, shadows, pattern or texture, select Background from the Format menu. In the Background dialog box that follows, click the list arrow.

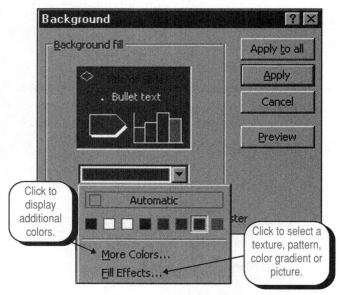

■ To change the background color, select a new color from the drop-down palette. Or click More Colors from the drop-down list to select from additional background color options.

- To apply a color gradient, texture, pattern or picture to the slide background, click Fill Effects from the drop-down list. In the Fill Effects dialog box that follows, click the appropriate tab and select the desired options. A preview window displays the result of your selection.

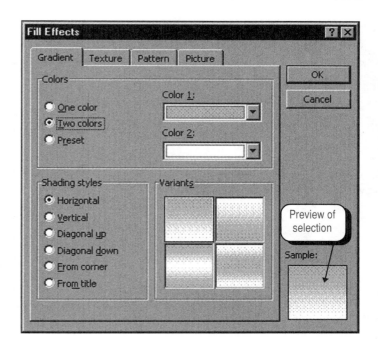

In this exercise, you will change the size and color of text on slides. Check your changes with the Desired Result shown on the following pages.

EXERCISE DIRECTIONS

1. Open 📠 **RECRUIT**, or open 💾 **09RECRUIT**.

2. Using Slide view, replace the font faces on all slides to Brisk (or any other decorative font). Use the Decrease Font Size button on the Formatting toolbar to reduce font sizes as necessary, so all text fits properly on each slide.

   ✓ *Replacing the fonts may also change the default bullet shape in your presentation so that your bullets may not match those illustrated in the Desired Result.*

3. Left-align the titles in Slides 2-7.

4. Use the Decrease Font Size button to reduce the size of bulleted text on Slide 5 (1997 Recruiting…) and Slide 7 (Corporate Recruiters).

5. Italicize sub-titles on Slide 1.

6. Switch to Outline view; use the Show Formatting button on the Outlining toolbar to turn formatting off and on.

7. Insert a new slide after Slide 6 that reads:

   New Hires Should Be…
   - energetic
   - articulate
   - quantitatively capable
   - motivated
   - outgoing

8. Switch to Slide view.

9. Apply the Bulleted List layout to the new slide, if necessary. Apply the same font face to the new slide as you did to the other slides, if necessary.

10. Apply a custom color scheme to all slides as follows:
    - Background   Dark Green
    - Accent   Purple
    - Fills   Light Blue

11. Switch to Slide Sorter view.

12. Compare your presentation to the Desired Result on the following page. Change the order of your slides to match, if necessary.

13. Print one copy as Handouts (3 slides per page) in Black and White.

14. Close the file; save the changes.

DESIRED RESULT

Corporate Recruiting

Undergraduate Hiring
September 9, 1997

1

Undergraduate Training Program

- 18 month program
- Formal classroom training
- Practical rotational experience
- Broad exposure and experience before placement

2

Recruiting Initiatives

- Ways to make company more appealing to undergraduates
- Women's panels
- On-campus interviewing
- Internet home page

3

1996 Recruiting Results

- 18 women and 16 men hired into training program
- 25% from West Coast
- 23% from Midwest
- 30% from East Coast
- 22% international
- 50% of hires former summer interns

4

1997 Recruiting Season

- Received 2578 resumes
- Interviewed 68 candidates
- Extended 2 offers
- 1997 target of 25 new hires

5

Internal Recruiting Initiatives

- Conduct interviewing skills workshops for group leaders who interview candidates
- Set up "round robin" interview format
- Create BA video to be shown on campuses
- Create network of mentors for new hires

6

New Hires Should Be...

- energetic
- articulate
- quantitatively capable
- motivated
- outgoing

7

Corporate Recruiters

- Amy Williams, Managing Director
- MBA Recruiting
  - Roberta Salto, VP
- BA Recruiting
  - Carmen Vasquez, VP
- Corporate Home Page
  - http://www.recruit.com

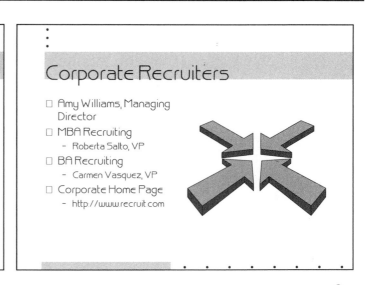

8

KEYSTROKES

ALIGN TEXT

1. Position insertion point in text to align.
OR
Select text to align.
2. Click desired Alignment button on Formatting toolbar:
   - Click **Left** .... [icon]
   - Click **Right** .... [icon]
   - Click **Center** .... [icon]

OR

a. Click **Format** .... [Alt]+[O], [A]
   Alignment.
b. Select desired alignment:
   - **Left** .... [L]
   - **Center** .... [C]
   - **Right** .... [R]
   - **Justify** .... [J]

REPLACE FONT FACES

1. Click **Format** .... [Alt]+[O]
2. Click **Replace Fonts** .... [R]
3. Select font face to **Replace** .... [Alt]+[P]
4. Select font face .... [Alt]+[W]
   to replace **With**.
5. Click **Replace** .... [Alt]+[R]

CHANGE FONT FACE

✓ *The following procedures can only be performed in Slide view.*

1. Position insertion point in word to format.
OR
Select text to format.
2. Select .... [Times New Roman ▼]
   desired font from Formatting toolbar
   Font Face drop-down menu.

OR

a. Click **Format, Font** ...... [Alt]+[O], [F]
b. Click the **Font** box .... [Alt]+[F]
   and select desired font face.
c. Click **OK** .... [Enter]

CHANGE FONT SIZE

1. Position insertion point in word to format.
OR
Select text to change.
2. Select desired size .... [24 ▼]
   from Formatting toolbar
   Font Size drop-down menu.

OR

1. Click **Format, Font** .... [Alt]+[O], [F]
2. Click the **Size** box .... [Alt]+[S]
   and select desired font size.
3. Click **OK** .... [Enter]

OR

Click [A˄ A˅] on the Formatting toolbar to increase/decrease font size incrementally.

CHANGE EMPHASIS (BOLD, ITALICS, SHADOW, UNDERLINE, COLOR)

1. Position insertion point in word to change.
OR
Select text to change.
2. Click desired emphasis button on Formatting toolbar:
   - **Bold** .... [B]
   - **Italic** .... [I]
   - **Underline** .... [U]

OR

a. Click **Format, Font** ...... [Alt]+[O], [F]
b. Click **Font Style** .... [Alt]+[O]
c. Select desired options.
d. Select desired emphasis style(s) from the Effects section of the dialog box:
   - **Underline** .... [Alt]+[U]
   - **Shadow** .... [Alt]+[A]
   - **Emboss** .... [Alt]+[E]
   - **Superscript** .... [Alt]+[R]
   - **Subscript** .... [Alt]+[B]
e. Click **Color** .... [Alt]+[C]
   drop-down list box and select a new font color, if desired.
f. Click **OK** .... [Enter]

CHANGE CASE

1. Select text to change.
2. Click **F<u>o</u>rmat** .... `Alt`+`O`
3. Click **Change Cas<u>e</u>** .... `E`
4. Select desired case:
   - **<u>S</u>entence case** .... `S`
   - **<u>l</u>owercase** .... `L`
   - **<u>U</u>PPERCASE** .... `U`
   - **<u>T</u>itle Case** .... `T`
   - **tO<u>G</u>GLE cASE** .... `G`

CHANGE SLIDE COLOR SCHEME

1. Click **F<u>o</u>rmat** .... `Alt`+`O`
2. Click **Slide <u>C</u>olor Scheme** .... `C`
3. Click Standard tab and select desired color schemes.

   OR

   a. Click **Custom** tab.
   b. Click item to change (Background, Text and Lines, etc.)
   c. Click **Change C<u>o</u>lor** .... `Alt`+`O`
   d. Select desired color.
   e. Click **OK** .... `Enter`
   f. Repeat for other items to change.
4. Click **Apply <u>t</u>o All** .... `Alt`+`T`

   OR

   Click **<u>A</u>pply** .... `Alt`+`A`
   to apply changes to
   current slide only.

CHANGE SLIDE BACKGROUND

1. Click **F<u>o</u>rmat, Background** .... `Alt`+`O`, `K`
2. Click the **<u>B</u>ackground fill** .... `Alt`+`B`
   drop-down arrow.
3. Select a new background fill color from the drop-down list.

   OR

   a. Select **<u>M</u>ore Colors** .... `M`
      from the drop-down list.
   b. Click the **Standard** or **Custom** tab and select a different fill color from the additional options.

   OR

   a. Select **<u>F</u>ill Effects** .... `F`
      from the drop-down list.
   b. Select desired options from appropriate tabs.
   c. Click **OK** .... `Enter`
4. Click **Apply <u>t</u>o all** .... `Alt`+`T`
   to apply background settings
   to the entire presentation.

   OR

   Click **<u>A</u>pply** .... `Alt`+`A`
   to apply the background setting
   to only the selected slide(s).

Exercise

10

■ **Copy Text Formatting** ■ **Move and Copy Text**
■ **Increase/Decrease Paragraph Spacing**

Standard and Formatting Toolbars

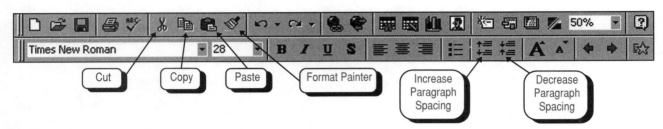

NOTES

Copy Text Formatting (Format Painter)

■ The Format Painter feature may be used in PowerPoint to copy formatting, such as font face, style, size, and color, from one part of text to another.

■ To copy formatting from one location to another, select the text that contains the format you wish to copy. Then, click the Format Painter button on the Standard toolbar (the I-beam displays a paintbrush) and select the text to receive the format.

■ To copy formatting from one location to several locations, select the text that contains the format you wish to copy, then double-click the Format Painter button. Select the text to receive the format, release the mouse button, and select additional text anywhere in the document.

■ To turn off this feature and return the mouse pointer to an I-beam, click the Format Painter button or press Escape.

■ When you use the Format Painter in Outline view, some formatting will not appear until you return to Slide view.

Move and Copy Text on a Slide

■ You can move text only in Slide or Outline views. However, it is more efficient to use Outline view to move or copy text from one slide to another.

■ To select bulleted items to move or copy in Outline view, position the mouse pointer on the bullet until it turns to a four-headed arrow and click once. The bulleted item, as well as all its subitems, will be highlighted. To select text to move in Slide view, click and drag across it to highlight it.

■ To move or copy text in Slide or Outline view, select the text, then select Cut or Copy and then Paste from the Edit menu, click the Cut, Copy or Paste buttons on the Formatting toolbar, or select and drag and drop the text. In addition, you may position the pointer in the text and then use the Move Up or Move Down buttons on the Outlining toolbar to reposition text up or down one line at a time in Outline view.

■ You can also cut, copy and paste text by selecting the text, then right-clicking the mouse. The shortcut menu will appear, from which you can select the option you wish to perform.

- To move selected text using drag and drop, place the mouse pointer in the selection and drag it until you see a horizontal or vertical line positioned where you want to insert the text. Release the mouse button, and your text will drop into place. To copy selected text, press the Ctrl key while you drag and drop text.

  ✓ Note: You can only copy text using drag and drop in Slide view. It does not work in Outline view.

- Use cut/copy and paste techniques to copy text to more than one new location or to copy text to a different presentation. Use the drag-and-drop technique in Outline view to move or copy text to a different slide or to rearrange bulleted items. Use the drag-and-drop feature in Slide view to move text on one slide.

Increase/Decrease Paragraph Spacing

- The space between paragraphs may be adjusted incrementally by selecting the paragraphs to be affected and clicking the Increase ⬛ or Decrease ⬛ Paragraph Spacing button on the Formatting toolbar.

- You may also adjust paragraph spacing by a specific amount by selecting Line Spacing from the Format menu. In the Line Spacing dialog box that follows, click in the Before paragraph and After paragraph increment boxes and type in desired number of lines or points to place before and after each paragraph. Then click the drop-down list arrow and select a unit of measurement: points or lines.

  ✓ Note: Paragraph spacing can be changed only in Slide view.

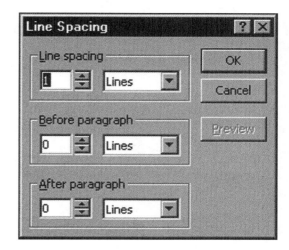

In this exercise, you will change the size, color and paragraph spacing of text on slides. Check your changes with the Desired Result shown on the following pages.

EXERCISE DIRECTIONS

1. Open ⌨ **HORSE**, or open 💾 **10HORSE**.

2. Switch to Slide view.

3. Apply a new template design: Whirlpool.

4. Change the font face on all slides to Jester or any other decorative font.

5. Using Format Painter, italicize all slide titles.

6. Display Slide 2 (Equestrian Events) and change to Outline view. Display slide miniature.

   - Move the second bulleted item (Dressage) down to become the last bulleted item.
   - Change the color of the subitems under the first bulleted item to green.

7. Create a custom color scheme on all slides as follows:
   - Text and lines: Green
   - Title text: Yellow
   - Fills: Purple
   - Accent: Pink

8. Switch to Slide view.

9. Display Slide 3 (Dressage).
   - Change the layout to Clip Art & Text.
   - Insert a relevant picture into the clip art placeholder.

10. Display Slide 5 (Three-Day Eventing).
    - Change the layout to Clip Art & Text.
    - Insert a relevant picture into the clip art placeholder.

11. Display Slide 8 (Riding Attire).
    - Increase the bulleted text font size to 48 point and increase the paragraph spacing so the text fills the placeholder vertically.
    - Highlight the bulleted text and double-click Format Painter.

12. Display Slide 10 (Riding Levels).
    - Use Format Painter to increase the bulleted text font size and paragraph spacing.

13. Display Slide 9 (Tacking Up).
    - Use Format Painter to increase the bulleted text font size and paragraph spacing.

14. Display Slide 6 (Care of the Horse).
    - Increase the bulleted text font size to 36 point.

15. Display Slide 4 (Show Jumping).
    - Increase the bulleted text font size to 48 point.

16. Switch to Slide Sorter view.

17. View the presentation in Black and White.

18. Compare your presentation to the Desired Result on the following page. Change the order of your slides if necessary.

19. Print one copy as Handouts (6 slides per page) in Pure Black and White.

20. Close the file; save the changes.

The Equestrian Sport

A Guide to Horseback Riding
Gallop Riding Academy

1

Equestrian Events in the Olympics

- Equestrian Events in the Olympics for the first time in 1912
  - Held in Stockholm, Sweden
  - 88 horses competed from 8 different nations
- Three-day Eventing
- Show Jumping
- Dressage

2

Dressage

- Originates from Ancient Greece
- Tests horse's physique and ability
- Demonstrates high degree of understanding between horse and rider

3

Show Jumping

- Must complete course in designated time
- Rider accumulates "faults" for errors

4

Three-day Eventing

- Dressage phase
- Endurance phase
- Stadium jumping phase

5

Care of the Horse

- Grooming Tools
- Veterinary Supplies
- Health and Maintenance

6

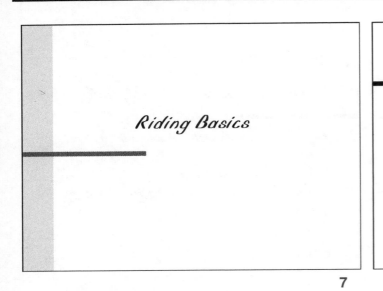

Riding Basics

7

Riding Attire

■*English riding hard hat*

■*Hunt boots*

■*Paddock boots*

8

Tacking Up

■*Saddle*

■*Bridle*

■*Girth*

9

Riding Levels

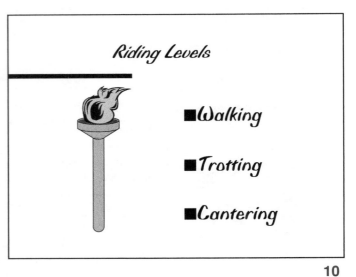

■*Walking*

■*Trotting*

■*Cantering*

10

Conclusion

■ *Ride at Gallop Riding Academy*
- *Expert riding instructors*
- *Modern boarding facilities*
- *Indoor riding arena*

11

KEYSTROKES

COPY TEXT FORMATTING

1. Position insertion point in text containing formatting to copy.

2. Click the **Format Painter** button....... 🖌 on the Standard toolbar.

   ✓ *Double-click the button if formatting is to be applied to multiple selections of text.*

3. Select text that you want to change or click to apply format to a word.

4. Press **Esc** to drop the .... Esc paintbrush, if necessary.

COPY

CTRL + C

1. Select the text to copy.

2. Click 📋 .... Alt + E , C

   OR

   Right-click and select **Copy**............. C from the shortcut menu.

MOVE (CUT)

CTRL + X

1. Select the text to move (cut).

2. Click ✂ .... Alt + E , T

   OR

   Right-click and select **Cut** .... T from the shortcut menu.

PASTE

CTRL + V

1. Position cursor where text is to be inserted.

2. Click 📋........................ Alt + E , P

   OR

   Right-click and select **Paste**............. P from the shortcut menu.

DRAG AND DROP

1. Select text or bulleted section to copy or move.

2. Position mouse pointer on selected text.

   ✓ *Mouse pointer must be a white pointer arrow ▢ and box.*

3. Click and drag text until vertical bar (or horizontal bar, if in Outline view) appears in desired new text position.

   ✓ *To copy text using this process, hold down Ctrl ▢ while dragging the text. You can only copy using this method in Slide view.*

4. Release mouse button.

INCREASE/DECREASE PARAGRAPH SPACING

1. Select paragraphs to be affected.

2. Click **Increase** 📶 or **Decrease** 📶 buttons on the Formatting toolbar to incrementally adjust spacing.

   OR

   a. Click **Format**...................... Alt + O

   b. Click **Line Spacing** .... S

   c. Enter in **Before** ..... Alt + B ,*number* **paragraph** text box the desired amount.

      AND/OR

      Enter in **After**........ Alt + A ,*number* **paragraph** text box the desired amount.

   d. Click **OK**................................... Enter

Exercise

11

■ **Change Paragraph Indent** ■ **Set Tabs**

NOTES

Change Paragraph Indent

■ Placeholder text can be indented from the left edge of the placeholder.

■ You can change an indent or the space between the bullet and the text by manipulating indent markers on the Ruler. You must display the Ruler to do this (select Ruler from the View menu).

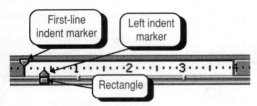

■ The top triangle on the indent marker is called the first-line indent marker. Drag this to indent the first line of the paragraph. This will increase or decrease the distance between the bullet and the text for the first line only.

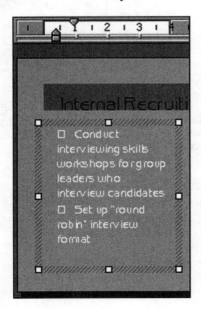

■ The bottom triangle is called the left indent marker. Drag this to indent all lines of the paragraph. This will increase or decrease the distance between the bullet and all lines of text in the bulleted paragraph.

■ The rectangle below the left indent marker moves the first-line indent marker and the left indent marker together. Drag this to indent all lines in the paragraph with the bullet.

■ If text is bulleted at more than one level, indent markers will appear on the Ruler for each level.

Set Tabs

■ Tab stops are defaulted at 1". This means that any time you select Tab from the Insert menu in PowerPoint, your text will advance 1".

■ To increase or decrease the distance between tab stops, you can click and drag any one of the tab stops (displayed on the bottom of the Ruler as vertical gray tick marks).

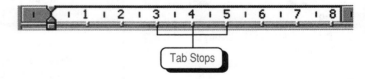

■ Dragging a tick mark to the right will increase the width of the tab, while dragging a tick mark to the left will reduce it.

■ Default settings are left aligned. This means that text typed at such a setting will align at the left and move text to the right of the tab as you type.

- The left-aligned tab type icon is located on the left of the horizontal Ruler and is displayed as an **L**.

Tab Type icon

- To set a new left-aligned tab, click anywhere on the bottom of the Ruler where a new tab is desired; a new tab marker is inserted. When a new tab is set, the preset tabs that precede it are deleted.

- To set a center-, right-, or decimal-aligned tab, click the Tab Type icon until the appropriate tab symbol appears, and then click the location on the bottom of the Ruler where you want the tab to appear.

- If you set a left-aligned tab 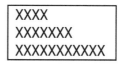, text will align as follows:

> XXXX
> XXXXXXX
> XXXXXXXXXX

- If you set a center-aligned tab , text will align as follows:

> XXXX
> XXXXXXX
> XXXXXXXXXX

- If you set a right-aligned tab , text will align as follows:

> XXXX
> XXXXXXX
> XXXXXXXXXX

- If you set a decimal-aligned tab, text will align at the decimal point as follows:

> XX.XX
> XXX.XX
> XXXX.XXX

In this exercise you will modify paragraph and bullet indentations and change tab settings on slides in a previously created presentation.

EXERCISE DIRECTIONS

1. Open ⌨ **RECRUIT**, or open 💾 **11RECRUIT**.

2. Switch to Slide view.

3. Select Ruler from the View menu.

4. Display Slide 2 (Undergraduate Training Program).
   - Click on the bulleted text to reveal the text placeholder.
   - Move the left-indent marker (bottom triangle) 0.5" to the right.

5. Display Slide 5 (1997 Recruiting Season).
   - Click on the bulleted text to reveal the text placeholder.
   - Drag the rectangle marker below the left indent marker to the right so that the bullets and the corresponding text are centered on the slide.

6. Display Slide 6 (Internal Recruiting Initiatives).
   - Click on the left column of text to reveal the left text placeholder.
   - Move the first-line indent marker (top triangle) so that it is .5" to the right of the left indent marker (bottom triangle).
   - Do the same for the right column of text.

7. Display Slide 8 (Corporate Recruiters).
   - Change the slide layout to Bulleted List.
   - Delete the clip art graphic.
   - Click on the bulleted text to reveal the text placeholder.
   - Move the second-level bulleted text to begin at 2" by dragging the appropriate rectangle marker to the right.
   - Set a left-aligned tab at 6.5".
   - Insert tabs and add phone numbers and "Visit Us!" as displayed in Illustration A.

8. Display Slide 7 (New Hires Should Be…).
   - Click on the bulleted text to reveal the text placeholder.
   - Set a right-aligned tab at 7.5".
   - Insert tabs and add text as displayed in Illustration B.

9. Switch to Slide Sorter view. Compare your presentation to the Desired Result on the following two pages. Reorder your slides to match the Desired Result if necessary.

10. Print one copy as Handouts (6 slides per page) in Pure Black and White.

11. Close the file; save the changes.

ILLUSTRATION A

Corporate Recruiters

☐ Amy Williams, Managing Director	555-6437
☐ MBA Recruiting	
– Roberta Salto, VP	555-6236
☐ BA Recruiting	
– Carmen Vasquez, VP	555-5286
☐ Corporate Home Page	
– http://www.recruit.com	Visit Us!

ILLUSTRATION B

New Hires Should Be...

☐ energetic	Importance Rank: 1
☐ articulate	2
☐ quantitatively capable	3
☐ motivated	4
☐ outgoing	5

Slide 1

Corporate Recruiting

Undergraduate Hiring
September 9, 1997

1

Slide 2

Undergraduate Training Program

- 18 month program
- Formal classroom training
- Practical rotational experience
- Broad exposure and experience before placement

2

Slide 3

Recruiting Initiatives

- Ways to make company more appealing to undergraduates
- Women's panels
- On-campus interviewing
- Internet home page

3

Slide 4

1996 Recruiting Results

- 18 women and 16 men hired into training program
- 25% from West Coast
- 23% from Midwest
- 30% from East Coast
- 22% international
- 50% of hires former summer interns

4

Slide 5

1997 Recruiting Season

- Received 2578 resumes
- Interviewed 68 candidates
- Extended 2 offers
- 1997 target of 25 new hires

5

Slide 6

Internal Recruiting Initiatives

- Conduct interviewing skills workshops for group leaders who interview candidates
- Set up "round robin" interview format
- Create BA video to be shown on campuses
- Create network of mentors for new hires

6

New Hires Should Be...

	energetic	Importance Rank: 1
	articulate	2
	quantitatively capable	3
	motivated	4
	outgoing	5

7

Corporate Recruiters

☐ Amy Williams, Managing Director   555-6437
☐ MBA Recruiting
   – Roberta Salto, VP   555-6236
☐ BA Recruiting
   – Carmen Vasquez, VP   555-5286
☐ Corporate Home Page
   – http://www.recruit.com   Visit Us!

8

KEYSTROKES

INSERT A TAB

1. Place insertion point in line of text where you want to insert tab.
2. Press the **Tab** key .... `Tab`
   OR
   To insert a tab at the beginning of a line:
   Click **Insert**, **Tab** .... `Alt`+`I`,`A`

CHANGE DEFAULT TAB SETTINGS

1. Click **Tab Type** icon .... `L`
   until the tab type desired appears.
2. Click on the bottom of the Ruler where tab is to be set.

TO DELETE TAB

Drag tab off Ruler to delete it.

INDENT TEXT FROM THE LEFT MARGIN

1. Place insertion point in paragraph or bulleted list to indent.

   ✓ *All bullets of the same sublevel in the active placeholder will be indented.*

2. Drag left-indent ... marker (rectangle) to desired position on Ruler to indent all lines, as well as the bullet itself.
   OR
   Drag first-line indent marker (top triangle) to desired position on Ruler to change the distance between the bullet and text for the first line of the paragraph only.
   OR
   Drag left-indent marker (bottom triangle) to desired position on the Ruler to indent all lines of text, but not the bullet itself.

NEXT EXERCISE

Exercise

12

- ■ **Create a Text Box**
- ■ **Move, Size, Copy, and Delete Placeholders and Other Objects**

Drawing Toolbar

Text Box

NOTES

Create a Text Box

- ■ If you wish to add text to a slide in a location other than a given placeholder, you may create a text box. A text box serves as a text placeholder, allowing you to insert text anywhere on a slide, depending on where it is drawn.

- ■ Like all other objects, text boxes can only be created in Slide view. To draw a text box, click the Text Box button 🔲 on the Drawing toolbar. Click and drag the mouse diagonally on the slide to create the desired size of the box. After releasing the mouse, type your text. If the text box is not located where you want it or is not the size you desire, you can move and/or resize it. *(See Move, Size, Copy and Delete Placeholders and Other Objects, below.)*

- ■ Text boxes do not appear in Outline view.

Move, Size, Copy, and Delete Placeholders and Other Objects

- ■ Text, clip art, and object placeholders, as well as objects created without a placeholder (such as text boxes, clip art pictures, tables and charts), can be moved, copied, sized, and deleted.

- ■ To move, copy, size, or delete a placeholder or an object created without a placeholder, you must first display handles to put the object into edit mode. To display an object or placeholder's handles, click inside it.

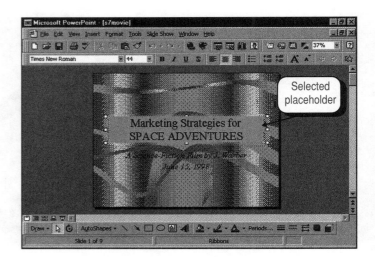

Selected placeholder

- ■ When handles appear, you can **size** the placeholder or object. Drag a top or bottom middle handle to change the vertical size (height); drag a left or right middle handle to change the horizontal size (width); drag a corner handle to size the placeholder proportionally. When you size a text placeholder, the text within it will adjust to the new borders.

- ■ You can **move** an object or a placeholder and its contents by displaying the handles, placing the pointer on the border (not on a handle) until the pointer changes to a four-headed arrow, and clicking and holding the left mouse button while dragging the object or placeholder to a desired location.

- Displaying the Rulers and guides when moving or sizing objects will allow you to determine the size and position of the object in relation to the slide.

- As you drag an object sizing handle the object's new borders are marked by a line on the horizontal and/or vertical Ruler, so you can easily see the new width or height of the object as you size it .

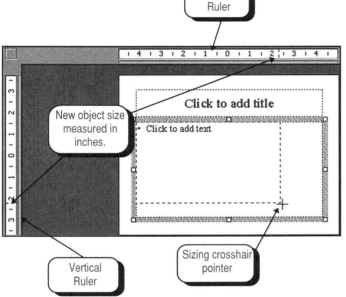

- As you drag an object across a slide, its location is marked by lines on the vertical and horizontal Rulers, so you can easily see its exact location as you move it.

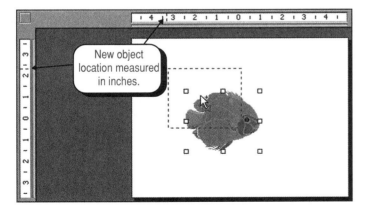

- To **copy** an object or placeholder to another location, press Ctrl while you drag the object or placeholder to the other location.

- To **delete** an object, click on it to select it and press the Delete key.

- To delete an object placeholder, display its handles and press the Delete key twice. (The first time you press Delete, the contents of the placeholder are deleted. The second time deletes the placeholder itself.)

- To delete a text placeholder, display its handles, click on a border (not on a handle) and press the Delete key twice. (The first time you press Delete, the contents of the placeholder are deleted. The second time deletes the placeholder itself.)

In this exercise, you will manipulate placeholders and add text boxes to your slides.

EXERCISE DIRECTIONS

1. Open 🎞 **MOVIE**, or open 💾 **12MOVIE**.

2. Switch to Slide view.

3. Display Rulers and Guides (View, Rulers; View, Guides).

4. Display Slide 1 (Marketing Strategies).
   - Move the placeholder containing the text "Marketing Strategies for SPACE ADVENTURES" to the bottom half of the slide.
   - Move the placeholder containing the text "A Science-Fiction Film…" to the top half of the slide as shown in the Desired Result on the following page.

5. Display Slide 2 (Goals and Objectives)
   - Change the layout to Clip Art & Text.
   - Resize the text placeholder to span the width of the slide and use the vertical Ruler to size it to a height of approximately 1". Position it below the slide title.
   - Resize the clip art placeholder to span the width of the slide and use the vertical Ruler to size it to a height of approximately 1". Position it below the text placeholder.
   - Insert any desired clip art image into the clip art placeholder at the bottom of the slide.

6. Display Slide 6 (The Sound Track).
   - Change the layout to Clip Art & Text.
   - Delete the text placeholder and the existing clip art.
   - Insert a relevant picture from the Clip Gallery into the clip art placeholder. Move the image to the center of the slide and size it proportionally, so it fills the remainder of the slide below the title text.
   - Create a text box and insert the words "Music to Remember" in Times New Roman 32-point bold. Color the text purple. Resize the text box so that the text fits on one line. Position the text box in the center of the clip art as shown.

7. Display Slide 5 (The Space Adventures).
   - Reduce the size of the title text placeholder, so the title breaks into two lines as shown in the Desired Result on the following page.
   - Move the title placeholder to the center of the top of the slide as shown in the Desired Result.

8. Switch to Slide Sorter view.

9. View the presentation in Black and White.

10. Compare your presentation to the Desired Result on the following two pages. Make any necessary adjustments to placeholders and/or font sizes so that all text fits properly on each slide.

11. Print one copy as Handouts (6 slides per page) in Pure Black and White.

12. Close the file; save the changes.

A Science-Fiction Film by J. Warber
June 15, 1998

Marketing Strategies for
SPACE ADVENTURES

1

Goals and Objectives

- International support/recognition for the film
- Profitable franchising
- Financial returns

2

Trilogy's Vision

- Widespread name recognition
- An animated TV series following the release of the film
- An expanding marketing and franchising department

3

Positioning our Product

- Internet Web site development
- Release of the soundtrack to the film
- Toys and stuffed animals
- Clothing and hats

4

The Space Adventures Web Site

- http://www.space.com
- Latest news on the feature film
- Ability to purchase Space Adventures paraphernalia
- Profile of a character each month
- Chat Channel for fans
- Interactive games with the characters

5

The Soundtrack

Music to Remember

6

Toys and Dolls

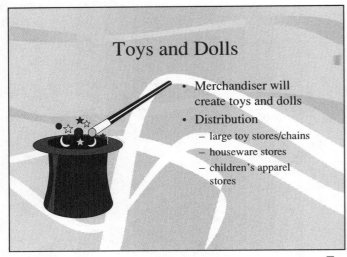

- Merchandiser will create toys and dolls
- Distribution
  - large toy stores/chains
  - houseware stores
  - children's apparel stores

7

Clothing and Hats

- Use as promotional items before release of film
- Adult and Children's sizes
- Distribution
  - large toy stores/chains
  - houseware stores
  - apparel stores (that sell similar merchandise)

8

Summary

- 30 years of marketing experience
- Past record of successful film marketing
  - The Wave -- grossed $35 million
  - Money Makes Us Move -- grossed $75 million
  - Spaced Out -- grossed $108 million

9

KEYSTROKES

CREATE A TEXT BOX

1. Click the **Text Box** button ....
   on the Drawing toolbar.
2. Click in slide and drag diagonally
   down to draw the box.
3. Type your text.

DISPLAY PLACEHOLDER OR OBJECT HANDLES

Click inside the placeholder or object.

MOVE PLACEHOLDERS AND OTHER OBJECTS

1. Display handles.
2. Position mouse pointer on a border
   (not on a handle).
3. Hold down left mouse button and drag
   object or placeholder to new location.
4. Release mouse button.

COPY PLACEHOLDERS AND OTHER OBJECTS

1. Display handles.
2. Position mouse pointer on a border
   (not on a handle).
3. Press **Ctrl** and hold down mouse
   button and drag object or placeholder
   to new location.
4. Release mouse button.

SIZE PLACEHOLDERS AND OTHER OBJECTS

1. Display handles.
2. Position mouse pointer on a top or
   bottom middle handle to change
   height, a left or right handle to change
   width, or a corner handle to change
   size proportionally.
3. Drag the handle until the placeholder
   or object is the desired size.

DELETE AN OBJECT CREATED WITHOUT A PLACEHOLDER

1. Display handles.
2. Press **Delete** ....

DELETE A PLACEHOLDER

1. Display handles.
   If deleting a text placeholder:
   Click on a border (not on a handle).
2. Press **Delete** ....
   to delete placeholder contents.
3. Press **Delete** again ....
   to delete placeholder.

Exercise 13

- Use Slide and Title Master ■ Save as Template
- Insert Slide Numbers, Date and Time, and Other Footer Text
- Format Bullets

NOTES

Use Slide and Title Master

- The **Slide Master** contains the default settings for all the slides in a presentation, except the Title slide. The **Title Master** contains the default settings for the format of the Title slide.

- By changing the content or formatting (font style, font size, color, position, tabs, indents, background, color scheme, template, etc.) of text or object placeholders on Slide Masters, all slides are automatically reformatted uniformly throughout the presentation. If, for example, you wanted to include clip art as your company's logo or a saying or quote on all slides in your presentation, you would include it on the Slide Master, and it would appear on all slides of your presentation.

Slide Master

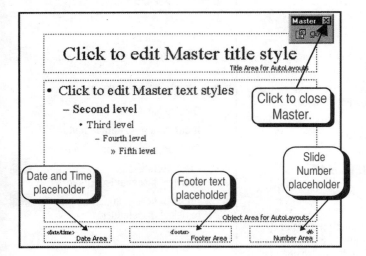

- Changes made on the Slide Master affect *all* slides in a presentation *except* those using the Title slide AutoLayout. Changes to the Slide Master affect only the active presentation.

- Formatting changes made to individual slides after the Slide Master has been created override changes made on the Slide Master.

- Slide Master may be accessed by selecting Master from the View menu, and then selecting Slide Master. Or, you can hold down the Shift key as you click the Slide View button.

- After making the desired changes on the Slide Master, click the Slide View button and display each slide in the presentation to see the effects. You may need to make adjustments to the Slide Master after seeing the results on individual slides.

- If you do not want to include Slide Master objects on a particular slide, display that slide and select Background from the Format menu. In the Background dialog box that follows, select the Omit background graphics from the Master check box and click Apply.

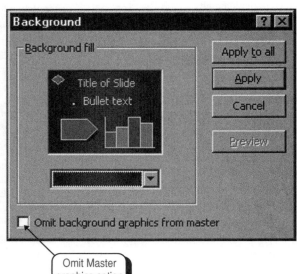

Save As Template

- The changes made to a presentation or to Masters can be saved as a new template. The template can then be used to create new presentations, or can be applied to other existing presentations.

- To save your presentation as a template, select Save As from the File menu and then select Presentation Template from the Save as type drop-down list. Type a template name in the File name text box and select the drive and other template folder where you want to store the template.

Insert Slide Numbers, Date and Time, and Footer Text

- Slide numbers, the date and/or time, and other text that you designate may be included in the footer area on individual or all slides. To do so, select Header and Footer from the View menu. In the Header and Footer dialog box that follows, click the appropriate check box to indicate whether you wish the Date and time, Slide number or Footer text to be on the current slide (Apply) or on all slides (Apply to All).

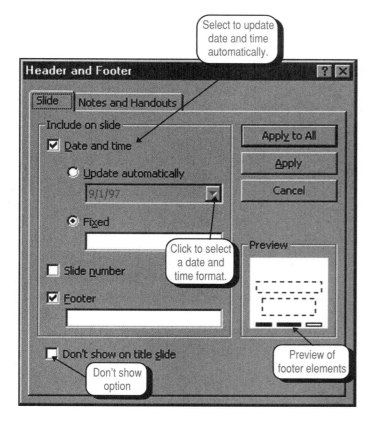

- If you wish to include the date and time or just the time and have it update automatically each time the presentation is accessed, click the Update automatically option. Then click the list arrow to select a desired format for the date and/or time. To insert a date and/or time that does not change, select Fixed and type the date/time you want displayed.

- If you do not wish to have slide numbers, the date and time, or any other footer text appear on the title slide, select the Don't show on title slide option.

- Since the Slide Master contains the default settings for the format of a slide, date and time, slide number and footer placeholders have already been created and positioned on it by PowerPoint. (See Slide Master illustration on previous page.) The preview window in the Header and Footer dialog box also lets you see how these items appear on the slide. The date and time appear on the bottom left of the slide, footer text appears in the middle of the slide and the slide number appears on the bottom right of the slide.

- If you wish to change the location of any of these items on the slide, you must make the changes on the Slide Master. To move the slide number, for example, select the slide number placeholder (so handles appear) and drag it to a new location on the Slide Master. If you wish to center the slide number on the bottom of the slide, delete the footer placeholder and move the slide number placeholder into the bottom center position.

- You may format the slide number, date and time, and footer text just like all other text within a text placeholder.

- The actual slide number will appear on your slides when you print and during a slide show. (Presenting slide shows will be covered in Exercise 29.)

Format Bullets

- Many AutoLayout formats include bulleted body text. The bullet styles and shapes are set in the Slide Master. You can change the bullet style, size, and shape individually for each bulleted item on each slide, or you can save time and keep the format consistent by formatting bullets on the Slide Master. Bullets formatted individually after the Slide Master has been created will override formatting set in the Slide Master.

Slide Master

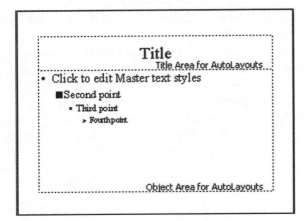

- If you wish to include text below bulleted items but would prefer no bullet on the explanatory text, you can remove the bullets. Click the Bullet On/Off button ▤ on the Formatting toolbar to turn bullets on and off on individual items or on selected text. You can also turn the bullet feature on or off by selecting or deselecting the Use a Bullet check box in the Bullet dialog box.

- To change the format and size of bullets, display the slide or Slide Master and position the insertion point in the bulleted item or bullet list level you want to change. Then select Bullet from the Format menu or right-click the mouse and select Bullet from the shortcut menu. If the insertion point is not positioned in bulleted text, and no bulleted items are selected, the option will not be available.

- In the Bullet dialog box which appears, select a desired bullet shape, Size, and Color.

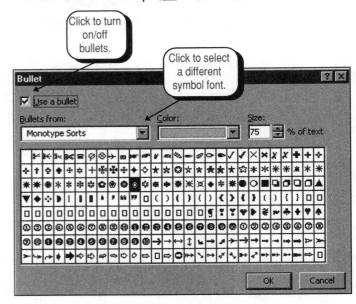

- You can select a bullet style from several character sets containing symbols and shapes (Wingdings, SymbolsA, etc). Click the Bullets from drop-down list box and select a symbol font to use.

In this exercise, you will use the Slide Master to add a graphic, change the bullets, and insert page numbers, affecting all slides in the presentation. See the Desired Result on page 87.

EXERCISE DIRECTIONS

1. Open ⌨ **INVEST**, or open 💾 **13INVEST**.

2. Change the slide template to Serene.

3. Display Rulers and Guides.

4. Switch to Title Master view.

5. Format the Title Master as follows:
   - Insert any relevant clip art to represent the company's logo. Move it to the upper left corner of the slide, as shown in the Title Master illustration on the following page. Size the image to fit in the corner as shown.
   - Delete the date/time and footer placeholders and insert a slide number (centered within its placeholder) on the bottom middle of the slide as shown.

6. Switch to Slide Master view.

7. Format the Slide Master as follows:
   - Insert the same clip art used on the Title Master. Position and size it to fit in the upper left corner of the slide as shown in the Slide Master illustration on the following page.
   - Decrease the width of the Master title style placeholder so that it does not overlap the clip art logo. Move it to the right so that its right border aligns above the right border of the body text placeholder as shown.
   - Delete the date/time and footer placeholders and insert a slide number (centered within its placeholder) on the bottom middle of the slide as shown.

8. Change the format of the bullets as follows:
   - main bullet to an envelope (Wingdings character set).
   - first subitem bullet to a mailbox (Wingdings character set).
   - fourth-level bullet to a green arrow.

9. Switch to Slide view.

10. Display Slide 2. (INVESTMENT TYPES).
    a. Move the clip art image to the far right of the slide, as shown in the Desired Result on page 87.
    b. Widen the body text placeholder by approximately .5".
    c. Select all the bulleted text and increase the paragraph spacing so that the text fills the placeholder vertically.
    d. Change the case of the slide title to title case.
    e. Use the the Decrease Font Size button on the Formatting toolbar to reduce the font size of the title text, if necessary, so that the title fits on one line.

11. Display Slide 5 (Invest Your Money...).
    - Select title text and click the Decrease Font Size button on the Formatting toolbar to reduce the title font size so that the title fits on one line.

12. Display Slide 3 (PORTFOLIO MANAGEMENT).
    a. Select all bulleted text and decrease its font size using the Decrease Font Size button on the Formatting toolbar.
    b. Change the case of the slide title to title case.
    c. Decrease the font size of the title text, if necessary, so that the title fits on one line.

13. Display Slide 4 (SERVICES INCLUDE).
    a. Change the case of the slide title to title case.
    b. Decrease the font size of the title text, if necessary, so that the title fits on one line.

14. View the presentation in Black and White.

15. Switch to Slide Sorter view and compare your presentation to the Desired Result on page 87.

16. Print one copy as Handouts (6 slides per page) in Black and White.

17. Close the file; save the changes.

TITLE MASTER

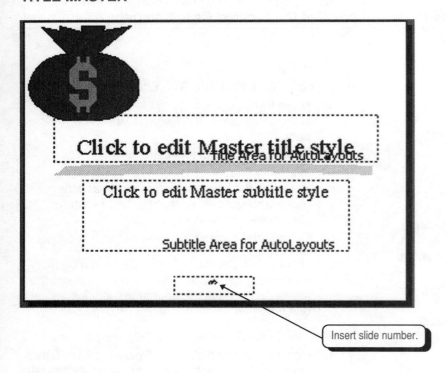

SLIDE MASTER

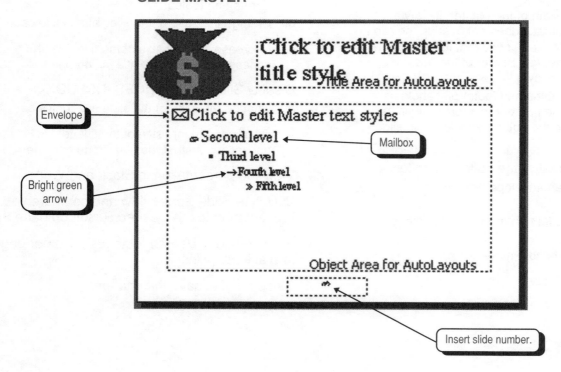

Bull Market Investments

Caroline Murphy, President

1

1

Investment Types

⊠Fixed Income

⊠Equities

⊠Mutual Funds

⊠Commodity Funds

⊠Emerging Market Funds

2

2

Portfolio Management

⊠Minimum of $250,000 invested

⊠Personal risk analysis

⊠Diversified portfolio strategy

⊠Quarterly account statements

3

3

Services Include

⊠Private financial evaluation

⊠Various mutual fund investments

⊠Retirement savings planning

⊠Tax-deferred investment options

4

4

Invest Your Money with Us

⊠Proven growth track record

⊠25% returns per year for past three years

⊠Estate planning

⊠Diversified investment planning

5

5

KEYSTROKES

FORMAT TEXT ON SLIDE OR TITLE MASTER

1. Open the desired presentation or create a new presentation.
2. Click **V**iew .... `Alt`+`V`
3. Click **M**aster .... `M`
4. Click **S**lide Master .... `S`
   OR
   Click **T**itle Master .... `T`
5. Select placeholder to change.
   OR
   Select text level to change.
6. Format font, size, alignment, enhancements, slide background, color scheme, template and other elements as desired.
7. Click `⊟` .... `Alt`+`V`, `S`
   to switch to Slide view.

OMIT MASTER SLIDE OBJECTS

1. Display slide on which to omit Slide Master objects.
2. Click **F**ormat .... `Alt`+`O`, `K`
   Background.
3. Select **Omit background** .... `Alt`+`G`
   graphics from the Master.
4. Click **A**pply .... `Alt`+`A`

SAVE A PRESENTATION OR MASTER AS TEMPLATE

1. Click **F**ile .... `Alt`+`F`
2. Click Save **A**s .... `A`
3. Select Save as **t**ype .... `Alt`+`T`
4. Select Presentation Template .... `↑` `↓`
5. Select File **n**ame .... `Alt`+`N`
6. Type a file name .... *name*
   for the template.
7. Click **S**ave .... `Enter`

INSERT PAGE NUMBERS, DATE AND TIME, AND OTHER FOOTER TEXT

1. Click **V**iew .... `Alt`+`V`
2. Click **H**eader and Footer .... `H`
3. Click **Slide** tab.
4. Click **D**ate and time .... `Alt`+`D`
   to insert date and/or time.
   a. Select **U**pdate .... `Alt`+`U`
      automatically to have date/time update each time you open the presentation.
   b. Click the drop-down list arrow and select a date/time format.
   OR
   a. Select Fi**x**ed .... `Alt`+`X`
      to insert a fixed date/time.
   b. Type date/time you want ..... *date/time* displayed in text box.
5. Click **Slide n**umber .... `Alt`+`N`
   to add slide numbers.
6. Click **F**ooter .... `Alt`+`F`
   and type footer text in text box, if desired.
7. Click **Don't show on** .... `Alt`+`S`
   title slide to omit footer contents on the Title slide.
8. Click App**l**y to all .... `Alt`+`Y`
   OR
   Click **A**pply .... `Alt`+`A`

   ✓ *Actual slide numbers will display when printing or during a slide show.*

TURN BULLETS ON/OFF

1. Position insertion point in bulleted item.
   OR
   Select multiple bulleted items.
2. Click the **Bullets** button `▤` on the Formatting toolbar.
   OR
   a. Click F**o**rmat, **B**ullet ... `Alt`+`O`, `B`
   b. Click **U**se a Bullet .... `Alt`+`U`
   c. Click **OK** .... `Enter`

   ✓ *An X in the box beside Use a Bullet indicates that the feature is active. An empty box means the feature is inactive and no bullet will appear.*

CHANGE BULLET CHARACTER

1. Position insertion point in desired bulleted item or select several bulleted items.
2. Right-click and select **B**ullet .... `B`
   from the shortcut menu.
   OR
   a. Click F**o**rmat .... `Alt`+`O`
   b. Click **B**ullet .... `B`
3. Click **B**ullets from .... `Alt`+`B`
   list to select desired character set.
4. Select desired bullet character.
5. Click **OK** .... `Enter`

CHANGE BULLET SIZE/COLOR

1. Position insertion point in bulleted item to change or select several bulleted items.
2. Right-click and select **B**ullet .... `B`
   from the shortcut menu.
   OR
   a. Click F**o**rmat .... `Alt`+`O`
   b. Click **B**ullet .... `B`
   To change bullet size:
   a. Select **S**ize box .... `Alt`+`S`
      in upper right corner.
   b. Type desired percentage .... *number* of original size.
   OR
   Click `⬍` to increase or decrease bullet size.
   To change bullet color:
   a. Click in the **C**olor .... `Alt`+`C`
      drop-down list box.
   b. Select the desired color.
3. Click **OK** .... `Enter`

NEXT EXERCISE

Exercise 14

■ Summary

In this exercise, you will create a logo using clip art and a text box and place them on the Slide Master. You will then view each slide in your presentation to see their effects. See the Desired Result on page 92.

EXERCISE DIRECTIONS

1. Open ⌨ **GYM**, or open 💾 **14GYM**.

2. Switch to Slide Master view.

3. Display Rulers and Guides.

4. Format the Slide Master as shown in Illustration A on the following page. Illustration B shows results of any changes made on the Slide Master.

   a. Shorten the title placeholder so that it is approximately 5½" wide and center it on the slide. Reduce the title text font size, if necessary, so that the title fits on the slide properly.

   b. Insert a relevant picture from the Clip Gallery. Position it and size it to fit in the upper right corner of the slide, as shown.

   c. Using the Text Box button, create a text placeholder and insert the words, "New World," in sans serif 24-point bold italics. Resize the text box so that the text fits on one line. Color the text yellow and position it in the middle of the clip art image as shown.

   d. Using the Text Box button, create a text placeholder with the words, "A New Way of Life," (include the quotation marks with the text) in sans serif 28 point. Resize the text placeholder so that all text fits on one line. Color the text green and position it at the bottom center of the slide as shown.

   e. Change the format of the main bullet to a green smiling face (Wingdings character set).

5. Switch to Slide view.

6. Display Slide 3 (New World Gym Membership).
   - Reduce the size of the text placeholder so that the text appears centered on the slide.

7. Display Slide 1 (New World Gym).
   - Delete the sub-title placeholder.

8. Compare your presentation to the Desired Result on page 92. Make any necessary adjustments to text placeholders and/or font sizes so that all text fits properly on each slide.

9. Print one copy as Handouts (6 slides per page) in Black and White.

10. Close the file; save the changes.

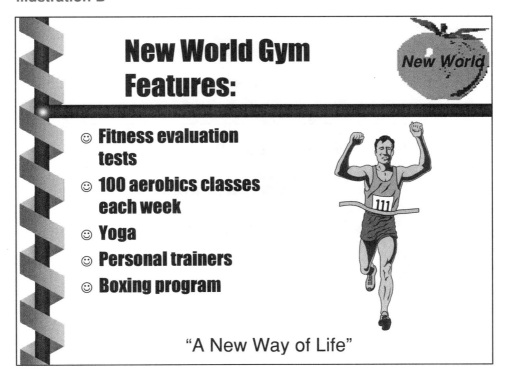

DESIRED RESULT

1

2

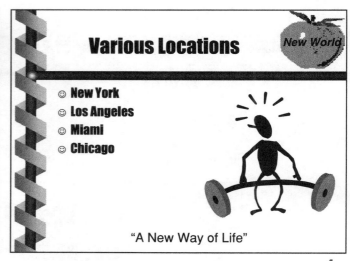

3

Slide 4 content (Various Locations):

Various Locations

New World

☺ New York
☺ Los Angeles
☺ Miami
☺ Chicago

"A New Way of Life"

4

What Makes Us Different...

New World

☺ Open 24 hours each day
☺ Spa café with nutrition clinics

"A New Way of Life"

5

NEXT EXERCISE

Exercise

15

■ **Summary**

In this exercise, you will create a logo using clip art and a text box and place them on the Slide Master. You will then view each slide in your presentation to see their effects. See the Desired Result on page 96.

EXERCISE DIRECTIONS

1. Open ⌨ **DENVER**, or open 💾 **15DENVER**.

2. Switch to Slide Master view.

3. Display Rulers and Guides.

4. Format the Slide Master as shown in Illustration A on the following page. Illustration B shows the results of changes made on the Slide Master.

   a. Shorten the title placeholder so that it is approximately 5" wide. Move it to the right side of the slide so that its right border is aligned above the right border of the body text placeholder, as shown.

   b. Insert a relevant picture from the Clip Gallery. Position it and resize it to fit in the upper left corner of the slide, as shown.

   c. Using the Text Box button, create a text placeholder and insert "Visit Us Out West!" in serif 28-point bold. Resize the placeholder so that text fits on one or two lines. Center the text within the graphic as shown and color it pink.

   d. Using the Text Box button, create a text placeholder with the words, "Denver, the vacation you've been searching for…" in 28-point serif bold italics. Color the text pink. Resize the text placeholder so that all text fits on one line. Position the placeholder at the bottom center of the slide as shown.

   e. Change the format of the main bullet to a pink flag (Wingdings character set).

5. Switch to Slide Sorter view.

6. Compare your presentation to the Desired Result on page 96. Make any necessary adjustments to text placeholders and/or font sizes so that all text fits properly on each slide.

7. Print one copy as Handouts (6 slides per page) in Pure Black and White.

8. Close the file; save the changes.

Illustration A

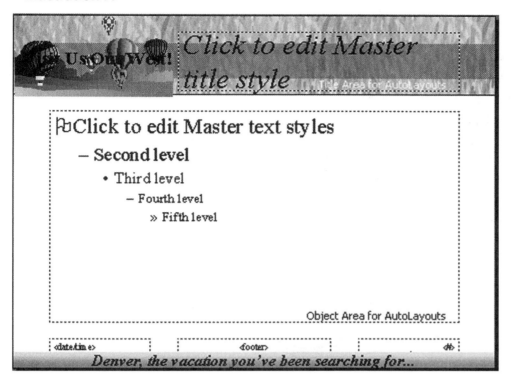

Illustration B

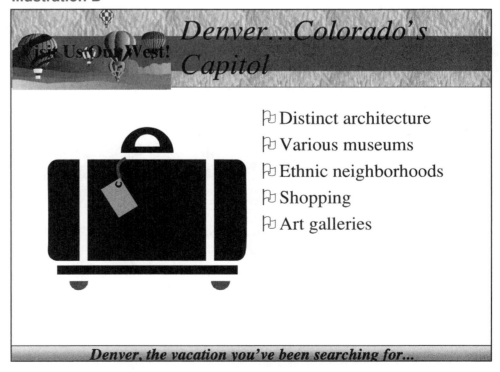

Desired Result

1

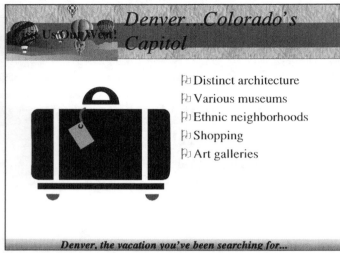

2

Museums

🐾Denver Art Museum
🐾Colorado History Museum
🐾Museum of Western Art

Denver, the vacation you've been searching for...

3

Denver's Architecture

🐾Colorado State Capitol
was built in Federal
Revival style
🐾Denver City and
County Building was
built in 1932 in
Neoclassical style
🐾90% of the structures
in the LoDo region of
Denver are historic

Denver, the vacation you've been searching for...

4

Shopping

🐾 Contemporary folk art
🐾 Spanish colonial and
southwestern antiques
🐾 Southwestern pottery
🐾 Turquoise jewelry

Denver, the vacation you've been searching for...

5

Lesson 3
Object Slides;
Linking and Embedding Slide Objects

Exercise 16

■ Insert a Chart

Standard Toolbar

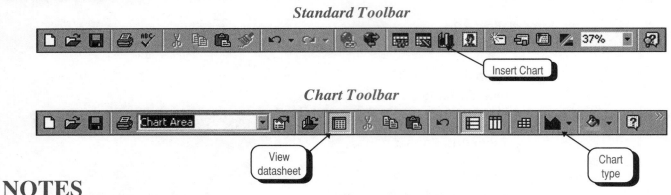

Chart Toolbar

NOTES

Insert a Chart

■ A chart may be added to a PowerPoint slide by importing one that was already created in Excel *(importing objects from other programs will be covered in Exercise 19),* or by using the Chart feature in PowerPoint to create one.

　✓ *Note: PowerPoint charts are created in MS Graph, a program that comes with Office 97. MS Graph must be installed for the chart feature to work.*

■ To create a chart in PowerPoint, double-click a graph placeholder on an AutoLayout slide.

■ Or to insert a chart without using a placeholder, select Chart from the Insert menu, or click the Insert Chart button 📊 on the Standard toolbar.

■ A datasheet window displays (see below) along with a Chart toolbar (see above) that replaces the Standard toolbar. Several charting features will also appear on the Formatting toolbar.

■ Enter the data you wish to chart (and delete the sample data) in the datasheet. The chart will reflect the new data. Click on the slide (not the chart) to hide the datasheet. To see the datasheet again, double-click the chart.

Text and Chart AutoLayout Slide

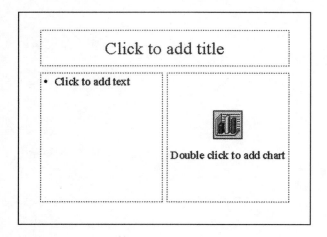

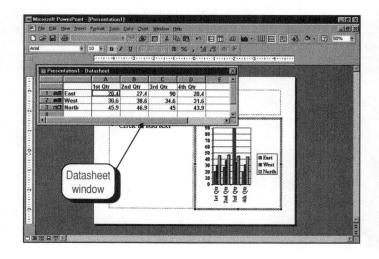

- The default chart type is 3-D Column. However, you may change the chart type before or after you enter data in the datasheet by clicking the chart on the slide and selecting Chart Type from the Chart menu, and then selecting either the Standard Types or Custom Types tab from the Chart Type dialog box.

Chart Type Dialog Box

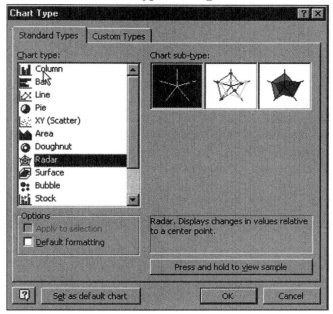

- Or, you can click the list arrow next to the Chart Type button [icon] on the Chart toolbar, and then select one of the chart types from the choices on the drop-down palette that appears.

- You may enhance your chart with a title and/or data labels. Data labels allow you to indicate the exact value of each data point. Follow the procedures outlined in the Keystrokes section on page 102 to insert and edit a chart title and data labels.

- You can also rotate and change the elevation of 3-D (three dimensional) graphs so that they present a different angle of the data. To do so, select the chart. Then, select 3-D View from the Chart menu. The preview area within the 3-D View dialog box displays the changes on the graph angle. Click Apply to apply the selected 3-D changes to your chart.

- You can resize and move a chart just like any other object. *(See Move, Size, Copy and Delete Placeholders and Other Objects in Exercise 12.)*

In this exercise, you will insert a chart slide into a previously created presentation.

EXERCISE DIRECTIONS

1. Open 🖮 **INVEST**, or open 💾 **16INVEST**.

2. Switch to Slide view.

3. Insert a New Slide and select the Chart AutoLayout.

4. Enter the slide title shown in Illustration A below and decrease the font size as needed to fit the title on one line.

5. Double-click the chart icon, delete the data from the datasheet and enter the new data shown below:

	1994	1995	1996	1997
Bull Stock Fund	10%	25%	30%	32%
Bull Bond Fund	2%	6%	7%	6%
Emerging Mkt Fund	10%	14%	16%	20%

6. Insert a chart title that reads: "Percent Return Over Four Years." Color the title text purple. Size the title text to 18 point and change the font face to Arial.

7. Include data labels in your chart (Show value).

8. Switch to Slide Sorter view.

9. Move this new slide to become Slide 4.

10. Switch to Slide Master view.

11. Move the slide number to the lower right corner of the slide.

12. Create a text placeholder and insert "Make Money!" in serif 28-point bold italics. Color the font red. Resize the text box so that text fits on one line. Position the text box as shown in the bottom center of the slide.

13. Switch to Slide view.

14. View the presentation in Black and White.

15. Print one copy as Handouts (6 slides per page) in Black and White.

16. Close the file; save the changes.

ILLUSTRATION A

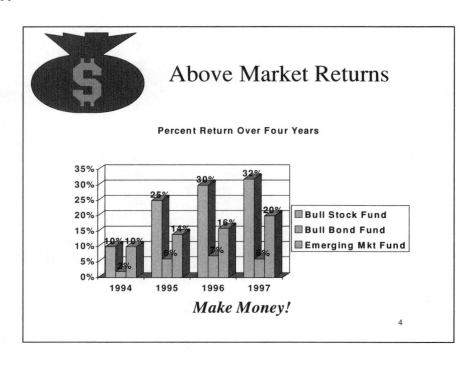

Bull Market Investments

Caroline Murphy, President

1

Investment Types

- ⌧Fixed Income
- ⌧Equities
- ⌧Mutual Funds
- ⌧Commodity Funds
- ⌧Emerging Market Funds

Make Money!

2

Portfolio Management

- ⌧Minimum of $250,000 invested
- ⌧Personal risk analysis
- ⌧Diversified portfolio strategy
- ⌧Quarterly account statements

Make Money!

3

Above Market Returns

Percent Return Over Four Years

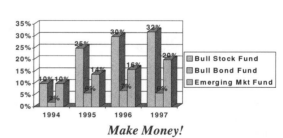

Make Money!

4

Services Include

- ⌧Private financial evaluation
- ⌧Various mutual fund investments
- ⌧Retirement savings planning
- ⌧Tax-deferred investment options

Make Money!

5

Invest Your Money with Us

- ⌧Proven growth track record
- ⌧25% returns per year for past three years
- ⌧Estate planning
- ⌧Diversified investment planning

Make Money!

6

KEYSTROKES

INSERT A CHART ON A SLIDE

1. Select a slide containing a chart placeholder from the Slide Layout dialog box and double-click the chart placeholder.

   OR

   To insert a chart without using a placeholder:

   Click the **Insert** menu ...... `Alt`+`I`, `H` and select **Chart**.

   OR

   Click **Insert Chart** .... `▦` on the Standard toolbar.

2. Delete the sample data and enter the data you wish to chart in the datasheet.

   To delete data in a Datasheet:

   a. Press **Ctrl + A** .... `Ctrl`+`A`

   b. Press **Delete** .... `Delete`

3. Click the graph to hide the datasheet.

   OR

   Click **View Datasheet** button .... `▦` in the Chart toolbar.

Select a chart type:

1. Click **Chart** .... `Alt`+`C`
2. Select **Chart Type** .... `T`
3. Select either the **Standard Types** tab or the **Custom Types** tab.
4. Select desired **Chart type** .... `Alt`+`C`
5. Select desired **Chart sub-type** .... `Alt`+`T` if necessary.
6. Click **OK** .... `Enter`

Insert a Title:

1. Click **Chart** .... `Alt`+`C`
2. Click **Chart Options** .... `O`
3. Click **Titles** tab.
4. Click **Chart title** .... `Alt`+`T`
5. Type title .... *title*
6. Click **Category (X) axis** .... `Alt`+`C`
7. Type title for x axis .... *title*
8. Click **Value (Z) axis** .... `Alt`+`V`
9. Type title for z axis .... *title*
10. Click **OK** .... `Enter`

Color Chart Title:

1. Right-click chart title.
2. Click **Format Chart Title** .... `O`
3. Click **Font** tab .... `F`
4. Click **Color** .... `Alt`+`C`
5. Select desired color.
6. Click **OK** .... `Enter`

Insert Data Labels:

1. Click **Chart** .... `Alt`+`C`
2. Click **Chart Options** .... `O`
3. Click **Data Labels** tab.
4. Select desired label type.
5. Click **OK** .... `Enter`

Change legend position:

1. Click **Chart** .... `Alt`+`C`
2. Click **Chart Options** .... `O`
3. Click **Legend** tab.
4. Select desired placement option.

   To hide the legend:

   Deselect the **Show legend** ...... `Alt`+`S` check box.

5. Click **OK** .... `Enter`

CHANGE FONT

1. Right-click chart item to be changed.
2. Click **Format Legend** .... `O` or **Format Axis**, or **Format Chart Title**, or **Format Data Labels**.
3. Click **Font** tab .... `Ctrl`+`Tab`
4. Select desired font options.
5. Click **OK** .... `Enter`

NEXT EXERCISE

<table>
<tr><td rowspan="2">Exercise

17</td><td>■ **Insert a Table** ■ **Insert and Delete Columns and Rows**
■ **Change Column Width** ■ **Table AutoFormat**</td></tr>
</table>

Standard Toolbar

NOTES

Insert a Table

- A Table may be added to a PowerPoint slide by importing one that was created in Microsoft Word *(importing objects from other programs will be covered in Exercise 19),* or by using the Table feature in PowerPoint to create one.

  ✓ *Note:* *MS Word must be installed to import a table created in Word.*

- To create a Table on a slide, double-click a table placeholder on a Table AutoLayout slide. PowerPoint offers one AutoLayout slide containing a table format.

Table AutoLayout Slide

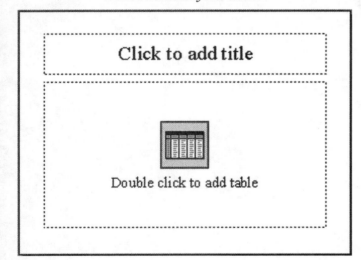

- Or, to insert a table without using a placeholder, click the Insert Word Table button 🖾 on the Standard toolbar, or select Microsoft Word Table from the Picture submenu on the Insert menu.

- After double-clicking the table placeholder or selecting Picture, Microsoft Word Table from the Insert menu, the Insert Word Table dialog box displays for you to indicate how many columns and rows you need for your table.

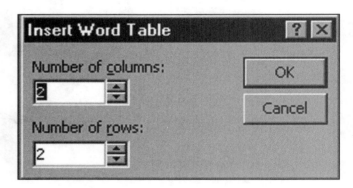

- Or, if you are using the Insert Microsoft Word Table button 🖾 on the Standard toolbar, you can drag the mouse across the grid to indicate the number of rows and columns you desire.

- Once you have selected the number of rows and columns, a table displays on your slide, and PowerPoint's toolbars and Menu bar are temporarily replaced by Word's toolbars and Menu bar. This enables you to use Word's table editing features inside PowerPoint.

- Click in a cell and enter the desired text. Press the Tab key to move the insertion point from cell to cell.

- After you have entered all table text, click on the slide containing the table to return to PowerPoint, or press Escape. You can return to the table and make changes at any time by double-clicking inside the table.

- If you use a Table AutoLayout slide to insert your table, the columns and rows will be evenly spaced within the table placeholder. You can also adjust the column widths if you choose *(see Change Column Width, in this exercise).*

- If you create your table on a slide not containing a table placeholder and use the grid to create the columns and rows, you may need to reposition or resize the table on the slide. To reposition the table, click within the table and drag it to the desired position. To resize a table, drag a handle. You may also need to adjust column widths *(see Change Column Width, in this exercise).*

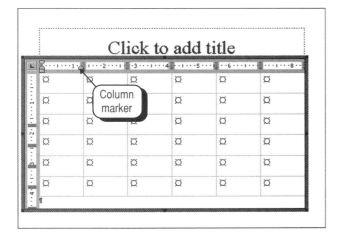

Insert and Delete Columns and Rows

- To insert a row, select Insert Rows from the Table menu or right-click a cell and select Insert Rows. A new row will be inserted above the insertion point position.

- To insert a column, highlight the column to the right of the column to be inserted. Then, select Insert Columns from the Table menu or right-click and select Insert Columns.

- To delete a column, highlight the column to be deleted, right-click and select Delete Columns.

- To delete a row, click in the row to delete, right-click and select Delete Cells. In the Delete Cells dialog box that follows, select Delete entire row.

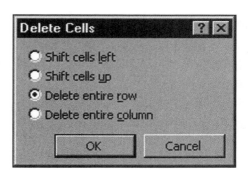

Change Column Width

- Column width may be changed using a specific measurement or by dragging the column marker located on the Ruler in the Table window *(see illustration to the left)* to the desired width.

- To adjust column widths and see the immediate effect of the change on the table as it is being made, position the mouse pointer on the column marker. When the mouse pointer changes to a double-headed arrow, press and hold the mouse as you drag the column marker left or right to the desired width or table size.

- You can also adjust column widths and margins within the table using a specific measurement. Select Cell Height and Width from the Table menu. In the Cell Height and Width dialog box that follows, click the Column tab and type the desired measurement in the Width box.

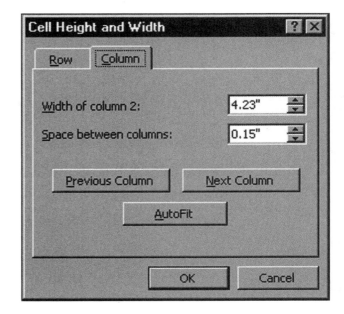

Table AutoFormat

■ The AutoFormat feature within Microsoft Word provides predefined formatting styles to apply to your table.

■ Select Table AutoFormat from the Table menu to access AutoFormat. In the Table AutoFormat dialog box that follows, available styles are listed on the left, and a preview window displays the selected style on the right. Click OK to apply the selected format to your table.

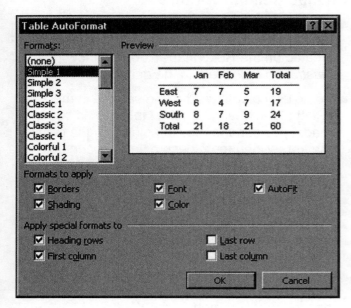

EXERCISE DIRECTIONS

1. Open ⌨ **HORSE**, or open 💾 **17HORSE**.

2. Display Slide 5 (Three Day Eventing).

3. Delete the clip art placeholder and the text placeholder.

4. Apply the Table Slide AutoLayout to Slide 5.

5. Enter the table data as shown in Illustration A, below.
   a. Create 3 columns and 4 rows.
   b. Set text to Jester or any other decorative font. Use 32-point bold for Row 1; set rows 2-4 to 28 point (without bold).
   c. Color all the table text red.
   d. Center column headings.
   e. Set column widths as follows:
      - Columns 1 and 2: 2.8"
      - Column 3: 3.7"
   f. Apply an AutoFormat to the table.

6. Undo the Table AutoFormat.

7. Reposition the table, if necessary, so that it is centered on the slide as shown.

8. Switch to Slide Master view.

9. Change the format of the main bullet to a light green smiling face (Wingdings character set).

10. Insert a slide number in the bottom right corner of every slide.

11. Switch to Slide view.

12. View the presentation in Black and White.

13. Print one copy as Handouts (6 slides per page) in Black and White.

14. Close the file; save the changes.

Illustration A

Three-day Eventing		
Phase	**Event**	**Objective**
Phase 1	Dressage	To demonstrate harmony between horse and rider.
Phase 2	Endurance	To prove the speed, endurance and cross country jumping ability of horse.
Phase 3	Stadium Jumping	To test the horse's ability to perform after the endurance competition.

5

Desired Result

The Equestrian Sport

A Guide to Horseback Riding
Gallop Riding Academy

1

1

Equestrian Events in the Olympics

☺ Equestrian Events in the Olympics for the first time in 1912
   – Held in Stockholm, Sweden
   – 88 horses competed from 8 different nations
☺ Three-day Eventing
☺ Show Jumping
☺ Dressage

2

2

Dressage

☺ Originates from Ancient Greece
☺ Tests horse's physique and ability
☺ Demonstrates high degree of understanding between horse and rider

3

3

Show Jumping

☺Must complete course in designated time
☺Rider accumulates "faults" for errors

4

4

Three-day Eventing

Phase	Event	Objective
Phase 1	Dressage	To demonstrate harmony between horse and rider.
Phase 2	Endurance	To prove the speed, endurance and cross country jumping ability of horse.
Phase 3	Stadium Jumping	To test the horse's ability to perform after the endurance competition.

5

5

Care of the Horse

☺ Grooming Tools
☺ Veterinary Supplies
☺ Health and Maintenance

6

6

Riding Basics

7

Riding Attire

☺English riding hard hat

☺Hunt boots

☺Paddock boots

8

Tacking Up

☺Saddle

☺Bridle

☺Girth

9

Riding Levels

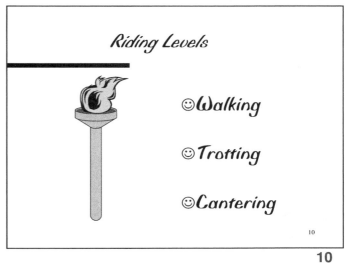

☺Walking

☺Trotting

☺Cantering

10

Conclusion

☺ Ride at Gallop Riding Academy
  – Expert riding instructors
  – Modern boarding facilities
  – Indoor riding arena

11

KEYSTROKES

INSERT A TABLE ON A SLIDE

1. Select a slide layout containing a table placeholder.
2. Enter the title in the title placeholder.
3. Double-click the table placeholder.
4. Enter desired **Number of columns**.
5. Enter desired **Number of rows**.
6. Click **OK**... `Enter`
7. Click the first cell and enter desired text.
8. Press **Tab** .... `Tab`
   to advance to the next cell.
   OR
   Press **Shift + Tab** .... `Shift`+`Tab`
   to move to the previous cell.
9. Click on slide to insert table and return to PowerPoint.

OR

To insert a table without using a placeholder:

1. Click the **Insert Microsoft Word Table** button ▦ on the Standard toolbar and drag to highlight desired number of columns and rows.
   OR
   a. Click **Insert** .... `Alt`+`I`
   b. Click **Picture** .... `P`
   c. Click **Microsoft Word Table** .... `T`
   d. Enter desired **Number of columns**.
   e. Enter desired **Number of rows**.
   f. Click **OK** .... `Enter`
2. Click the first cell and enter desired text.
3. Press **Tab** .... `Tab`
   to advance to the next cell.
   OR
   Press **Shift + Tab** .... `Shift`+`Tab`
   to move to the previous cell.
4. Click on slide to insert table and return to PowerPoint.

INSERT COLUMNS/ROWS

-COLUMNS-

1. Double-click the table in PowerPoint.
2. Select the column to the right of the new column you wish to insert.
   OR
   a. Click in the cell to the right of the new column you wish to insert.
   b. Click **Table** .... `Alt`+`A`
   c. Click **Select Column** .... `C`
3. Click **Table** .... `Alt`+`A`
4. Click **Insert Columns**...................... `I`

-ROWS-

1. Double-click the table in PowerPoint.
2. Click in the cell below the new row you wish to insert.
3. Click **Table** .... `Alt`+`A`
4. Click **Insert Rows** .... `I`

DELETE COLUMNS/ROWS

1. Double-click the table in PowerPoint.
2. Select the columns or rows to delete.
3. Click **Table** .... `Alt`+`A`
4. Click **Delete Columns** .... `D`
   OR
   Click **Delete Rows**......................... `D`

CHANGE COLUMN WIDTH

1. Double-click the table on the slide.
2. Select the column for which you want to change the width.
3. Click **Table** .... `Alt`+`A`
4. Click **Cell Height and Width**........... `W`
5. Click the **Column** tab .... `Alt`+`C`
6. Click the **Width** text box .... `Alt`+`W`
7. Type new width .... *number*
   OR
   Click arrow buttons to change width incrementally.
8. Click **OK**... `Enter`

TABLE AUTOFORMAT

1. Double-click the table in PowerPoint.
2. Click **Table** .... `Alt`+`A`
3. Click **Table AutoFormat** .... `F`
4. Make desired changes.
5. Click **OK**.. `Enter`

NEXT EXERCISE

Exercise 18

■ Insert an Organization Chart

Organization Chart Toolbar

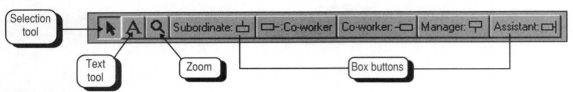

NOTES

- An **Organization Chart** is used to illustrate a company's hierarchy or structure.

- Organization charts may also be used to show the flow of a project or a family tree.

- PowerPoint contains an Organization Chart AutoLayout. To create an organization chart, select the organization chart AutoLayout and double-click on the organization chart placeholder icon.

Organization Chart AutoLayout

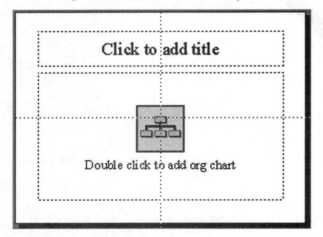

- Or, to create an organization chart without using a placeholder, click the Insert menu and select Picture, Organization Chart. The Microsoft Organization Chart window opens.

- By default, four boxes display. However, you can attach additional boxes to existing boxes using the box buttons on the Organization Chart toolbar *(see above).*

MS Organization Chart Window

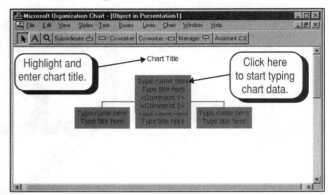

- Note that there are four box types: Manager, Subordinate, Co-Worker and Assistant; each box type attaches to the existing boxes differently. Click a box type button on the toolbar, then click in the box on the organization chart to which to attach it.

- You can also rearrange boxes. To do so, click the box you wish to move and select Cut from the Edit menu. Then, click in the box to which you wish to attach the cut box and select Paste from the Edit menu.

- You can enter up to four lines of text in each box. As you type, the box will adjust its size to fit the text. Click in each box to replace the sample text with your own.

- Each box can be formatted with different fonts, font sizes, fill colors and borders. In addition, text can be aligned left, center or right within each box.

- To change font attributes, highlight the text to receive the change, and select Font from the Text menu. In the Font dialog box that follows, make the desired changes.

- To change text alignment, click the box to receive the alignment change, then select Left, Right or Center from the Text menu.

- To change box colors, click in the box to receive the change, and select Color from the Boxes menu. Select a new color from the Color dialog box that follows. To change border colors, select Border Color from the Boxes menu and select a new color from the Color dialog box.

Color Dialog Box

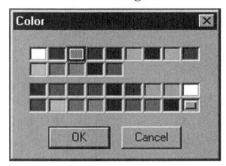

- To change box border style, select Border Style from the Boxes menu and select a new style from the submenu.

Border Style Drop-Down Menu

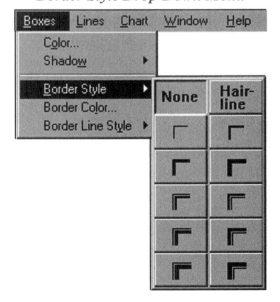

- Select Border Line Style from the Boxes menu to choose a dashed or solid border line style.

Border Line Style Drop-Down Menu

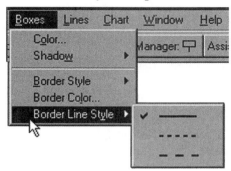

- When you are finished entering and editing data in your organization chart, click File, Exit and Return to Presentation. To return to the MS organization Chart window at any time, double-click on the chart.

In this exercise, you will insert an organization chart slide and a chart slide to a previously created presentation.

EXERCISE DIRECTIONS

1. Open ⌨ **RECRUIT**, or open 💾 **18RECRUIT**.

2. Switch to Slide view.

3. Display Slide 8 (Corporate Recruiters). Delete the bulleted list placeholder.

4. Apply the Organization Chart AutoLayout to Slide 8.

5. Enter the organization chart title and data shown in Illustration A. Use a sans serif font.

   ✓ *Note: Add Assistant boxes to include third-level information.*

6. Insert a New Slide and select the Chart AutoLayout.

7. Enter the slide title shown in Illustration B on the following page.

8. Delete the sample data from the datasheet and enter the following new data:

	1994	1995	1996	YTD 1997
No. Offers Made	50	37	40	2
No. Offers Accepted	25	30	34	0

9. Title the chart, "Number Offers Made vs. Number Offers Accepted."

10. Switch to Slide Sorter view.

11. Move the chart slide to become Slide 8 and the organization slide to become Slide 9 (the last slide).

12. Switch to Slide Master view.

13. Shorten the title placeholder to approximately 5 ½" wide. Position it on the top right of the slide so that its right border aligns above the right border of the body text placeholder.

14. Delete the date placeholder. Insert a black slide number at the bottom left on the slide.

15. Switch to Title Master view.

16. Shorten the title placeholder to approximately 5 ½". Position it on the top right of the slide so that the right border aligns above the right border of the sub-title placeholder.

17. Switch to Slide view.

18. Review each slide. If necessary, make adjustments to text placeholders so that text fits properly on each slide as shown in the Desired Result on pages 116 and 117.

19. Print one copy as Handouts (6 slides per page) in Black and White.

20. Close the file; save the changes.

Illustration A

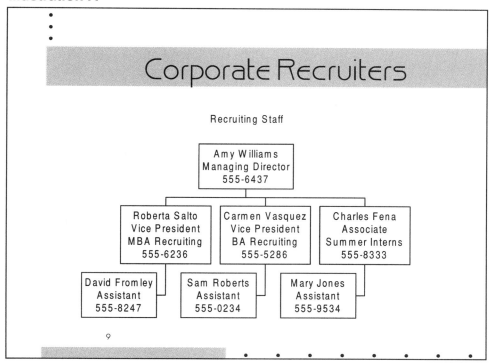

Illustration B

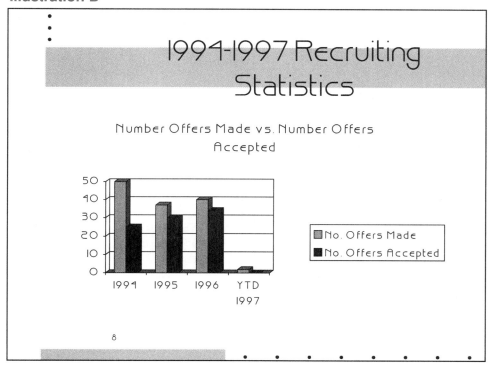

Desired Result

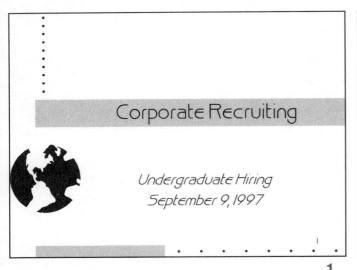

1

2

Recruiting Initiatives

☐ Ways to make company more appealing to undergraduates
☐ Women's panels
☐ On-campus interviewing
☐ Internet home page

3

3

1996 Recruiting Results

☐ 18 women and 16 men hired into training program
☐ 25% from West Coast
☐ 23% from Midwest
☐ 30% from East Coast
☐ 22% international
☐ 50% of hires former summer interns

4

4

1997 Recruiting Season

☐ Received 2578 resumes
☐ Interviewed 68 candidates
☐ Extended 2 offers
☐ 1997 target of 25 new hires

5

5

Internal Recruiting Initiatives

☐ Conduct interviewing skills workshops for group leaders who interview candidates

☐ Set up "round robin" interview format

☐ Create BA video to be shown on campuses

☐ Create network of mentors for new hires

6

6

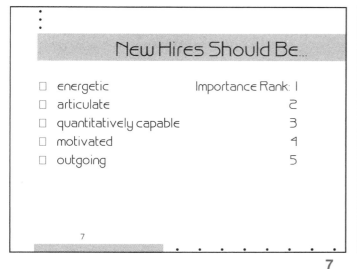

7

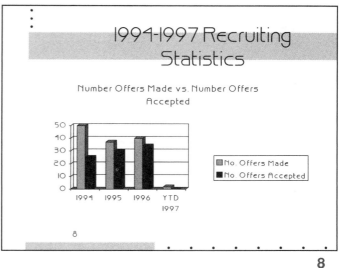

8

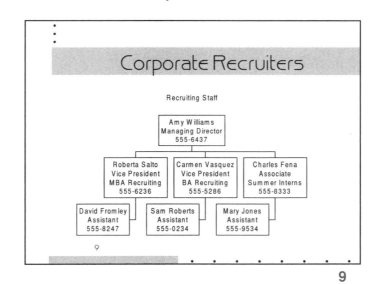

9

KEYSTROKES

INSERT AN ORGANIZATION CHART

1. Select a the Organization Chart Layout and double-click the Organization Chart placeholder icon.

   OR

   To insert an organization chart without using a placeholder:

   Click the **Insert**........ Alt + I , P , O menu and select **Picture**, **Organization Chart**.

2. Select box in which to enter text.

3. Type name and press **Enter**.......*name,* Enter

4. Type title and press **Enter**..........*name,* Enter

5. Type comment........................*text,* Enter (if desired) and press **Enter**.

6. Click another box and repeat steps 3-5.

   OR

Click outside the box to close box.

To Insert a Box:

a. Click the appropriate button on the Organization Chart toolbar for the box you wish to attach.

b. Click existing box to which you wish to attach new one.

To Rearrange Boxes:

a. Select the box to be moved.

b. Click **Edit**, **Cut**.............. Alt + E , T

c. Place cursor in box to which to attach cut box.

d. Click **Edit**, **Paste**......... Alt + E , P

7. Click **File**.............................. Alt + F

8. Click **Exit and Return** .... X to **Presentation**.

Exercise 19

■ Paste, Link and Embed Objects

NOTES

Paste, Link and Embed Objects

■ As indicated in the previous exercises, you can create a table and/or a chart (from worksheet data) in PowerPoint and place either on a PowerPoint slide, or you can import these and other objects from other programs.

■ The file that contains the original object is called the *source file.*

■ The file into which you are inserting the object is called the *destination file.*

■ There are three ways to add an object from another program to a slide: paste, link or embed it.

■ When you **paste** an object from another program into a slide, it is converted to a PowerPoint object and becomes part of the current presentation.

■ To paste an object from another program, you can cut or copy the object from one program and then paste it into a PowerPoint slide using the Cut, Copy and Paste buttons on the source and destination toolbars.

■ When you add an object to a slide and **link** it, the object maintains a connection to its source file and is not converted to a PowerPoint object. So any changes you make to the source file are automatically updated in the destination file. When you double-click the object, the source document opens, where you can edit the object.

■ To link a file, select the object in the source document you want to link, click the Copy button in the source document and switch to the presentation (the destination file). Select Paste Special from the Edit menu. In the Paste Special dialog box that follows, click Paste link.

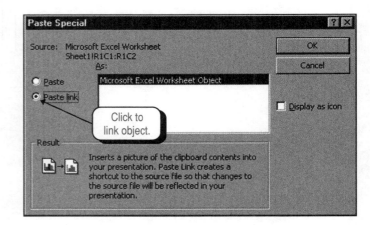

■ When you add an object to a slide and **embed** it, it does not maintain a link to its source document, so changes you make to the source file do not affect the destination file. But, unlike a pasted object, an embedded object is not converted to a PowerPoint object, so that when you double-click the object, the program of the source document is activated, where you can edit the object.

■ To embed an object created in another program, select Object from the Insert menu. In the Insert Object dialog box that follows, select the Create from file option button. Be sure the Link check box is not selected. Click Browse and select the file to insert and embed.

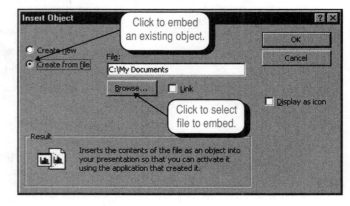

- You can also create a new object to embed by clicking the Create new option button in the Insert Object dialog box. Select the Object type to create from the list box and click OK. The program where you can create the selected object type will then open. For example, if you select a Bitmap Image, MS Paint opens. Create the object and click outside the source program window. The object is embedded and appears in the slide. You can double-click on it at any time to open the source program and edit the object.

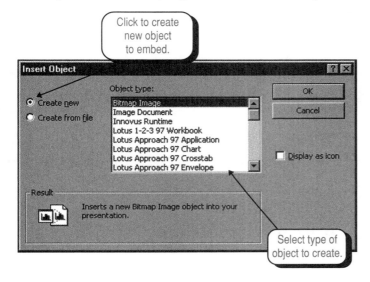

- **To embed *and* link** an object, select Object from the Insert menu, select the Create from file option button in the Insert Object dialog box, and select the Link check box. Click Browse and select the file to link and embed.

> *In this exercise you will link and embed an Excel worksheet, which has been created for you and is located on the data disk.*

EXERCISE DIRECTIONS

1. Open ⌨ **DENVER**, or open 💾 **19DENVER**.

2. Switch to Slide view.

3. Insert a New Slide and select the Bulleted List layout.

4. Insert the slide title as shown in Illustration A.

5. Delete the Bulleted List text placeholder.

6. Embed and link the worksheet from 💾 **19DENVER.XLS**, located on the data disk. A graph of the growth in visitors to Denver over the past 5 years should appear on your slide as shown in Illustration A. Reposition and resize the graph as necessary.

7. Double-click the graph to open **19DENVER.XLS**.

8. Click the Sheet 1 tab at the bottom of the Excel window.

9. Change the number of visitors in 1994 from 1,598,763 to 200 and the number of visitors in 1995 from 1,689,742 to 100.

10. Switch back to PowerPoint. Note the change in the Excel graph.

11. Double-click the graph to open **19DENVER.XLS**.

12. Switch the data in the Excel worksheet back to the original figures. Click the close button ☒ in the Excel window to close Excel.

13. Switch to Slide Sorter view.

14. Move the new slide to become Slide 6.

15. Switch to Slide Master view.

16. Insert slide numbers in the bottom right corner of each slide.

17. Switch to Slide view.

18. View the presentation in Black and White.

19. If necessary, make adjustments to text placeholders and/or font sizes so that all text fits properly on each slide as shown in the Desired Result on the following page.

20. Print one copy as Handouts (6 slides per page) in Black and White.

21. Close the file; save the changes.

Illustration A

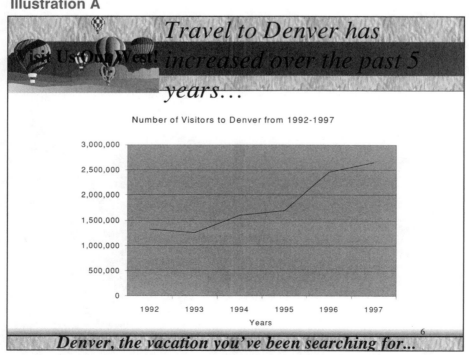

120

Desired Result

1

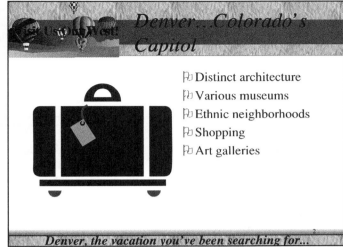

2

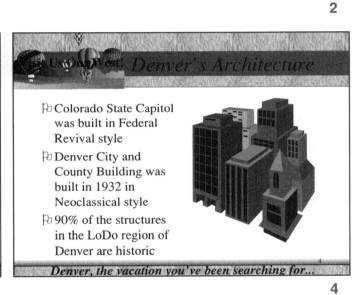

3

4

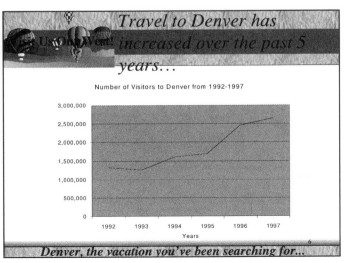

5

6

KEYSTROKES

PASTE AN OBJECT

1. Select the object to paste from the source file.
2. Click the **Copy** button .... 🔲

   OR

   a. Click **E**dit .... Ctrl + E

   b. Click **C**opy C

   OR

   a. Right-click mouse.

   b. Click **C**opy C

3. Display the slide on which to paste the object.
4. Click the **Paste** button .... 🔲

   OR

   a. Click **E**dit .... Ctrl + E

   b. Click **P**aste .... P

   OR

   a. Right-click mouse where you want object placed.

   b. Click **P**aste .... P

LINK AN OBJECT

1. Select the object to link from the source file.
2. Click the **Copy** button .... 🔲

   OR

   a. Click **E**dit .... Ctrl + E

   b. Click **C**opy C

   OR

   a. Right-click mouse.

   b. Click **C**opy C

3. Display the slide on which to place the object.
4. Click **E**dit .... Alt + E
5. Click **Paste Special** .... S
6. Click **Paste link** button .... Alt + L
7. Select from **As** box .... Alt + A
   the appropriate paste object.
8. Click **OK** .... Enter

EMBED AN OBJECT

Create New:

1. Click **I**nsert .... Alt + I
2. Click **O**bject .... O
3. Click **Create new** .... Alt + N
4. Click **Object type** list box .... Alt + T
5. Select application from which to create object.
6. Click **OK** .... Enter

   ✓ *The selected application will open.*

7. Create desired information.
8. Click outside the object to return to original application.

   ✓ *The object will appear on current slide.*

Create from File:

1. Click **I**nsert .... Alt + I
2. Click **O**bject .... O
3. Click **Create from file** .... Alt + F
4. Click **B**rowse .... Alt + B
5. Click **Look in** .... Alt + I
   drop-down list box.
6. Select drive containing file you want to insert.
7. Double-click folder in directories list containing file you want to insert.
8. Click file icon .... Alt + N ,*name*
   or type filename in
   File name box.
9. Click **OK** .... Enter

   To also link the object:

   Select the **Link** .... Alt + L
   check box.
10. Click **OK** .... Enter

NEXT EXERCISE

Exercise 20

■ **Summary**

In this exercise, you will create a presentation for Home Finders Realty, a real estate brokerage firm that wants real estate investors to use its services. This presentation will include table, chart, and organization chart slides. You will use the Slide and Title Masters to include information on all slides. Note: If you do not have Excel installed on your computer, do not create Slide 6.

EXERCISE DIRECTIONS

1. Create a new Template presentation; use the Serene template design.

2. Switch to Title Master view.

   a. Delete the date placeholder and insert a slide number in the bottom left corner of the slide as shown in Illustration A on the following page.

   b. Create the logos shown in Illustration A on the top and bottom right corners.
      - Color the HF logo orange.
   ✔ *Note: To create the HF logo on the top right, create two separate text boxes and enter the letter H in one and F in the other. Size "H" to 54 point and "F" to 40 point. Then move the text boxes to position the letters as shown in Illustration A.*

      - Insert any relevant graphic from the Clip Gallery as the bottom right logo. Position and resize the image to fit in the bottom right corner as shown.

   c. Copy the HF logo.
   ✔ *(Hint: Shift-click each text box to select both boxes, then click the Copy button on the Standard toolbar.)*

3. Switch to Slide Master view.
   - Paste the HF logo in the same position as on Slide 1.

4. Switch back to Title Master view.
   - Copy the clip art image.

5. Switch to Slide Master view.

   a. Delete the date placeholder and insert a slide number in the bottom left corner of the slide.

   b. Paste the clip art logo in the same position as on the Title Master.

   c. Change the first two default bullet styles to another desired style.

   d. Resize the title placeholder so it does not interfere with the HF logo.

6. Switch to Slide view.

7. Create the presentation shown in Illustration B on page 126, using the appropriate slide layouts. Note the special instructions below for Slides 3, 4 and 6.

   a. On Slide 3, use the names and titles below for the organization chart.
      - Walter James, President
      - Carmen Enton, Vice President
      - Henry Chu, Vice President
      - Jason LoBue, Vice President
      - Eileen Waters, Associate
      - Naomi Kahn, Associate
      - David Cohen, Associate
      - Resize and position the chart as necessary so that it does not overlap the logo.

b. On Slide 4, use the data below to create the chart. Include the following chart title: "Average Value of 1 & 2 Bedroom Apts in NYC ('000)."

	1993	1994	1995	1996	1997
1 BR	75	99	85	125	150
2 BR	100	125	115	150	175

c. On Slide 6, use a Title Only layout. Insert the slide title shown on Slide 6 in Illustration B.
   - Embed and link the pie chart from the 🖫 **20HOUSE.XLS** file provided on the data disk. The chart shown on Slide 6 in Illustration B should appear.
   - Resize and move the chart so that it is centered on the slide.

8. Display each slide.
   - Adjust the size and placement of placeholders and/or adjust the font size of the titles so that text fits properly on each slide and does not interfere with the logos.

9. Display Slide 7.
   - Color the bulleted text pink.

10. Open **20HOUSE.XLS** and click the Sheet 1 tab at the bottom of the window to display the Excel worksheet. Change the values to 5 for 1BR, 5 for 2BR, 5 for 3BR, 5 for 4BR, and 80 for Studio.

11. Display Slide 6. Note the changes in the pie chart.

12. Print one copy of Slide 6.

13. Change the values on the Excel worksheet back to their original numbers.

14. Display Slide 6. Note the changes in the pie chart.

15. Spell check.

16. Save the file; name it **HOUSE**. Accept the default summary information.

17. Print one copy of each slide as Handouts (6 slides per page) in Black and White.

18. Close the presentation window.

Illustration A

$$H_F$$

Home Finders Realty

New York Real Estate Brokerage
December 1997

Illustration B

Home Finders Realty

New York Real Estate Brokerage
December 1997

1

1

Let us find you a home...

- Offices in all 5 NYC boroughs
- Computerized searches of all apartments listed for sale
- Mortgage advising
- Listings of houses, cooperatives and condominiums
- Small commission fees

2

2

Set up an appointment with any member of our team...

```
                    Walter James
                     President
                         |
        ------------------------------------
        |                |                 |
  Carmen Enton      Henry Chu        Jason LoBue
  Vice President   Vice President   Vice President
        |                |                 |
  Eileen Waters     Naomi Kahn       David Cohen
   Associate        Associate         Associate
```

3

3

NY real estate has grown in value for the past 5 years...

Average Value of 1 & 2 Bedroom Apts in NYC
('000)

200
150
100
50
0
1993 1994 1995 1996 1997

■ 1 BR
■ 2 BR

4

4

Vacation properties also available...

- Hamptons
- Fire Island
- Long Island
- Connecticut
- Shelter Island

5

5

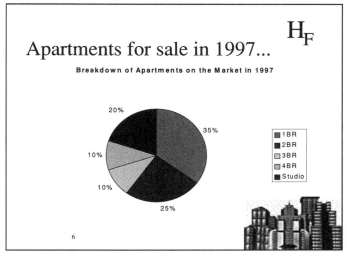

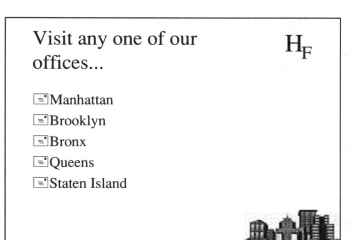

6

7

Exercise 21

■ Summary

You work for *The Food Giant Company* supermarket chain. You have been asked to create a presentation for the general public about the company's background, financial health, recent company developments and industry trends.

EXERCISE DIRECTIONS

1. Refer to the report shown in Illustration A on the following page.

2. Create a 10-slide presentation based on the information contained in the report.

3. Use any desired slide layouts to enter the information for your presentation. You must include at least one table slide, one chart slide and one organization chart slide.

4. Spell check.

5. Apply a relevant template design.

6. Include the following on the Slide and Title Master:
   - Company logo in the bottom left corner.
   - A page number in any desired position.
   - Relevant clip art in the upper right corner. (Size clip art to fit in the corner of slide as desired.)

7. Reformat all bullets and change their colors.

8. Move the slides into an appropriate order.

9. Print one copy of slides as Handouts (6 slides per page) in Black and White.

10. Save the file; name it **FOOD**.

11. Close the presentation window.

The Food Giant Company

The Industry

The supermarket industry is very mature and highly competitive. As a result, expansion in the industry is limited. Big, multi-regional food chains tend to dominate as smaller chains are increasingly being acquired by their larger competitors. The industry is experiencing a period of consolidation as mergers and acquisitions are moving the supermarket industry towards greater concentration. Big, multi-regional food chains have the advantage of geographic diversity, consumer franchises and strong cash flow. This is particularly true of supercenters. In the late 1980s and early 1990s, supercenters, stores of more than 150,000 square feet that sell both food and general merchandise, became increasingly popular. These supercenters threaten to drive smaller supermarkets out of business due to intense price and service competition. Only small chains that well utilize marketing and merchandising strategies can successfully compete with larger supermarket chains and supercenter stores. Larger chains can only compete by adapting to the development of supercenters by expanding their services.

The Company

Henry Mackler founded The Food Giant Company in 1918 when Mackler opened his first grocery store in Brooklyn, New York. Mackler expanded the company to 43 stores by the time of his death in 1942. His family has expanded the business on the East Coast since then and intends to open its first store in the West Coast next year. The Food Giant Company's headquarters remain in Brooklyn, NY and are located at 2456 Kings Highway. The Company currently operates 226 retail food stores in 6 northeastern states. It has recently made remodeling and remerchandising investments in most of its stores in an effort to improve company sales. The Food Giant Company has followed the industry trend of the supercenter and includes in most of its stores an on-site bakery, fish market, butcher, deli counter, and flower shop. Its earnings have grown each year for the past 5 years. In these years, the Company's competitors have suffered from higher operating costs and lower revenues.

Industry Comparables

Supermarket	Period	No. of Stores	Food Sales Per Store ($ Mil)	Net Sales ($ Mil)	% Change
The Food Giant	1997	226	18.1	4090	8.1
	1996	215	17.6	3784	7.6
Value-Rite	1997	144	29	4182	(0.2)
	1996	143	23	4189	(1.2)
Grocery King	1997	1014	10	10101	(2.2)
	1996	1108	9.3	10332	(0.5)
Peter's Inc.	1997	229	10.1	2308	(3.5)
	1996	231	10.4	2392	(3.5)

The Food Giant Management

Patsy Maher, Chairperson and CEO
James Rogen, President
Robert Hein, Vice Chairman
Rachel Wu, Chief Operating Officer
Frank DiGenaro, Chief Financial Officer
Jennifer Freehold, Treasurer

The Food Giant Financials

Year	No. of Stores	Net Sales($ Mil)
1993	167	2349
1994	205	3298
1995	200	3500
1996	215	3784
1997	226	4090

Lesson 4
Enhance Slides;
Work with Template Presentations

Exercise

22

- ■ **Floating Toolbars** ■ **Draw Graphic Objects**
- ■ **AutoShapes** ■ **Edit Objects** ■ **Snap to Grid/Shape**
- ■ **Nudge** ■ **Align or Distribute Objects**

Drawing Toolbar

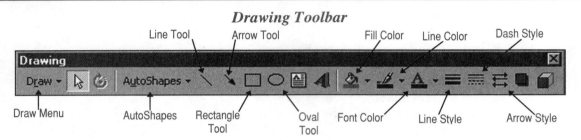

NOTES

Floating Toolbars

- If a submenu appears with a move handle, you can click and drag it away from the menu and leave it on screen. This is called a floating toolbar.

- To close a floating toolbar, click the close button on the toolbar.

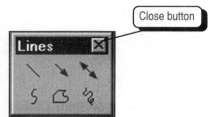

Draw Graphic Objects

- **Drawing tools** are used to create simple objects or designs on your slides. Drawing tools are found on the Drawing toolbar, which displays by default in Slide, Slide Master, and Notes Page views.

- Drawings created using the Drawing toolbar are considered objects. Drawing objects include lines, shapes, and freehand designs (objects learned earlier in this book include text boxes, clip art pictures, charts and tables). Closed shapes may be filled with a color or pattern.

- Drawings may be added to slides only in Slide or Slide Master views.

- To draw an object, click the Drawing toolbar button for the object you wish to draw. The insertion point changes to a crosshair (+). Position the crosshair where you want to start the object; click, hold, and drag the crosshair to the point where you want to end the object. After the object is drawn, it will appear with handles. To remove the handles, press the Escape key. To redisplay the handles, click on the object.

- Drawing objects can be sized, copied, and repositioned, like any other object. *(See Move, Size, Copy and Delete Placeholders and other Objects in Exercise 12.)*

- Displaying the Rulers and Guides when drawing objects will allow you to determine the object's size and position in relation to the slide's size.

- Some of the most commonly used line and shape tools are displayed on the Drawing toolbar. Many other designs are available on the AutoShapes menu *(see AutoShapes on the following page)*.

  - Use the **line tool** [] to draw a straight line. You can change the line style and color by selecting the line, then clicking the Line Style [], Dash Style [], or Line Color [] buttons on the Drawing toolbar and selecting a new style or color from the pop-up menu that appears.

  - Use the **arrow tool** [] to draw arrows. You can change the arrow style by selecting the arrow, clicking the Arrow style button [] on the Drawing toolbar, and selecting a different style. To change the color of the arrow, click More Arrows on the Arrow Style pop-up menu and select a new color.

  - Use the **rectangle tool** [] to draw squares or rectangles. To draw a perfect square, hold down the Shift key while dragging the mouse.

  - Use the **oval tool** [] to draw circles or ovals. To draw a perfect circle, hold down the Shift key while dragging the mouse.

AutoShapes

- When you select **AutoShapes** on the Drawing toolbar, several menus containing a variety of shapes (lines, connectors, flowchart elements, callouts, etc.) display. Each menu can be dragged away from the pop-up menu and made into a floating toolbar. To the right is an illustration of each category available on the AutoShapes menu, and an explanation of Lines, Connectors and Action Button AutoShapes.

Lines

Create curves, freeform, and scribble lines. The straight line and arrow tools are also available on this menu.

Connectors

Connect objects using a straight, angled, or curved line. Connector lines stay attached to objects when they are rearranged.

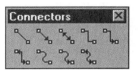

Action Buttons

Use to create a presentation for the Internet. Navigation buttons like Home, Help, Back, Next, etc. help you navigate a presentation.

Basic Shapes

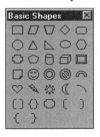

Callouts

Block Arrows

Flowchart

Stars and Banners

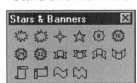

■ To draw an AutoShape, click the desired shape from a palette of shapes, then click and drag the mouse to expand the shape to the desired size. To draw a perfectly proportioned shape, hold down the Shift key while dragging the mouse.

■ Text can be added to an AutoShape. When it is, the text attaches to the shape and moves or rotates with the shape. To add text to an AutoShape, click the shape and type your text.

Edit Drawing Objects and AutoShapes

■ There are several ways to change the appearance of a shape or a drawing object.

✓ Note: Text boxes are shapes and can be edited in appearance just like any other shape.

■ You can change a shape's fill color or pattern, or you can change the color, pattern or thickness of the line surrounding the shape. You can also change the color, pattern or thickness of a line or arrow.

■ To change the color of a shape, select the shape, then click the Fill Color arrow ![fill color icon] (next to the fill color button) on the Drawing toolbar. Select the new color from the palette of options that appears.

■ The color choices that display are those that complement the color scheme of the presentation. To choose a color other than those displayed, select More Fill Colors. In the Color dialog box that follows, select the Standard tab and choose a color from the color palette. Clicking the Semitransparent check box will fill your shape with tiny holes. Therefore, if you place a semitransparent shape over other objects, you will be able to see the objects through the colored shape.

■ To fill the shape with a texture, pattern, color gradient or picture, select Fill Effects from the Fill Color pop-up menu and make your desired changes in the Fill Effects dialog box.

■ You can also use the Format dialog box to change a shape's color. To do so, select the shape and choose AutoShape (or Text Box if you are working with a text box) from the Format menu. Or, select the shape, right-click on it, and select Format AutoShape (or Text Box if you are working with a text box) from the shortcut menu.

■ In the Format dialog box that follows, click on the Colors and Lines Tab and use the Fill Color drop-down menu to make your desired changes.

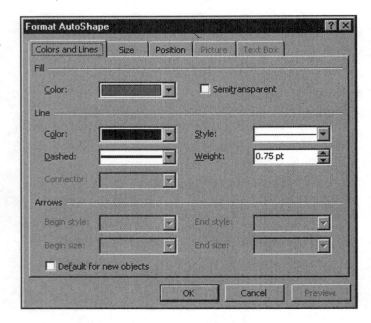

■ To change the color or pattern of a line, an arrow or the line surrounding a shape, select the shape, line or arrow, click the Line Color arrow ![line color icon] (next to the Line Color button) on the Drawing toolbar, and select a new color from the palette that displays.

■ The color choices that display are those that complement the color scheme of the presentation. To choose a color other than those displayed, select More Line Colors. In the Color dialog box that follows, select the Standard tab and choose a color from the Colors palette.

■ To give the line a pattern, select Patterned Lines after clicking the Line Color pop-up menu, and make your desired selections.

■ To change the style or thickness of a line, an arrow or the line surrounding a shape, click the Line Style button ![line style icon] on the Drawing toolbar and select from the choices. To choose a style other than those displayed, select More Lines. Then make your desired changes in the Line or Arrows section of the Format dialog box. To select a dashed line style, click the Dash Style button ![dash style icon] on the Drawing toolbar and select from the choices.

- To change the style of an arrow, click the Arrow Style button ⇄ on the Drawing toolbar and select a style from the palette. To choose a style other than those displayed, select More Arrows. Then make your desired changes in the Arrows section of the Format AutoShape dialog box.

- It is possible to change one AutoShape to another without changing its dimensions or color. To do so, click the Draw button on the Drawing toolbar and select Change AutoShape. From the pop-up menu, select the category of AutoShapes you wish use and then click on a new shape to replace the old one.

Snap to Grid/Shape

- The Snap to Grid option allows you to position an object on an invisible grid. When the snap to grid option is turned on, and the object is moved, the object will snap to the nearest point on the grid. To snap objects to the grid, select Snap, To Grid from the Draw menu before moving the object.

- You can also snap objects to other shapes by selecting Snap, To Shape from the Draw menu.

Nudge

- The nudge feature allows you to slightly move objects left, right, up and/or down. To nudge an object, select the object, then select Nudge, and either Up, Down, Left or Right from the Draw menu.

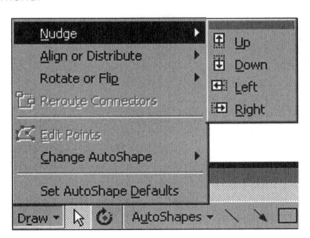

Align or Distribute Objects

- The Align or Distribute option allows you to align similar objects in relation to each other and/or distribute them evenly on the slide. You can distribute objects horizontally and vertically across the entire slide or within the space occupied by the objects. In the illustration below, the heart AutoShapes are aligned at the top of the slide and distributed horizontally in relation to the slide.

- To align or distribute objects, you must first select each object you wish to align or distribute. To do so, press the Shift key while clicking on each object. This allows you to select more than one object at a time. Then select Align or Distribute from the Draw menu and select the desired option from the submenu that follows.

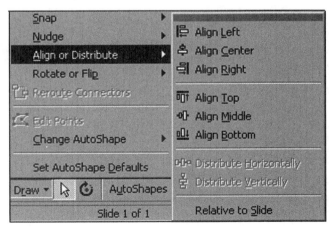

In this exercise, you will use various drawing tools to create shapes, change the color of those shapes, and then reposition them.

EXERCISE DIRECTIONS

1. Create a new presentation using the Serene template design.

2. Display the Drawing toolbar.

3. Display Rulers and Guides.

4. Insert a Title slide as the first slide.

5. Switch to Title Master view.

   a. Using the AutoShapes tool, draw a heart.
   - Use the Rulers to size it to approximately 2" by 2".
   - Position it in the top center of the slide as shown in Slide 1 in Illustration A.
   - Fill it pink and color the line around it green.
   - ✓ *Note: Use the colors suggested, which complement the slide's color scheme.*
   - Insert the words "Say Yes…" in the heart using the default font and size.
   - Insert a line break after "Say" as shown.
   - Change the text color to dark blue.

   b. Insert a slide number in the bottom right corner of the slide.

   c. Copy the heart to the clipboard.
   - ✓ *(Hint: Click on the heart to display its handles, then click on a border and copy it.)*

6. Switch to Slide Master view.

   a. Paste two copies of the heart and position them in the top left and right corners of the slide as shown in Slide 2 of Illustration A.

   b. Shorten the title placeholder and position it in the middle of the top of the slide so that it does not overlap the hearts.

   c. Change the text in the heart located on the upper right corner of the slide to read: "…and Leave the Rest to Us!" Insert line breaks where necessary.

   d. Change the first-level bullet to a red heart.

7. Switch to Slide view.

8. Create the presentation shown in Illustration A on the following two pages using the appropriate slide layouts and relevant clip art. Adjust the font size of the title text where necessary so that titles fit properly on each slide as shown.

9. On Slide 4, increase the paragraph spacing of the bulleted lists using the Formatting toolbar.

10. On Slide 6, insert a pie chart using the following data:
    - Age 18-21   10
    - Age 22-25   25
    - Age 26-30   30
    - Age 31-35   25
    - Over 35   10

11. Use the Blank Slide AutoLayout to create the last slide in the presentation as shown in Illustration B.

    a. Omit background graphics from the Slide Master.

    b. Create three hearts.
    - Use the Rulers to size them to approximately 2" by 2".
    - Position them across the top of the slide as shown in Illustration B.
    - Align them at the top.
    - Distribute them horizontally relative to the slide.
    - Color the first and last ones pink.
    - Fill the middle one with a checkered pattern in pink and white.

    c. Using the Text Box button, center the text "SAY YES" on one line in the middle of the Slide as shown, and apply a 72-point script font.

    d. Create an exclamation point.
    - Draw a thin approximately 1" high rectangle and color it pink.
    - Draw a small heart and color it pink.
    - Use the nudge feature to make the two objects line up appropriately to form an exclamation point.
    - Create a text box and insert and center the text shown at the bottom center of the slide in Illustration B. Use the default font face and size. Resize the placeholder so that the text breaks as shown.

12. Correct spelling errors.

13. Save the file; name it **WEDDING**.

14. Print one copy of each slide in Black and White. Compare your slides with those in Illustration A.

15. Close the presentation window.

Illustration A

Slide 1

Say Yes...

How to Plan the Perfect Wedding

Say Yes Wedding Consultants
Miami, Florida

1

Slide 2

Say Yes...   ...and Leave the Rest to Us!

Things to Consider:

- ♥ Prenuptial Activities and Festivities
- ♥ Wedding Attire and Flowers
- ♥ Ceremony and Rehearsal
- ♥ The Reception
- ♥ The Honeymoon

2

Slide 3

Say Yes...   ...and Leave the Rest to Us!

Prenuptial Activities...

- ♥ Newspaper announcements
- ♥ Invitations
- ♥ Stationery
- ♥ Party favors

3

Slide 4

Say Yes...   ...and Leave the Rest to Us!

Say Yes Wedding Consultants Can Help...

- ♥ Register for gifts.
- ♥ Select a band.
- ♥ Select a florist.
- ♥ Choose the menu at your wedding.
- ♥ Select invitations.
- ♥ Stick to your budget.
- ♥ Plan your honeymoon.
- ♥ Design your wedding gown.
- ♥ Pick gifts for the wedding party.

4

Slide 5

Say Yes...   ...and Leave the Rest to Us!

The Reception Requires the Most Preparation...

- ♥ Traditional Reception
  - Food is served.
  - Wedding toasts are made.
  - Bride and groom have first dance.
  - Wedding cake is cut with champagne toast.

5

Slide 6

Say Yes...   ...and Leave the Rest to Us!

The Average Age of Brides is Rising...

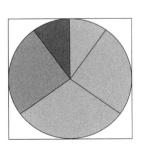

- ☐ Age 18-21
- ☐ Age 22-25
- ☐ Age 26-30
- ☐ Age 31-35
- ■ Over 35

6

We Advise Couples of Any Age...

♥ Our fees depend on the number of wedding guests in attendance.
♥ Consultants will advise on any and all aspects of your wedding.

7

8

Illustration B

KEYSTROKES

DRAW AUTOSHAPES

1. Click **AutoShapes**................. `Alt`+`U`
   on the Drawing toolbar.
2. Click desired shape from pop-up menu:
   - **Lines**..`L`
   - **Connectors** ....`N`
   - **Basic Shapes**.........................`B`
   - **Block Arrows** ....`A`
   - **Flowchart**................................`F`
   - **Stars and Banners**.................`S`
   - **Callouts** ....`C`
   - **Action Buttons** ....`O`
3. Position crosshair (+) at point where shape will start.
4. Click and drag to desired end point.

   ✓ *Most drawing shapes require the same procedure. You click, hold, and drag the mouse point to the right and down. Some shapes require additional actions to get the desired result. The distance and drag direction determine the size and shape of the object.*

DRAW A PERFECT CIRCLE/SQUARE

1. Click `□` or `○` on the Drawing toolbar.
2. Position crosshair (+) at point where shape will start.
3. Press the **Shift** key while dragging mouse diagonally to ending point.
4. Release mouse button.

DRAW ARROWS

1. Click the **Arrow** button .... `↖`
   on the Drawing toolbar.
2. Position the crosshair (+) at start point.
3. Click and drag to end point.

DRAW LINES AND FREEFORM SHAPES

1. Click **AutoShapes**................. `Alt`+`U`
   on the Drawing toolbar.
2. Click **Lines**..................................`L`
   from the pop-up menu.
3. Select a line, arrow, scribble line, or freeform shape.
4. Move pointer to draw line or shape, clicking to change direction or angle, if necessary.
5. Double-click to stop drawing.

CHANGE AUTOSHAPES

1. Select Shape to be changed.
2. Click **Draw** .... `Alt`+`R`
3. Click **Change AutoShape**....`C`
4. Click desired shape category from submenu with which to replace the existing one.
   - **Basic Shapes**.........................`B`
   - **Block Arrows** ....`A`
   - **Flowchart**................................`F`
   - **Stars and Banners**.................`S`
   - **Callouts** ....`C`
5. Select desired replacement shape.

SNAP TO GRID/SHAPE

1. Click **Draw** .... `Alt`+`R`
2. Click **Snap**.................................`S`
3. Click **To Grid** ....`G`
   OR
   Click **To Shape**...........................`S`

NUDGE

1. Select object to be moved.
2. Click **Draw**............................ `Alt`+`R`
3. Click **Nudge** ....`N`
4. Click desired direction:
   - **Up** ....`U`
   - **Down**.......................................`D`
   - **Left** ....`L`
   - **Right** ....`R`

ALIGN OBJECTS

1. Press and hold down the **Shift** key and select each object to be aligned.
2. Click **Draw**............................ `Alt`+`R`
3. Click **Align or Distribute** ....`A`
4. Click desired alignment:
   - Align **Left** ....`L`
   - Align **Center** ....`C`
   - Align **Right** ....`R`
   - Align **Top** ....`T`
   - Align **Middle** ....`M`
   - Align **Bottom** ....`B`

DISTRIBUTE OBJECTS

1. Press and hold down the **Shift** key and select each object to be distributed.
2. Click **Draw**............................ `Alt`+`R`
3. Click **Align or Distribute** ....`A`
4. Click **Distribute Horizontally**...........`H`
   OR
   Click **Distribute Vertically**...............`V`
   To distribute objects evenly across the slide:
   a. Select the objects to be distributed.
   b. Click **Draw**........................ `Alt`+`R`
   c. Click **Align**...............................`A`
      or Distribute.
   d. Click **Relative to Slide** ....`S`

   ✓ *Note: A check mark will indicate that it is selected.*

Exercise 23

■ **Create Shadows** ■ **Create 3-D Objects**

Drawing Toolbar

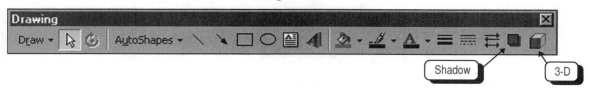

NOTES

Create Shadows

■ PowerPoint allows you to add a shadow effect to text or a graphic object. PowerPoint provides several predesigned shadow options.

■ To add a predesigned shadow to an object or text, select the object or text, then click the Shadow button ▣ on the Drawing toolbar. A menu of shadow options appears. Select the desired shadow.

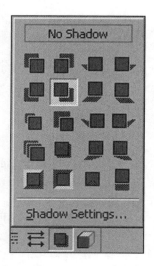

■ The preset shadow options add gray shadows to drawing objects. However, it is possible to change the color of the shadow. To do so, select the object and click the Shadow button on the Drawing toolbar. Select <u>S</u>hadow Settings from the menu. A floating toolbar displays. Click the arrow next to the Shadow Color button ▣▾ and select the color you wish to use.

Shadow Settings Floating Toolbar

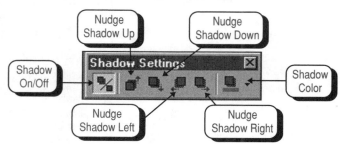

■ Using the options on the Shadow Settings toolbar, you can also adjust the position of the shadow by clicking the appropriate button.

Create 3-D Objects

■ PowerPoint also allows you to add three dimensions to an object. To do so, select the object, then click the 3-D button ▣ on the Drawing toolbar. A 3-D menu appears for you to make a selection.

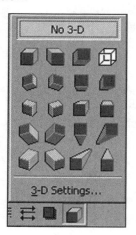

- Clicking the 3-D Settings option will create a 3-D Settings floating toolbar.

3-D Settings Floating Toolbar

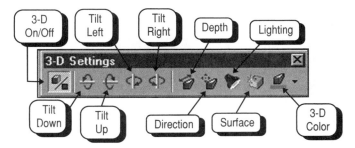

- Using the options on the 3-D Settings toolbar, you can adjust the color, the effect, the perspective and the tilt of the 3-D effect.

> *In this exercise, you will use various drawing tools to create shapes, change the color of those shapes, add shadow and 3-D effects to them, and reposition them.*

EXERCISE DIRECTIONS

1. Open ⌨ **HOUSE**, or open 💾 **23HOUSE**.

2. Display Rulers and Guides.

3. Switch to Title Master view.
   a. Delete the HF logo.
   b. Using the AutoShapes tool, insert an up ribbon banner from the Stars and Banners submenu in the upper right corner of the slide. Use the Rulers to size the banner to approximately 2" wide and 1.5" high.
   c. Color the banner light blue.
   d. Insert a shadow to the left of the banner as shown in Illustration A on the following page. Nudge the shadow to the left and down.
   e. Color the shadow orange.
   f. Select the banner.
   g. Type the letters "HF" on the banner.
   h. Color the text orange.
   i. Set the "H" to a 40-point bold serif and the "F" to 24-point bold serif.

4. Switch to Slide Master view.
   a. Repeat the above instructions.
   b. Color the banner purple.
   c. Add the same shadow to the banner as above.

5. Switch to Slide view.

6. Display Slide 5 (Vacation properties).

7. Using the AutoShapes tool, insert a circle approximately 2" in diameter anywhere to the right of the bulleted text. Color it orange.

8. Apply 3-D Style 19 to the circle so that it forms a cylinder extending from the HF banner as shown in Illustration A. Reposition the shape as necessary.
   a. Select the circle and type the words "Buy a second home!" in bold 28-point serif as shown in Illustration A. Color the text yellow. Insert line breaks where necessary.
   b. Change the color of the slide title text to purple.

9. Display Slide 6 (Apartments for sale…).
   a. Double-click on the pie chart to open Excel. Select the Sheet 1 tab at the bottom of the Excel window.
   b. Change the data in the linked Excel worksheet to the following and save it:
      - 1BR   10
      - 2BR   10
      - 3BR   5
      - 4BR   5
      - Studio   70
   c. Switch back to PowerPoint.
   d. Note the changes to the chart on Slide 6.

10. Display Slide 7 (Visit any one of our offices…).
    a. Using the AutoShapes tool, insert an Explosion 2 shape from the Stars and Banners submenu.
       - Use the Rulers to size it to approximately 4" wide by 3" high.
       - Position it to the right of the bulleted text as shown in Illustration B on the following page.
       - Color it green.
    b. Select the explosion shape, and type the words "Offices in all 5 boroughs!" in 28-point bold serif as shown in Illustration B.
       - Color the text dark blue. Insert line breaks where necessary.
    c. Apply Shadow Style 13 to the explosion shape.
       - Nudge the shadow to the left.
       - Color the shadow pink.

11. Correct spelling errors.

12. Switch to Slide Sorter view.

13. Compare your presentation to the Desired Result on pages 144 and 145. Make any necessary adjustments to placeholders and font sizes so that text does not overlap the AutoShapes.

14. Print one copy as Handouts (6 slides per page) in Pure Black and White.

15. Close the file; save the changes.

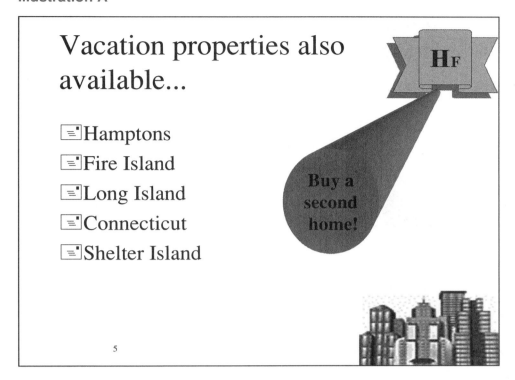

Desired Result

1

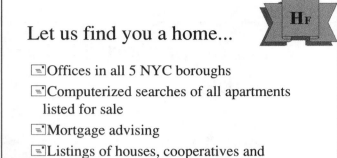

2

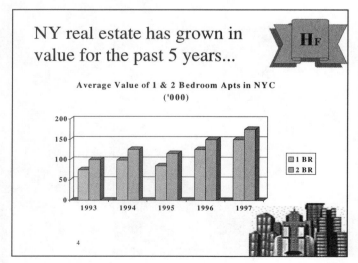

3

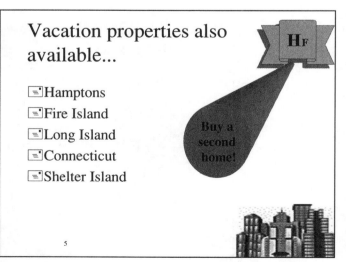

4

5

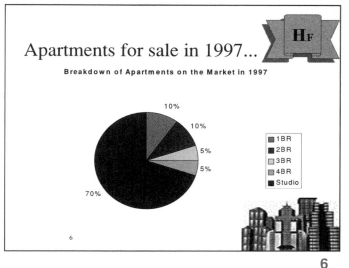

6

7

KEYSTROKES

ADD SHADOWS

1. Select the object on which to apply the shadow.
2. Click the **Shadow** button ....
   on the Drawing toolbar.
3. Click the desired shadow.

MOVE SHADOWS

1. Select the object on which to move the shadow.
2. Click the **Shadow** button ....
   on the Drawing toolbar.
3. Click **Shadow Settings** ....
4. Click the appropriate button to nudge the shadow:

   - **Left** ....
   - **Right** ....
   - **Up** ....
   - **Down** ....

CHANGE SHADOW COLOR

1. Select the object on which to change the shadow color.
2. Click the **Shadow** button ....
   on the Drawing toolbar.
3. Click **Shadow Settings** ....
4. Click the **Shadow Color** ....
   arrow button.
5. Select the desired color.

ADD 3-D

1. Select the object on which to apply 3-D.
2. Click the **3-D** button ....
   on the Drawing toolbar.
3. Click the desired 3-D effect.

CHANGE 3-D EFFECT

1. Select the object on which to change the 3-D effect.
2. Click the **3-D** button ....
   on the Drawing toolbar.
3. Click a different 3-D effect.

CHANGE TILT

1. Select the 3-D object on which to change its tilt.
2. Click the **3-D** button ....
   on the Drawing toolbar.
3. Click **3-D Settings** ....
4. Click the appropriate button to:

   - **Tilt Up** ....
   - **Tilt Down** ....
   - **Tilt Left** ....
   - **Tilt Right** ....

CHANGE 3-D PERSPECTIVE

1. Select the object on which to change its perspective.
2. Click the **3-D** button ....
   on the Drawing toolbar.
3. Click **3-D Settings** ....
4. Click the **Direction** button ....
5. Click **Perspective** ....
6. Click the **Direction** button ....
7. Select desired perspective direction.

CHANGE 3-D COLOR

1. Select the object on which to change the 3-D color.
2. Click the **3-D** button ....
   on the Drawing toolbar.
3. Click **3-D Settings** ....
4. Click the **3-D Color** arrow............
   button.
5. Click desired color.
   OR
   a. Click **More 3-D Colors** ....
   b. Select desired color.
   c. Click **OK** ....

Exercise 24

■ WordArt

Drawing Toolbar

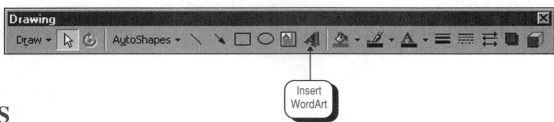

Insert WordArt

NOTES

WordArt

■ WordArt lets you create special effects with text. You may choose from a variety of effects to apply to text. Note several effects below:

■ WordArt pictures may be sized or positioned just like any other object. *(See Move, Size, Copy and Delete Placeholders and Other Objects in Exercise 12.)*

■ To access WordArt, click on the Insert WordArt button ◢ on the Drawing toolbar. (If the Drawing toolbar is not displayed, select Toolbars, Drawing from the View menu.)

■ In the WordArt Gallery dialog box that appears, select an effect to apply to your text.

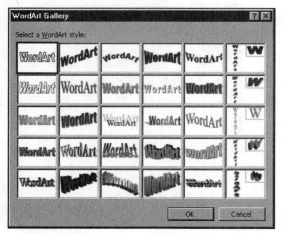

■ In the Edit WordArt Text dialog box that follows, type the text to become WordArt in the Text box and select the desired Font face, font Size and font style (bold or italic).

■ Once the WordArt is on the slide, you can edit it. When the WordArt is selected, the following floating toolbar appears and allows you to edit the WordArt.

■ To hide the floating toolbar, right-click the WordArt and select Hide WordArt Toolbar. If the toolbar is not available, right-click the WordArt and select Show WordArt Toolbar.

Edit WordArt

■ After the WordArt has been created you can
make changes to it using the buttons on the
WordArt floating toolbar. To begin the editing
process, first select the WordArt text. The chart
below explains the function of each button on the
floating toolbar.

Button	Use to
Edit Te_t...	change the font face, font size or font style, or edit the text.
	open the WordArt Gallery and change the WordArt effect.
	change the fill color, line color and width, and text size or position.
Abc	change the shape of the WordArt.
	rotate the WordArt. Use the round handles that appear around the WordArt and rotate as you desire.
Aa	make all letters the same height.
Ab	make WordArt text appear vertically.
	align text in WordArt if there is more than one line of text. Select Right, Left, Center, Word Justify, Letter Justify or Stretch Justify.
AV	change the space between the letters in your WordArt, or its kerning. Loose kerning allows more space between characters, while tight kerning allows less space. Select Very Tight, Tight, Normal, Loose, Very Loose, or Custom.

In this exercise, you will use WordArt and AutoShapes to enhance a previously created presentation.

EXERCISE DIRECTIONS

1. Open ⌨ **GYM**, or open 💾 **24GYM**.

2. Display Rulers and Guides.

3. Insert a new slide.

   a. Select the Organization Chart layout.

   b. Insert the slide title shown in Illustration A on the following page.

   c. Insert the chart title and data as shown in Illustration A.

   d. Resize and position the chart as necessary so that it does not overlap other text on the slide.

4. Insert a new slide.

   a. Select the Chart layout.

   b. Insert the slide title shown in Illustration B on the following page.

   c. Insert the following data in the chart datasheet:
   Growth in Membership Since 1992

1992	672
1993	784
1994	899
1995	1067
1996	1080
1997	1533

   d. Include the chart and x-axis titles as shown in Illustration B.

   e. Resize and position the chart as necessary so that it does not overlap other text on the slide.

5. Switch to Slide Sorter view.

   a. Move this new Chart slide to become Slide 6.

   b. Move the Organization Chart slide to become Slide 7.

6. Switch to Slide Master view.

   a. Delete the clip art and "New World" text.

   b. Using the AutoShapes tool, insert a 32-point star from the Stars and Banners submenu. Color it light green. Color the line around it pink. Position and size it to fit in the upper right corner of the slide as shown in Illustration B.

   c. Using the WordArt of your choice, insert the words "New World" in 24-point bold serif. Color the text purple. Position it in the center of the star as shown.

   d. Insert a slide number in the bottom right corner of each slide.

7. Switch to Title Master view.

   a. Using a different WordArt option than before, insert the words "A New Way of Life" in a 36-point sans serif font. Position it in the top center of the slide as shown in Slide 1 of the Desired Result on page 150.

   b. Use any desired fill color.

   c. Size the WordArt to approximately 1" high by 5" wide.

   d. Using the WordArt Shape button on the WordArt toolbar, change the shape of the text to wavy.

   e. Adjust the character spacing of the WordArt text to tight kerning.

8. Switch to Slide view.

9. Display Slide 4 (Various Locations).

   a. Change the slide title to read "4 Convenient Locations."

   b. Reduce the size of the title text using the Decrease Font Size button on the Formatting toolbar, if necessary, so that the title fits on one line.

   c. Delete the bulleted text placeholder.

   d. Using a vertical WordArt option, retype the gym locations to read Wall Street, Tribeca, East Side, and West Side, as shown in Illustration C on page 150.

   ✓ *(Hint: Press Enter after typing each location name in the Word Art text box.)*

   - Use a 36-point sans serif font.
   - Color the text light green and the line around it pink.
   - Size the WordArt to approximately 4 ½" high by 3 ½" wide.

   e. Reposition the WordArt to center it in the slide as shown in Illustration C.

10. Correct spelling errors.

11. Compare your presentation to the Desired Result on pages 150 and 151. Change the order of your slides if necessary.

12. Print one copy as Handouts (6 slides per page) in Pure Black and White.

13. Close the file; save the changes.

Illustration A

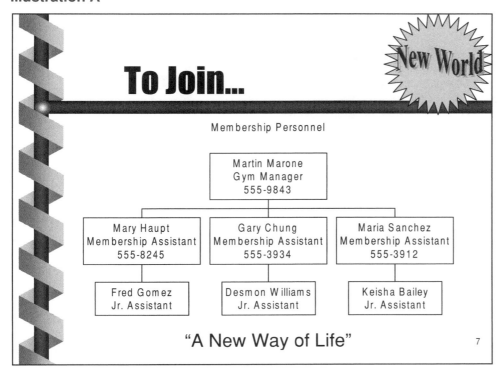

Illustration B

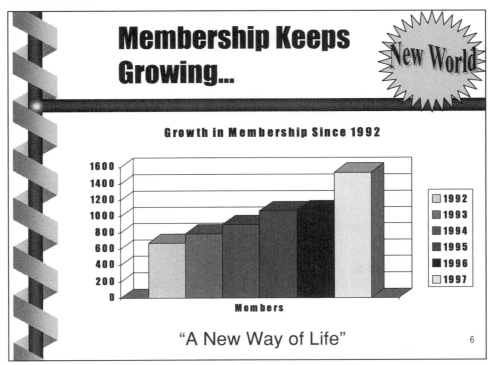

Illustration C

Desired Result

1

2

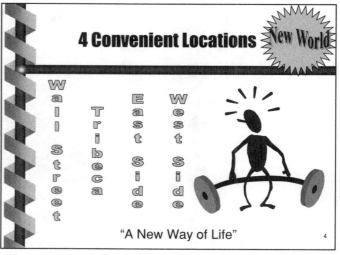

3

4

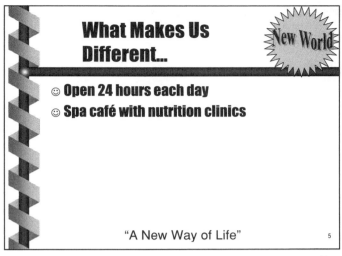

5

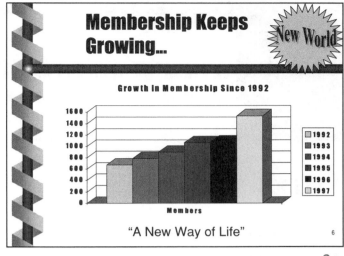

6

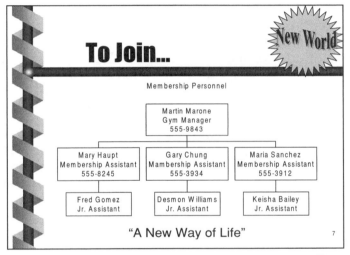

7

KEYSTROKES

INSERT WORDART

1. Click the **Insert WordArt** button ......
   on the Drawing toolbar.
2. Select desired **WordArt** .... Alt + W,
   Style.
3. Click **OK** .... Enter
4. Enter **Text** .... Alt + T, *text*
   on which to apply WordArt.
5. Click **OK**.

EDIT WORDART

1. Select WordArt to be edited.
2. Click **Edit Text** button............. Edit Text...
   OR
   a. Right-click WordArt.
   b. Select **Edit Text** X
3. Make desired changes.

FORMAT WORDART

1. Select WordArt to be formatted.
2. Click **Format WordArt** button ....
   on the WordArt toolbar.
   OR
   a. Click **Format** .... Alt + O
   b. Click **WordArt** .... O
   OR
   a. Right-click WordArt.
   b. Select **Format WordArt** .... O
3. Make desired changes.
4. Click **OK** .... Enter

Exercise 25

■ **Group, Ungroup and Regroup Objects**
■ **Flip and Rotate Objects** ■ **Layer Objects**

NOTES

Group, Ungroup, and Regroup Objects

■ When a drawing is comprised of several basic shapes, it is difficult to move, copy, or duplicate all the shapes as a whole object. **Grouping** allows you to select all the shapes in the group and treat them as a single object so that copying, duplicating, and moving the object become possible.

■ To group an object comprised of individual shapes, select each shape (hold the Shift key down while you click each shape). Select Group from the Draw menu. You can ungroup the grouped objects by selecting Ungroup from the Draw menu. You can also right-click on the selected object(s) and use the shortcut menu to execute these commands.

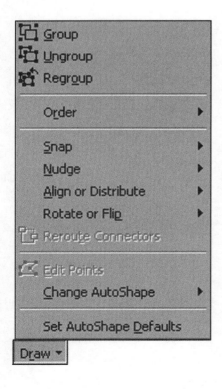

■ **Ungrouping** allows you to separate the objects you grouped. You can also use the Ungroup feature to alter a clip art image—that is, you can change the fill color or shape of individual parts that comprise the graphic. Select Ungroup from the Draw menu to separate the parts that comprise the graphic. Then, click on each part you wish to alter and change the fill and/or shape, or delete the graphic part.

■ When you ungroup a clip art image, PowerPoint asks if you want to convert the image to a PowerPoint drawing so that it can be manipulated. Converting an image to a PowerPoint drawing does not affect the image in the Clip Gallery; the conversion applies only to the image that appears on the slide in the active presentation. Select Yes to convert the image.

■ **Regrouping** allows you to group objects that had been separated using the Ungroup command. To do so, select Regroup from the Draw menu.

Flip and Rotate Objects

■ You can change the direction of a drawing by flipping the object horizontally (left/right) or vertically (top/bottom). You can also rotate an object to position it at an angle.

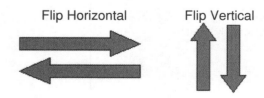

Flip Horizontal   Flip Vertical

- To flip an object, select the object and click the Draw button on the Drawing toolbar. Select Rotate or Flip and then click Flip Horizontal or Flip Vertical.

- You can rotate an object by 90-degree increments. To do so, select the object, select Rotate or Flip from the Draw menu, then click Rotate Right or Rotate Left.

- Free rotate allows you to turn an object to any degree by dragging a handle on the selected object. To rotate freely, select the object, then click the Free Rotate button ⟳ on the Drawing toolbar. Or, select Rotate or Flip, Free Rotate from the Draw menu.

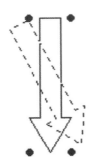

- To rotate an object to an exact degree, click the object you want to rotate. Then, select Object, Text Box, WordArt, or AutoShape from the Format menu. Or, right-click the object and select Format Object, Text Box, WordArt, or AutoShape from the shortcut menu. In the Format dialog box that appears, click on the Size tab. In the Rotation box, type in the number of degrees you wish to rotate the object.

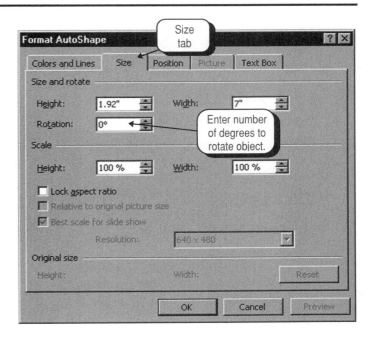

Layer Objects

- Shapes or objects can be layered or stacked on top of each other to create interesting effects. You may adjust the layers by moving them back or bringing them forward in the stack. To adjust the layers of shapes or objects, select a shape or object. Then select Send to Back, Bring to Front, Bring Forward or Send Backward from the Order submenu on the Draw menu.

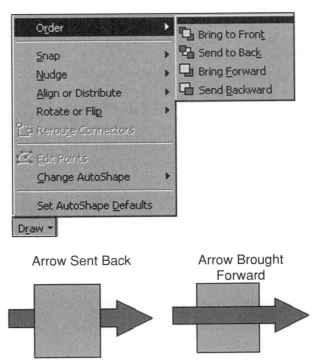

> *In this exercise, you will create a new presentation, in which you will group, rotate and layer objects.*

EXERCISE DIRECTIONS

1. Create a new Blank Presentation.

2. Accept the default Title Slide layout.

3. Display Rulers and Guides.

4. Create the presentation shown in Illustration A on pages 156 and 157 using the appropriate slide layouts and relevant clip art.

   a. To create the title slide:
      - Use WordArt to insert the words "Live Longer" in a 44-point sans serif font. Choose any horizontal WordArt option you desire.
      - Position and size it to fit in the upper left corner of the slide as shown. Use the Free Rotate tool to tilt the WordArt as shown.
      - Color the text light blue and the line around the text purple.

   b. Use the following data to create the chart on Slide 3 (Cholesterol Levels…).

Age 20-30	175
Age 30-40	190
Age 40-50	210
Age 50-60	215
Age 60-70	250

      - Use the x-axis title shown.

   c. Use a Table Slide layout to create Slide 6 (Vitamins Are Essential…).
      - Use three columns and six rows.
      - Bold and center the column headings.
      - Center the first column of text.
      - Change the color of the font to dark blue.
      - Adjust column widths so that text line breaks match those in Slide 6 in Illustration A on page 157.

5. Switch to Title Master view.

6. Display the Drawing toolbar.

7. Insert the five-point star from the Stars and Banners AutoShapes submenu. Position it at bottom center of the slide as shown in Illustration B on page 157. Size it to approximately 3" high by 4" wide.

8. Insert a rounded rectangle from the Basic Shapes AutoShapes submenu.

   a. Size it to approximately 5" wide by ½" high.

   b. Copy the rectangle, and paste it twice. Group the three rectangles and position them as shown in Illustration B on page 157. Center the rectangles over the star.

   c. Fill the rectangles yellow and color the outline dark blue.

   d. Send the rectangles to the back (behind the star).

9. Create a text box and enter the text: "Take Control of Your Health."

   a. Center the text in the text box and color it yellow.

   b. Center the text box in the star and size it so that it fits into the star.

10. Select the three objects and group them.

11. Copy the grouped object.

12. Switch to Slide Master view.

13. Paste the grouped object in the Slide Master, position it in the top left corner of the page and size it to fit in the corner of the slide as shown in Illustration C on page 157.

14. Use the Free Rotate tool to tilt the object.

15. Ungroup the object and delete the text box.

16. Regroup the star and rectangles.

17. Right-align the title text on all slides and color it dark blue.

18. Color all bulleted text dark blue.

19. Change the first-level bullet to a clover symbol.

20. Change the second-level bullet to a star symbol.

21. Switch to Slide view.

22. Change the background color on all slides to light blue.

23. Spell check the presentation.

24. Compare your presentation to Illustration A on the following two pages.

25. Resize and/or reposition objects and text placeholders and adjust font sizes, as necessary, on each slide to prevent overlap with the logo.

26. Print one copy as Handouts (2 slides per page) in Black and White.

27. Save the presentation; name it SILVER.

28. Close the presentation.

Illustration A

Live Longer

Silver Age Vitamins

Nutritional Supplements for Seniors

Take Control
of Your
Health

1

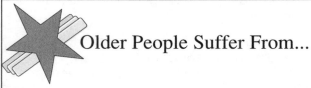

Older People Suffer From...

♣High cholesterol
♣High blood pressure
♣Reduced memory
♣Lower energy level
♣Arthritis
♣Osteoporosis

2

Cholesterol Levels
Increase with Age...

250	
200	
150	
100	
50	
0	

Total Cholesterol Level (mg/dL)

- Age 20-30
- Age 30-40
- Age 40-50
- Age 50-60
- Age 60-70

3

...But Silver Age
Vitamins Can Help...

♣ Reduce cholesterol
♣ Lower risk of heart attack
♣ Lower blood pressure
♣ Strengthen bones
♣ Sharpen memory
♣ Extend your life

4

Silver Age Vitamins
Contain...

♣Over 30 essential vitamins and minerals including:
  * Vitamins A, C, D, E, and K
  * Iron
  * Calcium
  * Zinc
  * Magnesium
  * Various anti-oxidants

5

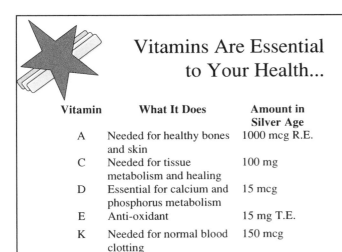

Vitamins Are Essential to Your Health...

Vitamin	What It Does	Amount in Silver Age
A	Needed for healthy bones and skin	1000 mcg R.E.
C	Needed for tissue metabolism and healing	100 mg
D	Essential for calcium and phosphorus metabolism	15 mcg
E	Anti-oxidant	15 mg T.E.
K	Needed for normal blood clotting	150 mcg

6

Where to Find Silver Age

- ♣ Call us directly at 1-800-455-9832
- ♣ Froemer's Pharmacy
- ♣ Beltway Drug Stores
- ♣ Wiggley Vitamin Shops
- ♣ Most health food stores

7

Illustration B

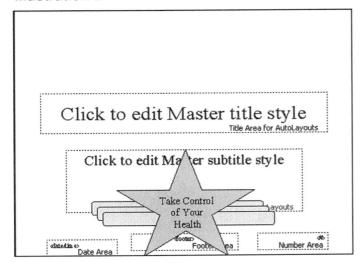

Illustration C

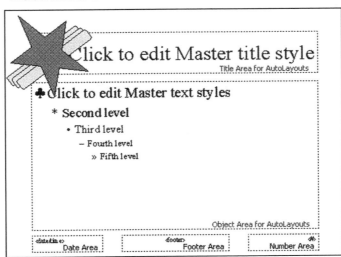

KEYSTROKES

GROUP OBJECTS

1. Hold down **Shift** while clicking objects to group.
2. Click **Draw**...........................![Alt]+![R]
3. Click **Group** ....![G]

UNGROUP OBJECTS

1. Select desired grouped object.
2. Click **Draw**...........................![Alt]+![R]
3. Click **Ungroup** ....![U]
4. Repeat to divide the object further.

REGROUP OBJECTS

✓ *Regroups most recently ungrouped object. If slide containing ungrouped object becomes inactive, object cannot be regrouped using this procedure. It will have to be grouped.*

1. Click **Draw**...........................![Alt]+![R]
2. Click **Regroup** ....![O]

FLIP AND ROTATE OBJECTS

1. Select desired object.
2. Click **Draw**...........................![Alt]+![R]
3. Click **Rotate or Flip** ....![P]
4. Select desired option:

OPTION	MOVEMENT
Free Rotate	Rotates object to any degree as you manipulate its handles. Remember to click the free rotate button when rotation is complete.
Rotate Left	Rotates an object counter-clockwise in 90-degree increments.
Rotate Right	Rotates an object clockwise in 90-degree increments.
Flip Horizontal	Flips an object left to right.
Flip Vertical	Flips an object top to bottom.

ROTATE OBJECTS TO AN EXACT DEGREE

1. Select desired object.
2. Click **Format**.........................![Alt]+![O]
3. Click **Object**, **Text Box** ....![O]
   AutoShape, or **WordArt**.
   OR
   a. Right-click object.
   b. Click **Format Object**..................![O]
      Text Box, **AutoShape**, or **WordArt**.
4. Click **Size** tab.
5. Click in **Rotation** box.............![Alt]+![T]
6. Type number of degrees .... *number* to rotate object.
7. Click **OK**.

LAYER OBJECTS

1. Select desired object ....![Alt]+![R] and click **Draw**.
2. Click **Order** ....![R]
3. Select desired option:

OPTION	MOVEMENT
Bring to Front	Places object on top of all other objects.
Send to Back	Places object beneath all other objects.
Bring Forward	Moves object one layer up on the stack.
Send Backward	Moves object one layer down on the stack.

CYCLE THROUGH OBJECTS

1. Press **Ctrl + A** ....![Ctrl]+![A] to select all objects.
2. Press **Tab** ....![A] until desired object is selected.

NEXT EXERCISE

Exercise 26

■ **Template Presentations** ■ **AutoContent Wizard**

NOTES

Template Presentations

■ PowerPoint provides sets of slides that relate to specific types of presentations. These template presentations are predesigned and include suggestions for the type of information that should be entered on each slide. To access these presentations, select <u>N</u>ew from the <u>F</u>ile menu. In the New Presentation dialog box that follows, select the Presentations tab and note the presentations that are available.

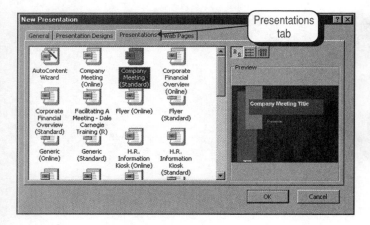

■ You will note that the first presentation type is the AutoContent Wizard *(see explanation, above right)*. The remaining presentations include two basic formats for each presentation type, Online and Standard. If you plan to use your presentation on the Web, select the Online option. *(Creating Web presentations will be covered in Exercise 40.)*

■ After you choose a presentation, it will open, and the number of slides in the presentation will be displayed on the Status bar. Select the sample text on each slide and replace it with your own.

AutoContent Wizard

■ The AutoContent Wizard is one of the presentation options under the Presentations tab in the New Presentation dialog box. It is also an option in the PowerPoint dialog box when you launch PowerPoint.

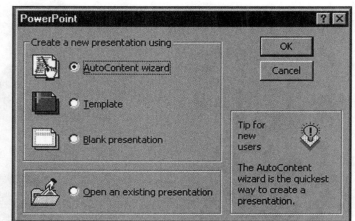

■ The Autocontent Wizard walks you through the presentation development process. Follow the prompts and select <u>F</u>inish when you are prompted to do so. Your presentation will display in Outline view, and a Slide view miniature will also display.

EXERCISE DIRECTIONS

1. Create a new presentation using the Product Overview (Standard) template.

2. Display Slide 1 (see illustration A below).

    a. Highlight the bracketed sample information and enter the product name: "Seaview Lecture Center."

    b. Delete the photograph placeholder and the sub-title placeholder and then insert a relevant graphic. Size it to fill the center of the slide as shown in Illustration A.

    c. Delete the company logo placeholder in the upper left corner of the slide and replace it with a logo you create as follows.

        • Use the horizontal scroll AutoShape from the Stars and Banners submenu. Color the scroll yellow. Size it to approximately 2" high by 2 ½" wide.

        • Using the WordArt of your choice, insert the words: "Challenge Your Mind." (Insert a line break after each word as you type it in the Edit WordArt Text dialog box.) Color the text purple. Use a 32-point font. Position and resize the WordArt to fit in the center of the scroll as shown.

        • Group the scroll AutoShape and the WordArt.

3. Switch to Slide Sorter view.

    • Move Slide 7 (Availability) to become Slide 6.

4. Switch back to Slide view.

5. Replace sample text with the text on the remaining slides as shown in Illustration B on the following page.

6. On Slide 7 (Pricing), select all text and insert a right-aligned tab at 7" to align the yearly costs for each membership.

7. Switch to Slide Master view.

    • Change the color of all bullets to complement the presentation. Change the first- and second-level bullets to any two desired symbols.

    • Insert slide numbers in the bottom right corner of each slide.

8. Switch to Slide view.

9. Spell check.

10. Print one copy of slides as Handouts (6 slides per page) in Black and White.

11. Save the file; name it **LECTURE**.

12. Close the presentation window.

Illustration A

Illustration B

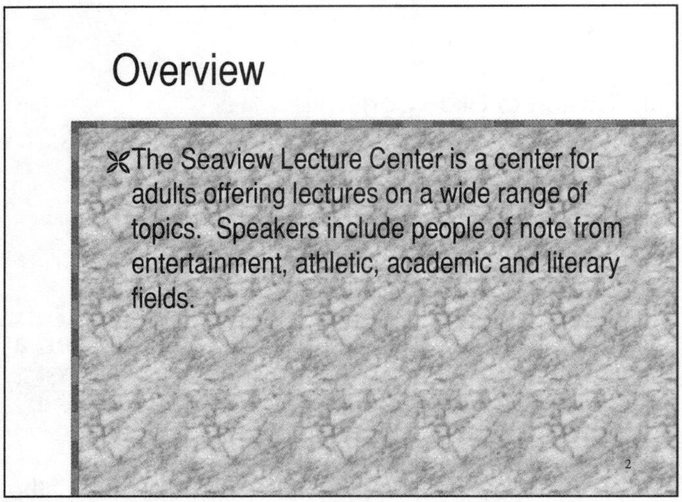

Overview

✂ The Seaview Lecture Center is a center for adults offering lectures on a wide range of topics. Speakers include people of note from entertainment, athletic, academic and literary fields.

2

2

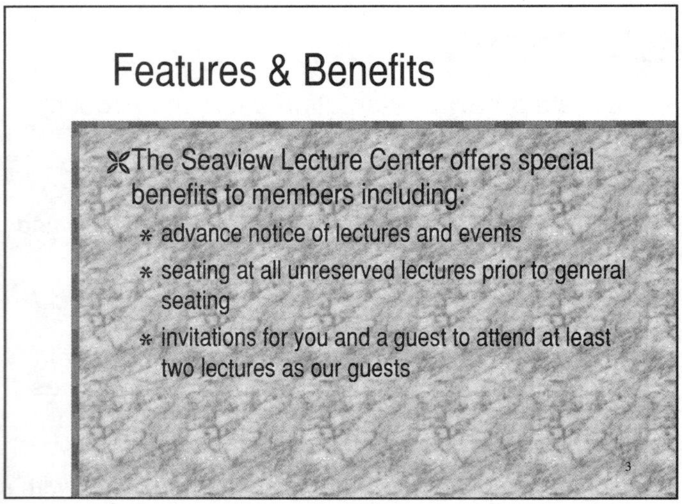

Features & Benefits

✂ The Seaview Lecture Center offers special benefits to members including:
  * advance notice of lectures and events
  * seating at all unreserved lectures prior to general seating
  * invitations for you and a guest to attend at least two lectures as our guests

3

3

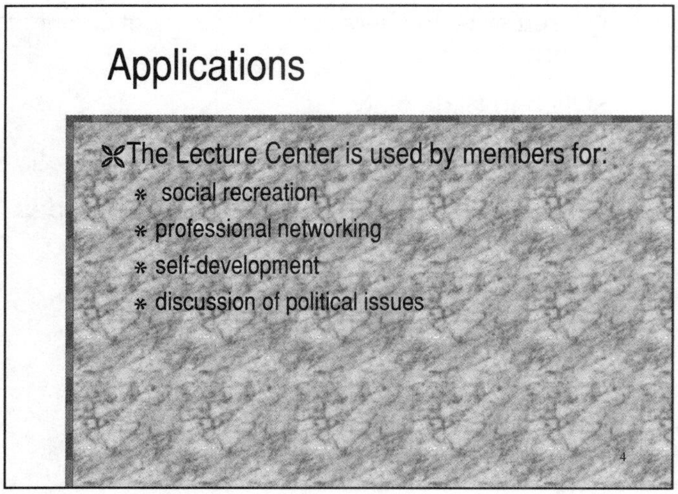

Applications

✂ The Lecture Center is used by members for:
  * social recreation
  * professional networking
  * self-development
  * discussion of political issues

4

4

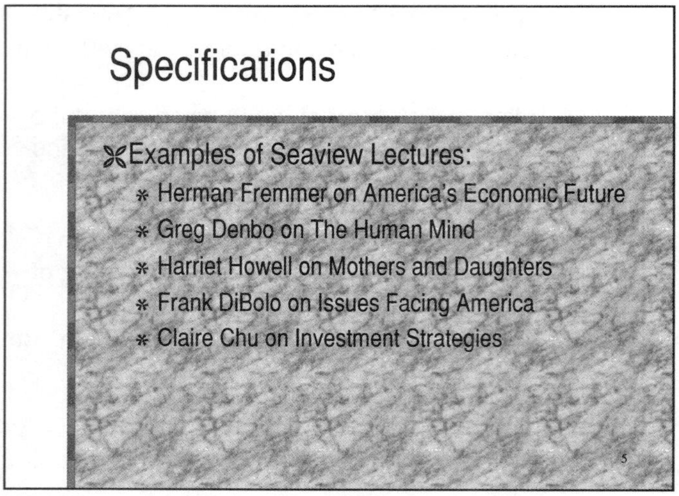

Specifications

✂ Examples of Seaview Lectures:
  * Herman Fremmer on America's Economic Future
  * Greg Denbo on The Human Mind
  * Harriet Howell on Mothers and Daughters
  * Frank DiBolo on Issues Facing America
  * Claire Chu on Investment Strategies

5

5

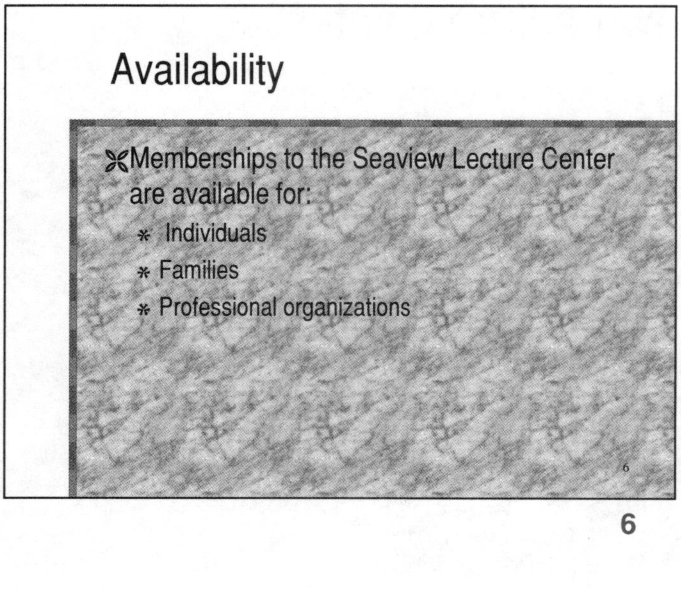

Availability

✂ Memberships to the Seaview Lecture Center are available for:
  * Individuals
  * Families
  * Professional organizations

6

6

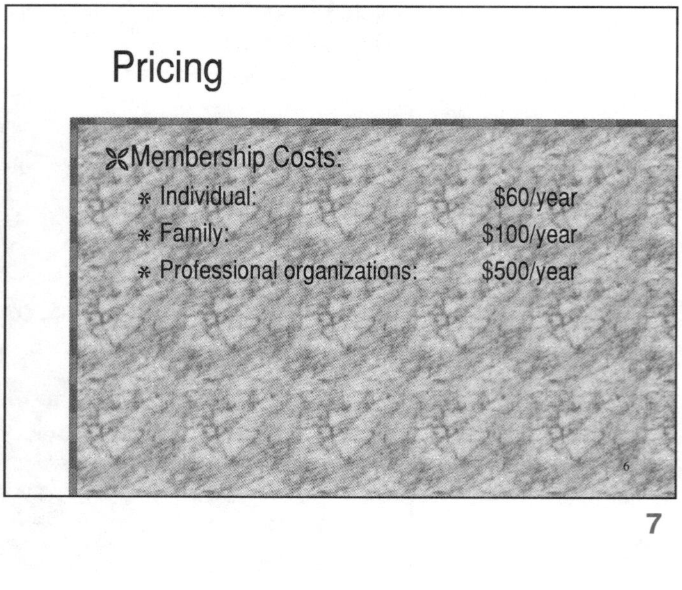

Pricing

✂ Membership Costs:
  * Individual: $60/year
  * Family: $100/year
  * Professional organizations: $500/year

6

7

KEYSTROKES

OPEN A TEMPLATE PRESENTATION

1. Click **File**, **New** .... Alt + F , N
   OR
   a. Click **Start** .... Start
   b. Click **New Office Document**.
2. Click **Presentations** tab.
3. Double-click desired stock presentation.
   OR
   a. Click desired stock presentation.
   b. Click **OK** .... Enter
4. Select sample text on each slide and replace it with your own.

AUTOCONTENT WIZARD

1. Click **File**, **New** .... Alt + F , N
   OR
   a. Click **Start** .... Start
   b. Click **New Office Document**.
2. Click **Presentations** tab.
3. Double-click **AutoContent** ....
   Wizard presentation icon.
   OR
   a. Click **AutoContent** ....
   Wizard presentation icon.
   b. Click **OK** .... Enter
4. Follow prompts to complete presentation template.

Exercise 27

■ **Summary**

You work for the Helsinki Travel Bureau. You have been asked to create a presentation for prospective visitors about travel to Helsinki during the summer, the history of the city, summer events, sightseeing highlights, hotel accommodations and restaurant choices.

EXERCISE DIRECTIONS

1. Refer to the report shown in Illustration A on the next two pages.

2. Create a 9-slide presentation based on the information contained in the report.

   a. Use any desired slide layouts to enter the information for your presentation. You must include at least one table slide and one chart slide.

   b. Apply a relevant template design.

   c. Use the Slide Master to include a city insignia and page number on each slide. The city insignia should be created using multiple AutoShapes, which are then grouped together using the Grouping feature.

   d. Utilize WordArt in two ways in the presentation. Change the color and shape of both WordArt designs from their original format.

   e. Reformat all bullets and change their colors.

   f. Move the slides into an appropriate order.

3. Print one copy of slides as Handouts (6 slides per page) in Black and White.

4. Save the file; name it **FINLAND**.

5. Close the presentation window.

Helsinki, Finland in the Summer

Helsinki comes to life in the summer when long hours of sunshine bring outdoor dining and arts festivals to the city. The city is in full bloom in the summer inspiring locals to play bocce, relax on park benches, sail or take motor boats to nearby islands. Galleries, bookstores, concert halls and theaters offer visitors many cultural events and performances. The Helsinki Festival, from August 22 to September 7, is the city's summer highlight and culminates in the Night of the Arts during which free performance art, readings, music and visual and decorative arts are offered to the public.

The City

King Gustavus I of Sweden, which then ruled Finland, founded Helsinki in 1550. The city passed from Swedish to Russian rule in 1809. In 1812, Czar Alexander I made Helsinki the capital of Finland. Finland gained independence from Russia in 1917 and the Helsinki region's population and commercial importance have grown since then. Helsinki is currently home to approximately 874,953 inhabitants. The center of the city's old section is Senate Square which has many buildings designed in the neoclassial style of the 1800s.

Events

As part of the Helsinki Festival, the Helsinki Filharmonia and Finnish Philharmonic Choir will present a music program beginning at 8 P.M. on August 24 at Huvila, a waterfront space near the Helsinki Theater. Tickets are $18-$24.

The 26.7-mile Helsinki Marathon lures thousands of spectators along its course, which spans the city's waterways and streets. It starts at 3 P.M. August 16 at Olympic Stadium at the statue of Paavo Nurmi, winner of nine Olympic gold medals for running.

Sightseeing

The quickest and least expensive way to see the city is on the tram 3T, which passes through the major areas in 50 minutes. There is an English-language guidebook available on board. Fare is $1.75.

Suomenlinna, a living historic island village surrounded by 18th-century fortifications, is a 13-minute ferry ride from downtown. The village contains numerous small museums, cafes, art galleries, and a beach. Tickets for the ferry are $3.50 round trip.

Helsinki has many outdoor markets. The most famous outdoor bazaar, Kauppatori, is made up of various stalls and boats where produce and crafts are sold. It is open Monday through Friday through August 29 from 7 A.M. to 2 P.M. and 3:30 P.M. to 8 P.M. It is on the South Harbor near the President's Palace.

The Helsinki Tourist Association (358-9) 601-966, offers guided walking tours in English by arrangement for $140 a person.

Where to Stay

Rates are approximately 50% lower in the summer than they are at other times of the year.

- *The Lord Hotel has 48 rooms and is decorated with Art Nouveau murals and unusual architectural features. Rooms are $92 for a double.*
- *Grand Marina is on the harbor east of Market Square. Its brick building dates back to 1912 and contains 420 rooms. Rates are $97 for a double.*
- *The 200 room Strand Inter-Continental is one of the most luxurious hotels in the city. It offers a view of the city from across a channel that leads to the Gulf of Finland. Rates are $196 for a double.*

Where to Eat

The following restaurants serve Finnish fare.

- *Valhalla is located on Suomenlinna, a short ferry ride from town. Dinner for two with wine averages about $120.*
- *Kosmos serves excellent Finnish, Russian and French dishes. Dinner for two with wine averages about $60.*
- *Elite serves the city's arts and theater crowd. There is outdoor seating in the summer. Dinner for two with wine averages about $55.*

Growth in Tourism

Year	Number of Visitors
1993	1,049,990
1994	1,297,649
1995	1,409,374
1996	1,693,745
1997	2,953,978

The following statistics might be helpful to the Helsinki visitor:

Population
Metro area: 874,953
Weather in August
High: 68
Low: 53
Days with rain: 15
Hotel
Room for two with tax: $285.00
Dinner for One
With tax and tip: $38.00
Taxi
Upon entry: $3.98
Each additional km. $1.05
From the airport: $28.30
Car Rental for a Day
Mid-sized, manual shift $148.25
Helsinki Travel Bureau   1-800-377-9334

NEXT EXERCISE

Exercise
28

■ **Summary**

You have been asked to create a business plan presentation for a group of prospective investors. The presentation should outline your industry, company profile and financial results. Your objective in making the presentation is to raise money to finance the expansion of your stores to supercenters. You will use information from the same report used in Exercise 21 and the Business Plan template to develop your business plan presentation.

EXERCISE DIRECTIONS

1. Refer to the report shown in Illustration A on the next page.

2. Create a 9-slide presentation based on the information contained in the report. Use the Business Plan (Standard) stock template presentation.

3. Open the Business Plan (Standard) template presentation.

4. Switch to Slide Sorter view.

5. Delete Slide 8 (Goal & Objectives), Slide 11 (Risks & Rewards) and Slide 12 (Key Issues).

6. Switch to Slide Master view.

7. Create a company logo in the upper right corner of the slide using AutoShapes and a text box. Group the components of the logo. Shorten the title placeholder as necessary.

8. Switch to Slide view.

   a. Fill in relevant information from the report on each slide as directed. Keep in mind your objective as stated above.

   b. The new Slide 8 (Financial Plan) should describe to your potential investors the project for which you hope to use their money. Be creative in describing the project as you see it. Change the title of the slide to read "Expansion Plan."

   c. Slide 9 (Resource Requirements) should inform your investors of how much money you require for the project.

9. Print one copy of slides as Handouts (6 slides per page) in Black and White.

10. Save the file; name it **PLAN**.

11. Close the presentation window.

The Food Giant Company

The Industry

The supermarket industry is very mature and highly competitive. As a result, expansion in the industry is limited. Big, multi-regional food chains tend to dominate as smaller chains are increasingly being acquired by their larger competitors. The industry is experiencing a period of consolidation as mergers and acquisitions are moving the supermarket industry towards greater concentration. Big, multi-regional food chains have the advantage of geographic diversity, consumer franchises and strong cash flow. This is particularly true of supercenters. In the late 1980s and early 1990s, supercenters, stores of more than 150,000 square feet that sell both food and general merchandise, became increasingly popular. These supercenters threaten to drive smaller supermarkets out of business due to intense price and service competition. Only small chains that well utilize marketing and merchandising strategies can successfully compete with larger supermarket chains and supercenter stores. Larger chains can only compete by adapting to the development of supercenters by expanding their services.

The Company

Henry Mackler founded The Food Giant Company in 1918 when Mackler opened his first grocery store in Brooklyn, New York. Mackler expanded the company to 43 stores by the time of his death in 1942. His family has expanded the business on the East Coast since then and intends to open its first store in the West Coast next year. The Food Giant Company's headquarters remain in Brooklyn, NY and are located at 2456 Kings Highway. The Company currently operates 226 retail food stores in 6 northeastern states. It has recently made remodeling and remerchandising investments in most of its stores in an effort to improve company sales. The Food Giant Company has followed the industry trend of the supercenter and includes in most of its stores an on-site bakery, fish market, butcher, deli counter, and flower shop. Its earnings have grown each year for the past 5 years. In these years, the Company's competitors have suffered from higher operating costs and lower revenues.

Industry Comparables

Supermarket	Period	No. of Stores	Food Sales Per Store ($ Mil)	Net Sales ($ Mil)	% Change
The Food Giant	1997	226	18.1	4090	8.1
	1996	215	17.6	3784	7.6
Value-Rite	1997	144	29	4182	(0.2)
	1996	143	23	4189	(1.2)
Grocery King	1997	1014	10	10101	(2.2)
	1996	1108	9.3	10332	(0.5)
Peter's Inc.	1997	229	10.1	2308	(3.5)
	1996	231	10.4	2392	(3.5)

The Food Giant Management

Patsy Maher, Chairperson and CEO
James Rogen, President
Robert Hein, Vice Chairman
Rachel Wu, Chief Operating Officer
Frank DiGenaro, Chief Financial Officer
Jennifer Freehold, Treasurer

The Food Giant Financials

Year	No. of Stores	Net Sales($ Mil)
1993	167	2349
1994	205	3298
1995	200	3500
1996	215	3784
1997	226	4090

Lesson 5
Work with Slide Shows

<table>
<tr><td>**Exercise**
29</td><td>■ **Show a Presentation** ■ **Check Slides before the Presentation**
■ **Add Slide Transitions** ■ **Add Sound** ■ **Set Transition Advance**</td></tr>
</table>

Slide Sorter Toolbar

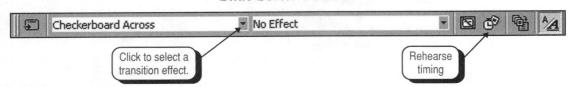

NOTES

Show a Presentation

■ PowerPoint enables you to show an on-screen presentation of your slides to an audience.

■ Slides may be shown one at a time as an oral report is given, or they may run continuously. The run continuously option is convenient if you want, for example, to have a demonstration at a trade show.

■ When a slide show is presented, each slide displays on the entire screen without showing the PowerPoint program (toolbars and menus).

■ You can advance slides by clicking the mouse or pressing a key.

> ✓ Note: If you plan to show your slide presentation to a large audience, you will need to project the computer image onto a large screen. This will require a projection device. See your local computer dealer for projection device information.

■ To activate a slide show, display the first slide to be shown, then click the Slide Show View button 🖵 on the lower left of the screen or select Slide Sho<u>w</u> from the <u>V</u>iew menu.

Check Slides Before the Presentation

■ The **Style Checker** feature within PowerPoint lets you check your slides for spelling errors, visual clarity (too many font styles used), and inconsistencies in case and punctuation before running the slide show. To do so, select St<u>y</u>le Checker from the <u>T</u>ools menu. In the Style Checker dialog box that follows, select what you wish PowerPoint to check and click <u>S</u>tart.

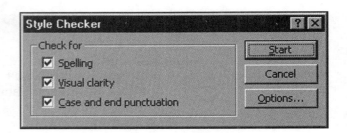

■ Clicking the <u>O</u>ptions button will allow you to set style checking options in the Style Checker Options dialog box.

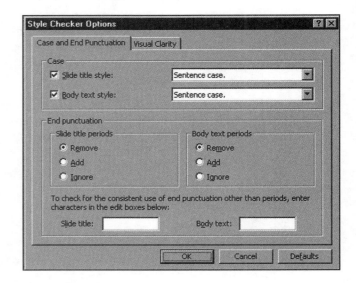

■ After checking the presentation, the Style Checker dialog box displays the Style Checker's findings for you to respond to. See the Keystrokes section of this exercise for specific procedures. You may then return to your presentation to make changes.

Add Slide Transitions

- **Transitions** control the way slides move on and off the screen during a slide show.

- Transitions may be added to slides in all views, but Slide Sorter view offers the quickest and easiest way to add transitions, because the Slide Sorter toolbar contains tools for performing these tasks *(see the Slide Sorter Toolbar illustration on the previous page)*.

- To add a transition in Slide Sorter view, select the slide to which to add a transition and then click the Effect drop-down menu on the Slide Sorter toolbar. A drop-down menu of transition choices appears. Select a transition effect. The effect is demonstrated on the selected slide.

- In Slide Sorter view, slides that contain transitions are marked by a slide icon, which appears below and to the left of the miniature slide image.

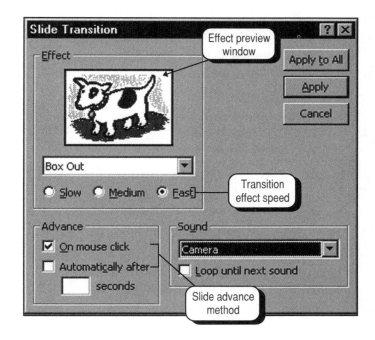

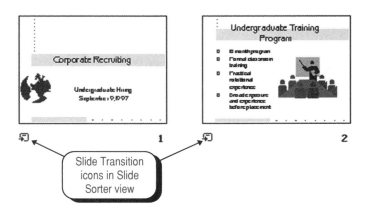

Slide Transition icons in Slide Sorter view

- To add transitions to slides in views other than Slide Sorter, display the slide to apply a transition to and select Slide Transition from the Slide Show menu. In the Slide Transition dialog box that follows, you can select a transition effect, the speed of the transition and how you wish to advance the slide (manually, with a mouse click or automatically, after a specified number of seconds). You can apply these settings to the selected slide (Apply) or to all slides in the presentation (Apply to all).

- Transitions include a number of special effects. Select a transition effect and note the result in the Effect preview window. A description of transition effects appears below and on the following page.

  - **Blinds:** creates an effect of opening and closing venetian blinds and can be set for horizontal or vertical.

  - **Box:** forms a box and opens from the center outward or the edges inward.

  - **Checkerboard:** creates a checkerboard effect by placing small black squares randomly on the screen to reveal the new slide.

  - **Cover:** replaces the slide with the next slide from the specified direction.

  - **Cut:** replaces the slide with the next slide without directional motion.

  - **Dissolve:** sprinkles the slide on and off the screen.

  - **Fade:** gradually darkens the slide to black before revealing the next slide.

- **Random Bars:** reveals the new slide gradually by placing horizontal or vertical bars on the screen.

- **Split:** reveals a new slide and removes the old slide from the center outward or inward, horizontally or vertically.

- **Strips:** reveals a new slide and removes the old slide from one corner of the screen to the other using a variety of directions.

- **Uncover:** reveals a new slide as the active slide is removed.

- **Wipe:** removes one slide from the screen in the specified direction, revealing the new slide.

- **Random:** assigns a random transition effect as you move from slide to slide. Assigning Random to numerous slides generates a random assortment of transitions.

Set Transition Effect Speed

- You can adjust the speed of the transition effect by clicking Slow, Medium or Fast in the Slide Transition dialog box.

Add Sound

- In addition to adding a visual transition for moving slides on and off screen, you may add a sound effect when moving from slide to slide. If you want the sound to affect a slide, select the slide to receive the sound effect, then select the effect from the Sound drop-down list in the Slide Transition dialog box and click Apply. If you wish the sound to remain until the next sound effect is encountered on a slide, click the Loop until next sound check box.

Set Transition Advance

- The Advance option allows you to specify how you wish to advance to the next slide. Select On mouse click to manually advance the slide, or select Automatically to have PowerPoint advance the slide for you. If you choose Automatically, you must specify the number of seconds you wish the slide to remain on screen before PowerPoint advances to the next slide.

- If you select an automatic advance, the timing you assign to the slide will appear below the slide in Slide Sorter view.

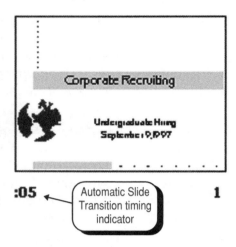

- Transition advance timings may be set individually for each slide (Apply) or collectively for all slides (Apply to All). Slides containing timings may, however, be advanced manually when necessary.

- The **Rehearse Timings** feature allows you to rehearse your presentation and set the advance timings for each slide as you do so. To rehearse a presentation, select Rehearse Timings from the Slide Show menu or click the Rehearse Timings button on the toolbar in Slide Sorter view. A slide show will begin with the following Rehearsal dialog box appearing on the screen. Click the advance button to stop the timing on one slide and restart it on the next slide.

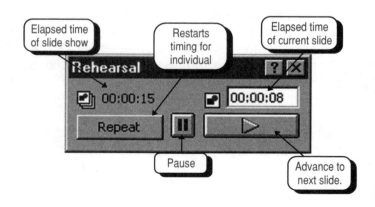

In this exercise, you will edit a previously created presentation by adding items to the Slide and Title Masters, inserting new slides, and adding transition effects, transition sounds, and transition advance timings to selected slides. You will also view your slide presentation.

EXERCISE DIRECTIONS

1. Open ⌨ **FOOD**.

2. Switch to Slide view.

3. Display Rulers and Guides.

4. Switch to Slide Master view.
   a. Delete the clip art in the upper right corner of the slide.
   b. Move the slide title placeholder to the right so that the upper left corner of the slide is empty and the right border of the title placeholder aligns above the right border of the body text placeholder.
   c. Move the company logo to the upper left corner of the slide.
   d. Insert an AutoShape on top of the logo and fill it with any desired color. Send the AutoShape to the back so that the logo is on top of the AutoShape.
   e. Make any necessary adjustments to the size of the logo and/or AutoShape so that the logo fits inside the AutoShape, and the AutoShape fits in the upper left corner of the slide. *(See sample in Illustration A on the following page.)*
   f. Group the AutoShape and the logo.
   g. Copy the new logo.

5. Switch to Title Master view.
   a. Delete the original company logo.
   b. Paste the new company logo from the Slide Master.
   c. Delete the clip art in the upper right corner of the slide.

6. Switch to Slide view.

7. Insert a New Slide and select the Table Slide AutoLayout.

8. Enter the Table information as shown in Illustration A on the following page. Format the title using the same font and style as were used on other slides in the presentation.
   • Center the first row text and set it to bold.
   • Set the text in each row to a different color.
   • Center the text in the second and third columns.

9. Switch to Slide Sorter view.

10. Move the new slide to become Slide 6.

11. Select Slides 1 and 4 and apply a slide transition effect from the Effect drop-down menu on the Slide Sorter toolbar.

12. Select Slide 1 and apply a sound effect using the Slide Transition dialog box.

13. Switch to Outline view and apply a slide transition and a sound effect as well as a transition speed for Slides 2 and 3 using the Slide Transition dialog box.

14. Save the changes to the presentation; do not close the file.

15. Using the Style Checker, check your presentation. Make suggested changes, if appropriate.

16. View the slide show.

17. Switch to Slide view.

18. Add slide transition advance timings to each slide, as you desire.

19. Change the advance method to advance slides automatically.

20. View each slide. Make any necessary adjustments to placeholders and/or font sizes so that text does not overlap the new logo.

21. View the slide show again.

22. Print one copy as Handouts (6 slides per page) in Black and White.

23. Close the file; save the changes.

Illustration A

The Food Giant Costs Less...

Item	Food Giant's Price	Competitor's Price
16 oz. Raisin Bran Cereal	$2.99	$3.99
Eggs	$1.99/dozen	$2.49/dozen
32 oz. Milk	$3.49	$3.99
32 oz. Orange Juice	$2.49	$2.99

6

KEYSTROKES

SHOW PRESENTATION

1. Display Slide 1.
2. Click the **Slide Show View** button...... 🖳
   OR
   a. Click **View** .... `Alt`+`V`
   b. Click **Slide Show** .... `W`

ADVANCE SLIDES

1. Start presentation slide show *(see directions above)*.
2. Click left mouse button.
   OR
   Press **Enter** .... `Enter`

CHECK SLIDES BEFORE THE PRESENTATION

1. Open desired presentation.
2. Click **Tools** .... `Alt`+`T`
3. Click **Style Checker** .... `Y`
4. Select desired elements to check.
5. Click **Start** .... `Alt`+`S`
6. For each suggested inconsistency, select one of the following buttons from the Style Checker dialog box:
   a. **Ignore** .... `Alt`+`I`
      to ignore the current occurrence of the inconsistency.
   b. **Ignore All** .... `Alt`+`G`
      to ignore all occurrences of the inconsistency in the presentation.
   c. **Change** .... `Alt`+`C`
      to have Style Checker correct the inconsistency.
   d. **Change All** .... `Alt`+`L`
      to have Style Checker correct all occurrences of the inconsistency in the presentation.

ADD TRANSITIONS

✓ *The following commands are available in Slide, Outline, and Notes Page views.*

1. Display slide to which to apply the transition.
2. Click **Slide Show** .... `Alt`+`D`
3. Click **Slide Transition** .... `T`
4. Click the **Effect** .... `Alt`+`E`
   drop-down arrow.

---

5. Click desired transition..... `↓` `↑` `Enter`
6. Click **Apply** .... `Alt`+`A`
   to apply transition to displayed slide.
   OR
   Click **Apply to All** .... `Alt`+`T`
   to apply transition to all slides.
   OR
1. Click **View** .... `Alt`+`V`
2. Click **Slide Sorter** .... `D`
   a. Click the **Transition Effect** drop-down menu 🔲 `No Transition` `▼` on **Slide Sorter** toolbar to display a list of effects.
   b. Select desired transition.
   OR
   a. Click 🔲 .... `Alt`+`E`
      on Slide Sorter toolbar and click the **Effect** drop-down list.
   b. Click desired transition ..... `↓` `↑` `Enter`
   c. Click **Apply** .... `Alt`+`A`
      to apply transition to displayed slide.
      OR
      Click **Apply to All**............... `Alt`+`T`
      to apply transition to all slides.

SET TRANSITION SPEED

1. Display slide to which to apply the transition.
2. Click **Slide Show** .... `Alt`+`D`
3. Click **Slide Transition** .... `T`
4. Select a transition effect. *(See Add Transitions, above.)*
5. Select desired speed for transition:
   - **Slow** .... `Alt`+`S`
   - **Medium** .... `Alt`+`M`
   - **Fast** .... `Alt`+`F`
6. Click **Apply** .... `Alt`+`A`
   to apply speed to current slide.
   OR
   Click **Apply to all** .... `Alt`+`T`
   to apply speed to all slides in presentation.

ADD TRANSITION SOUND

1. Display slide to which to apply the sound transition.
2. Click **Slide Show** .... `Alt`+`D`
3. Click **Slide Transition** .... `T`
4. Click the **Sound** .... `Alt`+`U`
   drop-down arrow.
5. Select a sound effect........ `↓` `↑` `Enter`
6. Click **Apply** .... `Alt`+`A`
   to apply sound transition to displayed slide.
   OR
   Click **Apply to All** .... `Alt`+`T`
   to apply sound transition to all slides.

SET SLIDE ADVANCE

1. Click **Slide Show** .... `Alt`+`D`
2. Click **Slide Transition** .... `T`
3. Select desired advance method:
   On mouse click..................... `Alt`+`O`
   OR
   a. **Automatically** .... `Alt`+`C`
   b. Enter number of seconds to display slide before advancing to the next one.
4. Click **Apply** .... `Alt`+`A`
   to apply advance method to displayed slide.
   OR
   Click **Apply to All** .... `Alt`+`T`
   to apply advance type to all slides.

REHEARSE TIMINGS

1. Click **Slide Show** .... `Alt`+`D`
2. Click **Rehearse Timings** .... `R`
   OR
   a. Click **View** .... `Alt`+`V`
   b. Click **Slide Sorter** .... `D`
   c. Click **Rehearse Timings**............ 🕑
3. Click the **Advance** button .... `▷`
   to stop timing and restart the timing for the next slide.

Exercise 30

■ **Preset Animation** ■ **Custom Animation**
■ **Change Animation Order**

NOTES

Preset Animation

■ You can use PowerPoint's **preset animation** feature to control the way text and objects appear on a slide during a slide show. For example, you can use different display effects to show one bulleted item at a time, such as having it fly in from the left of the slide. During the slide show, the items in the list will appear when you click the mouse, or automatically at the time interval you designate.

■ To use preset animation, select the text or object to animate and select Preset Animation from the Slide Show menu. Then, select an animation effect from the submenu that appears.

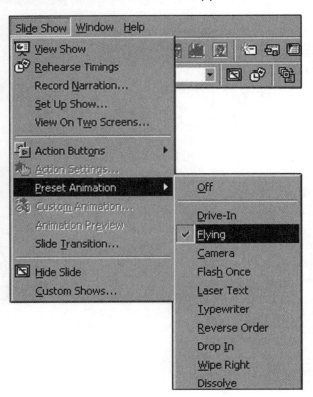

■ You can also add preset animation effects using the Animation Effects toolbar.

Animation Effects Toolbar

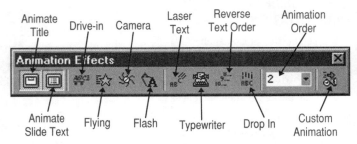

■ To display the Animation Effects toolbar, click the Animation Effects button 🟦 on the Formatting toolbar (the Animation Effects button is not available if you are in Slide Sorter view). Or, select Toolbars, Animation Effects from the View menu.

■ To preview how the animation will appear during a slide show, select Animation Preview from the Slide Show menu. A miniature slide will display and demonstrate how the animation will appear in the slide show. Click the close box ☒ on the miniature slide to remove it.

Custom Animation

- The **custom animation** feature allows you to create your own custom animation for the way text and/or objects appear on a slide during a slide show.

- **To create a custom animation effect for an object or text**, switch to Slide view and display the slide that contains the object or text to which you want to apply the animation. Right-click the object or text box and select Custo__m__ Animation, or select the object and then select Custo__m__ Animation from the Sli__de__ Show menu.

- In the Custom Animation dialog box that follows, select the Effects tab and choose from the following options:

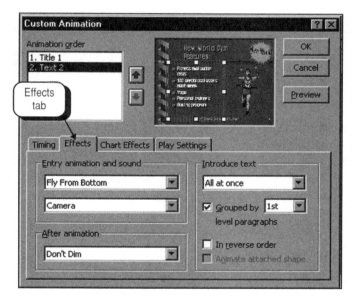

- *Entry animation and/or sound.* Click the drop-down list arrow and choose the way the text or object is introduced on the slide.

- *Introduce text.* Click the drop-down list arrow and choose how you want to introduce text on the slide: All at once (the default), by word, or by letter.

- *After animation.* Click the drop-down list arrow if you wish to dim the text or object after it appears on the slide. You can also give the text or object a different color after it displays on screen.

- *Grouped by.* Click the drop-down list arrow to select the level of text that will be animated (1st, 2nd, 3rd, etc.).

- *In reverse order.* Select the checkbox to have text appear in reverse order.

- **To animate chart elements**, right-click the chart, click Custo__m__ Animation, select the Chart Effects tab on the Custom Animation dialog box and choose from the following options:

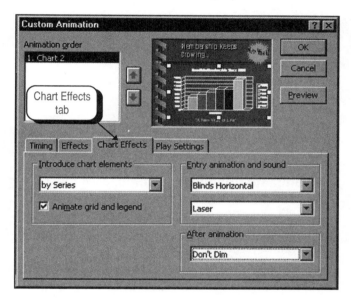

- *Introduce chart elements.* Click the drop-down list arrow to select the way you wish each chart element to be introduced: by Series, by Category, by Element in Series, or by Element in Category.

- *Animate grid and legend.* Select to animate chart grid, legend, text and axis separately.

- *Entry animation and sound.* Click the first drop-down list arrow to select the way you want to introduce each chart element. Click the second drop-down list arrow to choose an accompanying sound.

- *After animation.* Click the drop-down list arrow if you wish to dim the chart element after it appears on the slide. You can also give the chart element a different color after it displays on screen.

- The Timing tab in the Custom Animation dialog box lists text or objects that have not been animated.

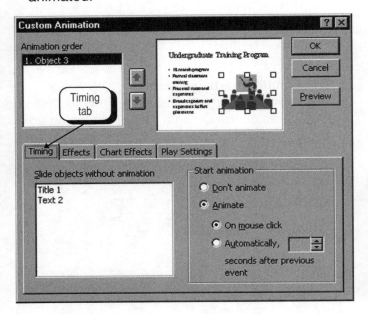

- **To animate unanimated items,** click the Timing tab, select the unanimated item(s) from the Slide objects without animation list box, and select the Animate option button. Then click the Effects tab and choose an animation effect.

- **To set the timing for animated items,** select the item from the Animation order list box, then click the Timing tab, select the Automatically button and indicate how many seconds after the previous event you wish the animation to start.

- The Play Settings tab in the Custom Animation dialog box allows you to set how audio and video clips play during a slide show.

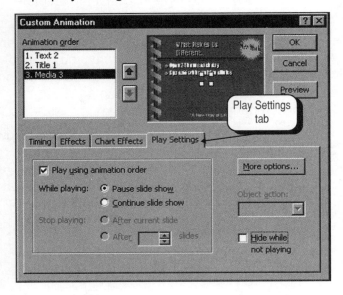

Change Animation Order

- The items on your slide that have been animated and the order in which they have been animated appear in the Animation order list box in the Custom Animation dialog box. You can change the animation order by selecting the object from the Animation order list that you wish to move and clicking the Up or Down arrow to move the object up or down in the animation order.

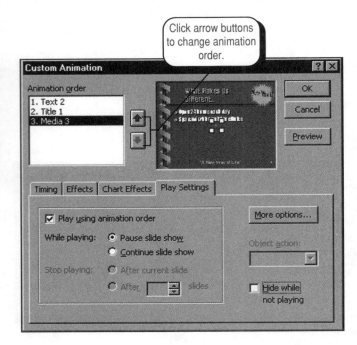

EXERCISE DIRECTIONS

1. Open ⌨ **HOUSE**, or open 💾 **30HOUSE**.

2. Switch to Slide view.

3. Insert a New Slide and select the Table Slide AutoLayout.

4. Enter the slide title as shown in Illustration A, below.

5. Enter the Table information as shown in Illustration A.
   - Use three columns and five rows.
   - Center the second two columns of text. Set the first row of text to bold.
   - Make any necessary adjustments so that the column text does not overlap the graphics.

6. Switch to Slide Sorter view.

7. Move the new slide to become Slide 5.

8. Create a desired transition effect for each slide.

9. Add a 5-second slide transition timing for Slide 4.

10. Switch to Slide view.

11. Create a preset animation transition for bulleted text on Slides 2, 6, and 8 using any desired option.

12. Animate the AutoShape on Slide 8 using any desired effect.

13. Display Slide 4 (NY real estate has grown...). Animate the bar chart by Category using any desired effect and add a sound effect.

14. Save the changes to the presentation; do not close the file.

15. Using the Style Checker, check your presentation. Make suggested changes, if appropriate.

16. View the slide show.

17. Change the advance method to advance all slides automatically, and set a transition time as desired.

18. View the slide show again.

19. Print one copy as Handouts (6 slides per page) in Black and White.

Illustration A

Average sale price of NY apartments per room

	Co-op	Condo
Studio	$39,579	$80,839
1 Bedroom	$57,621	$92,499
2 Bedrooms	$76,856	$138,752
3 Bedrooms	$237,973	$230,554

KEYSTROKES

APPLY PRESET ANIMATION TO LISTS, OBJECTS, OR CHARTS

✔ *Many of the following steps can be performed in other views, but all the features are available in Slide view.*

–FROM ANIMATION EFFECTS TOOLBAR–

1. Click the **Animation Effects** button ... 🌠 on the Formatting toolbar to display the Animation Effects toolbar.
2. Select the slide containing list, object, or chart that you want to animate.
3. Click anywhere inside list, object, or chart that you want to animate.
4. Click desired animation effect on the Animation Effects toolbar.

   To preview animation:

   a. Click **Slide Show** .... Alt + D
   b. Click **Animation Preview** .... E

   ✔ *A miniature of the slide with the selected animation effect appears on screen.*

–FROM SLIDE VIEW–

1. Select slide containing list, object, or chart that you want to animate.

   a. Click **Slide Show** .... Alt + D
   b. Click **Preset Animation** .... P
2. Select desired effect.

   OR

   Click **Off** .... O
   to turn off all effects.

   To preview animation:

   a. Click **Slide Show** .... Alt + D
   b. Click **Animation Preview** .... E

   ✔ *A miniature of the slide with the selected animation effect appears on screen.*

APPLY CUSTOM ANIMATION TO LISTS, OBJECTS OR CHARTS

✔ *Many of the following steps can be performed in other views, but all the features are available in Slide view.*

1. Select the slide containing list, object, or chart that you want to animate.
2. Click anywhere inside list, object, or chart that you want to animate.
3. Click **Custom Animation** .... 🕷 on Animation Effects toolbar.

   OR

   a. Click **Slide Show** .... Alt + D
   b. Click **Custom Animation** .... M
4. Select options for list, object, or chart that you want to animate:

   • **Animation order:** selects order for various animated items to appear on slide.

   • **Timing:** selects how, when and/or if elements will be animated on slide.

   • **Effects:** selects animation and sound effects.

   • **Chart Effects:** selects how chart elements will be introduced on a slide that contains a chart.

   • **Play Settings:** determines settings for audio and video clips on slide.

   ✔ *Options that are dimmed are not applicable to the currently selected item that you want to animate.*

   To preview animation:

   a. Click **Slide Show** .... Alt + D
   b. Click **Animation Preview** .... E

   ✔ *A miniature of the slide with the selected animation effect appears on screen.*

CHANGE ANIMATION ORDER

1. Select desired object to which to apply custom animation.
2. Click **Slide Show** .... Alt + D
3. Click **Custom Animation** .... M

   OR

   a. Right-click desired object.
   b. Click **Custom Animation** .... M

   OR

   a. Click **Animation Effects** button ... 🌠 on the Formatting toolbar.
   b. Click **Custom Animation** .... 🕷 button.
4. Click in **Animation Order** .... Alt + O list box.
5. Click on item to move.
6. Click **Up** or **Down** ⬇ arrow buttons to move item.
7. Click **OK** .... Enter

NEXT EXERCISE

Exercise 31

■ **Insert Comment** ■ **Create Handouts**
■ **Create Speaker Notes** ■ **Notes Master and Handouts Master**

Reviewing Toolbar

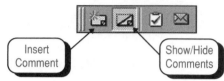

NOTES

Insert Comment

■ Comments are hidden notes or annotations that you or a reviewer can add to a presentation. These comments can be read on screen, hidden when the presentation is printed, printed with the presentation, or incorporated into the presentation. By default, PowerPoint uses information in the User Information Profile to identify the author of the comments inserted into a presentation.

■ To insert a comment, you must be in Slide view. Display the slide on which you wish to add a comment and select Comment from the Insert menu. A Reviewing toolbar, along with a comment box displays.

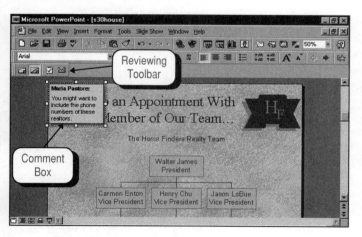

■ Enter the comment in the comment box. Click outside the comment box to resume work on your slide. Comment boxes are objects and can be moved and resized like any other objects.

■ A displayed comment box will print as part of the slide. To hide the comment, click the Show/Hide Comment button on the Reviewing toolbar. A hidden comment will not print with the slide. To delete a comment, display the comment, select the comment box and press the Del key.

Create Handouts

■ PowerPoint allows you to print your presentation as Handouts with 2, 3 or 6 slides on a page. These printouts may be distributed to the audience so that they can follow along with your on-screen presentation and have material to which they can refer at a later time.

■ In previous exercises, you printed your presentation as handouts with 2 or 6 slides per page. To print handouts with 3 slides per page, the same procedure is used. Select Print from the File menu, click the Print what drop-down arrow and select a desired handout option.

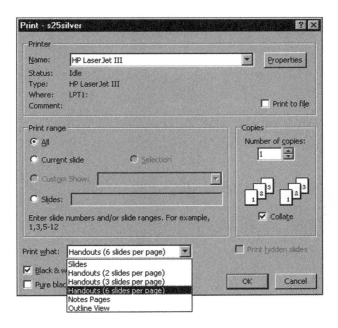

Create Speaker Notes

■ PowerPoint allows you to print your presentation showing a miniature slide image at the top of the page with a notes placeholder below the image to which you can add speaker's notes. These notes can assist the speaker in delivering the presentation. Or, the notes placeholder can be left blank so that the audience can use it for notetaking.

■ You can enter speaker notes in either Notes Page view or Slide view. In Notes Page view, display the slide on which you want to add notes. Select Notes Page from the View menu or click the Notes Page View button 🖵 Then, click the text placeholder and type your notes.

Note: You cannot edit the slide in Notes Page view.

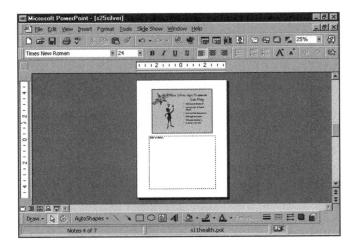

■ In Slide view, display the slide on which you want to add notes and select Speaker Notes from the View Menu. In the Speaker Notes dialog box that appears, you can type or edit your notes. To view your notes on the Notes page, click the Notes Page View button.

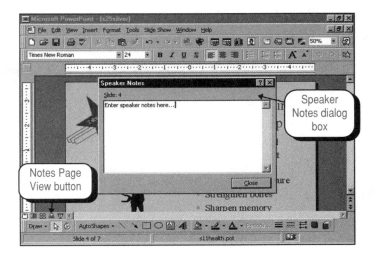

Format Notes Pages

■ You can format text on the Notes pages before or after you enter it. Use the commands on the Formatting toolbar, or the commands (Font, Line Spacing, Bullet, etc.) on the Format menu.

Print Notes Pages

■ Use the same procedures to print Notes pages that you used to print slides and handouts.

Notes Master and Handout Master

■ In Exercise 13, you learned to use the Slide Master to insert text or graphics on one slide and have it appear on all slides of your presentation. The Handout and Notes Masters allow you to customize your handouts or Notes pages. You can add a header or footer (which may include the date/time, page number, topic or speaker's name) to the Master and have it appear on all slides in the handouts or Notes pages.

■ To access Handout Master, select Master, Handout Master from the View menu. A Handout Master layout, along with a Handout Master floating toolbar appears *(see illustration on following page)*. Select the appropriate button on the Handout Master floating toolbar to indicate how many slides you desire on each page.

■ To add a header or footer, page number, etc., select <u>H</u>eader and Footer from the <u>V</u>iew menu and click the Notes and Handouts tab. Enter the header and footer information you wish to include on your Master. Headers and/or footers added to the Handout Master will also appear on Notes pages. *(See Insert Slide Numbers, Date and Time, and Footer Text in Exercise 13 for more information on headers and footers.)*

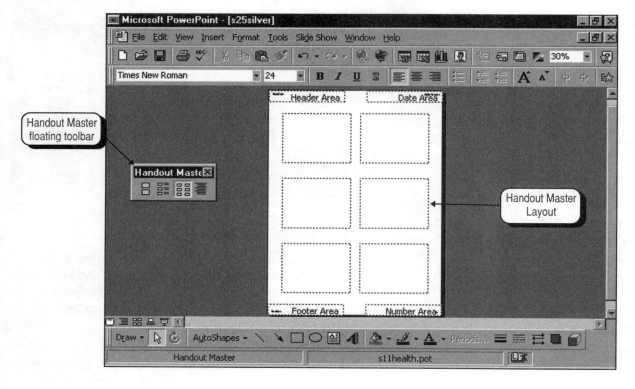

■ To access Notes Master, select <u>M</u>aster, <u>N</u>otes Master from the <u>V</u>iew menu. A Notes Master layout appears. Enter text or objects that you wish to appear on your Notes pages.

■ To add a header or footer, click the appropriate placeholder in the Notes Master and enter the related information. Placeholders may be moved or deleted, as desired.

Notes Master Layout

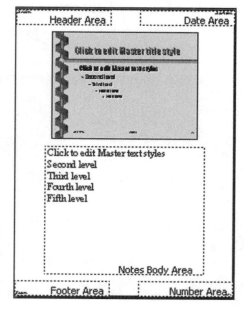

EXERCISE DIRECTIONS

1. Open ☞ **SILVER**, or open 🖫 **31SILVER**.

2. Switch to Slide view.

3. Create a desired transition effect for each slide.

4. Display Slide 3.
   - Animate the bar chart by Category and add any desired sound effect.

5. Display Slide 4.

6. Insert a comment that says, "You might want to add statistics as evidence of Silver Age's success."

7. Insert a new slide as Slide 5, and select the Chart AutoLayout.
   - Enter the following chart data:

Silver Age	84%
Young Forever	25%
Vitamins 2000	36%

   - Apply the Clustered Column chart (without 3-D effect).
   - Use the default font sizes, styles and colors.
   - Enter slide title and x-axis title as shown in Illustration A on the following page. Show the percentage values indicated.

8. Make any necessary adjustments to the chart and the slide title so that they do not overlap other slide elements.

9. Delete the comment on Slide 4.

10. Switch to Notes Page view. Add the following notes to the slides indicated using a bulleted 14-point font size (see example shown in Illustration B on the following page).
    - ✓ (Hint: Click the Bullet button on the Formatting toolbar to add bullets.)

11. Slide 1:
    - Introduce the purpose of the presentation.
    - Give a general overview of the items to be covered in the presentation.

12. Slide 3:
    - Review the different Silver Age vitamins and how each targets a specific age group.

13. Slide 5:
    - Studies show that Silver Age is the most effective of these vitamins.
    - Discuss similar statistics for blood-pressure reduction.

14. Switch to Notes Master view.
    - Enter the footer information and the date, (updating automatically), as shown in Illustration B.
    - Delete the page number placeholder.

15. Switch to Handout Master view.
    - Enter the same date and footer information as you did on the Notes pages.
    - Insert the page number as shown in Illustration C on page 189.

16. Print one copy of Notes pages 1-5 in Black and White.

17. Print one copy of the presentation as Handouts (3 slides per page) in Black and White.

18. Close the file; save the changes.

Illustration A

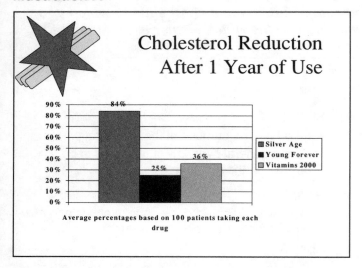

Illustration B

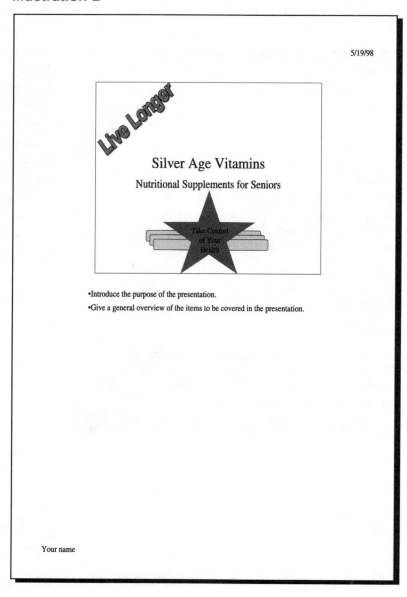

Illustration C

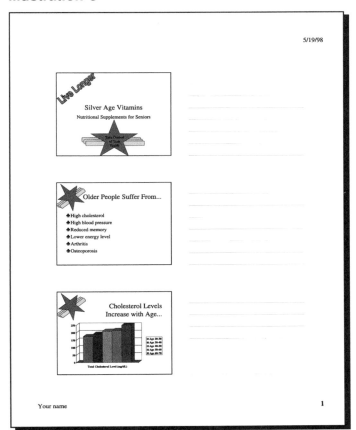

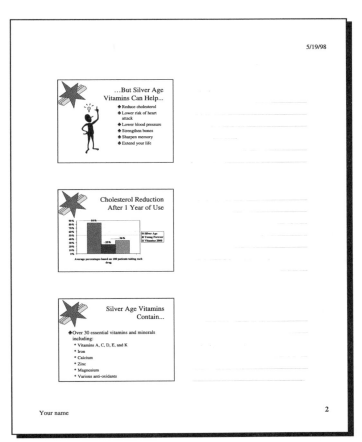

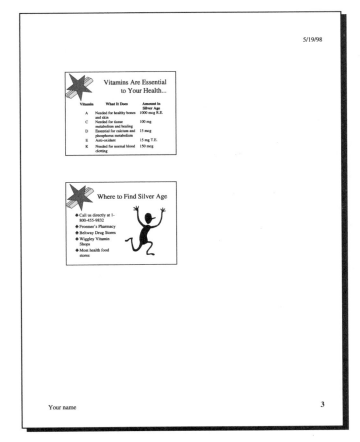

KEYSTROKES

INSERT COMMENT

✓ *You must be in Slide view to insert a comment.*

1. Display the slide on which to add a comment.
   a. Click **Insert** .... `Alt`+`I`
   b. Click **Comment** .... `M`
   OR
   a. Click **View** .... `Alt`+`V`
   b. Click **Toolbars** .... `T`
   c. Click **Reviewing**.
   d. Click **Insert Comment** button ..... 🖳 on the Reviewing toolbar.
2. Type comment in the comment box.

CREATE SPEAKER NOTES

1. Display slide on which to add notes.
2. Click 🖳 .... `Alt`+`V`, `N` to view Notes page.
3. Click on notes placeholder at bottom of page.
4. Type notes.

PRINT NOTES PAGES AND HANDOUTS

1. Click **File** .... `Alt`+`F`
2. Click **Print**................................ `P`
3. Click **Print what**.............. `Alt`+`W`, `↓` list arrow.
4. Click desired option.......... `↓` `↑`, `Enter`
5. Click **OK**............................... `OK`

HANDOUT AND NOTES MASTER

1. Click **View** .... `Alt`+`V`
2. Click **Master**................................. `M`
3. Click **Handout Master** .... `D`
OR
1. Click **Notes Master**....................... `N`
2. Make desired changes.
   To Return to Slide View
   a. Click **View**....................... `Alt`+`V`
   b. Click **Slide** .... `S`

INSERT HEADERS AND/OR FOOTERS ON NOTES PAGES AND HANDOUTS

1. Click **View** .... `Alt`+`V`
2. Click **Header and Footer**................ `H`
3. Select **Notes and Handouts** tab.
4. Make desired selections.

NEXT EXERCISE

<table>
<tr><td>**Exercise**
32</td><td>■ **Use the Annotation Pen**
■ **Create Continuously Running Presentations**</td></tr>
</table>

NOTES

Use the Annotation Pen

■ With the **Annotation Pen,** you can draw on slides during a slide show. Annotations made on the screen during a slide show do not alter the slide in any way and disappear when you move to another slide. Slide transition and animation timings are suspended when you are annotating, and begin again when you turn the Annotator off.

■ To erase annotations on the current slide, press the letter E on the keyboard.

■ The annotator pen can be accessed by clicking on the Menu icon 🖉 △ , which appears in the lower left corner of the screen during a slide show. Select Pen from the pop-up menu. Your mouse then becomes a pen point so you can write on the slide. To change the pen color, select Pointer Options, Pen color from the pop-up menu. To turn Annotator off, click the Menu icon and select Arrow from the pop-up menu.

✓ Note: *If the Menu icon doesn't appear, move the mouse to display it. You can also right-click and select Pen from the shortcut menu.*

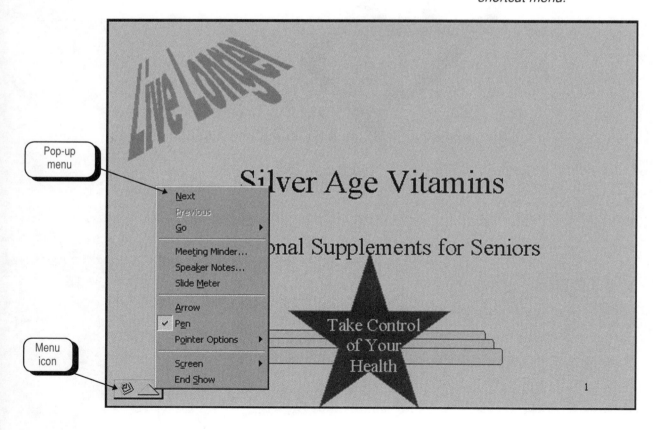

Create Continuously Running Presentations

■ Slide shows can be set to run continuously so that slides advance automatically, and the presentation automatically restarts. Continuously running slide shows are particularly useful when displayed at trade shows or on a sales counter.

■ When creating a continuously running presentation, slide transition timings must be set to allow enough time for people to review the information presented on each slide.

■ To create a continuously running presentation, select the timing for each slide transition as indicated in Exercise 29. Select Set Up show from the Slide Show menu. In the Set Up Show dialog box that follows, click the Loop Continuously Until 'Esc' check box. To stop a running slide show, press Esc.

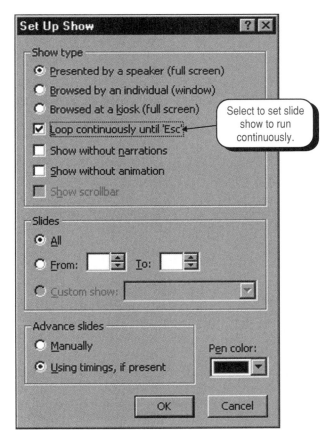

Select to set slide show to run continuously.

In this exercise, you will edit a previously created presentation by adding transitions, sound, and timings to selected sides. You will also use the Annotator during your slide presentation.

EXERCISE DIRECTIONS

1. Open ⌨ **WEDDING**, or open 💾 **32WEDDING**.

2. Switch to Slide view.

3. Apply a desired transition effect and a transition speed for each slide in the presentation in the Slide Transition dialog box.

4. Apply a desired animation effect to bulleted text on Slides 2, 3, 4, 5 and 7. Dim points after animation in any color.

5. Animate and add sound to the clip art graphics on Slides 3 and 5. Add a 5-second animation timing to each. Use any desired animation effect.

6. Display Slide 6 (graph slide). Animate the chart by category and add any desired sound effect.

7. Save the changes to the presentation.

8. View the slide show. Use the Annotator to circle Things to Consider on Slide 2 and the Traditional Reception paragraph on Slide 5.

9. Add slide transition timings to each slide and change the advance method to advance automatically.

10. Set the slide show to run continuously and view the slide show again.

11. After viewing the entire presentation once, stop the presentation.

12. Close the file; save the changes.

KEYSTROKES

ANNOTATE DURING SLIDE SHOWS

1. Click **Slide Show View** button .... 🖥
   OR
   a. Click **View** .... `Alt`+`V`
   b. Click **Slide Sho̲w** .... `W`
2. Click the **Menu** icon .... 📷△
   in lower left corner of screen.
3. Click **Pen** .... `E`
   to turn Annotator on.
4. Press left mouse button and write on
   slide with the "pen."

   To turn Annotator off:
   a. Click the **Menu** icon .... 📷△
      in the lower left corner of screen.
      OR
      Right-click on screen.
   b. Click **A̲rrow** .... `A`

   To change annotator pen color:
   a. Click the **Menu** icon .... 📷△
   b. Select **Po̲inter Options** .... `O`
   c. Click **P̲en color** .... `P`
      and select desired color.

CREATE A CONTINUOUSLY RUNNING SLIDE SHOW

1. Click **Sli̲de Show** .... `Alt`+`D`
2. Click **Slide T̲ransition** .... `T`
3. Select **Automati̲cally** .... `Alt`+`C`
4. Enter number of seconds........... *number*
   to display slide before advancing to
   the next one.
5. Click **A̲pply** .... `Alt`+`A`
   to apply advance type to displayed
   slide.
   OR
   Click **Apply t̲o All** .... `Alt`+`T`
   to apply advance type to all slides.
6. Click **Sli̲de Show** .... `Alt`+`D`
7. Click **S̲et Up Show** .... `S`
8. Click **L̲oop Continuously** .... `Alt`+`L`
   Until 'Esc'.
9. Click **OK** .... `Enter`
10. Click **Slide Show View** button .... 🖥
    to run the slide show.

    To stop Continuous Run of Slide Show:
    Press **Esc** .... `Esc`

Exercise

33

- ■ **Pack and Go**
- ■ **Unpack a Presentation and View It with PowerPoint Viewer**
- ■ **Meeting Minder**

NOTES

Pack and Go

- ■ The Pack and Go Wizard feature lets you save your presentation so that you can show it on another computer that does not have PowerPoint installed. When you save your presentation with Pack and Go, PowerPoint Viewer (the small program that allows you to view your presentation on another computer that does not have PowerPoint installed), is saved along with your presentation. Pack and Go also compresses large files so that you can fit your presentation on one or two floppy disks.

- ■ To access the Pack and Go Wizard, select Pac**k** and Go from the **F**ile menu. In the Pack and Go Wizard dialog box, click the **N**ext button and follow the prompts that step you through the procedure for packing up your presentation.

Unpack a Presentation and View It with PowerPoint Viewer

- ■ Before showing your presentation on another computer, you must unpack it. To do so, open Windows Explorer, then open the folder containing your packed presentation. Double-click PNGSETUP. Then, in the Pack and Go Setup dialog box that follows, enter the path to the folder to which you plan to copy your presentation files.

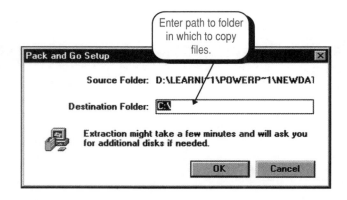

- ■ To view your presentation using the PowerPoint viewer, use Windows Explorer to open the folder that contains the unpacked presentation, and double-click PPVIEW 32 to start the Viewer program. In the Microsoft PowerPoint Viewer dialog box that follows, enter the name of the presentation you wish to show, and click the **S**how button.

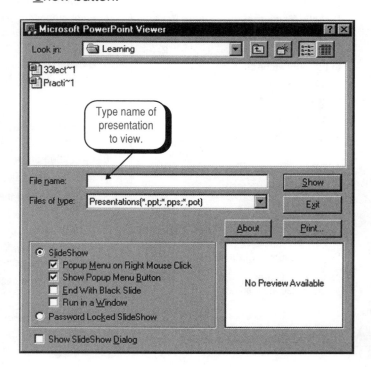

Meeting Minder

- The Meeting Minder feature allows you to record any ideas that are generated during the slide show. To record notes when a slide is on screen, right-click and select Meeting Minder. In the Meeting Minder dialog box that follows, select the Meeting Minutes tab and enter those ideas or notations into the Meeting Minutes box. You can export your notations to a Microsoft Word file by clicking the Export button on the Meeting Minder dialog box.

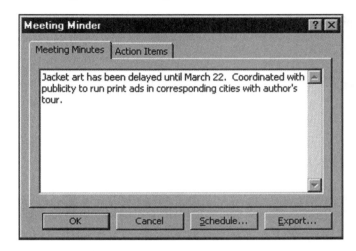

- Once exported, your ideas or notes are automatically formatted into a Meeting Minutes template document, which includes the date, time, and title of the presentation.

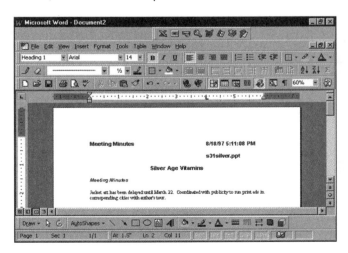

- If you have follow-up items that you wish to record, click the Action Items tab and fill out the information in the dialog box that appears.

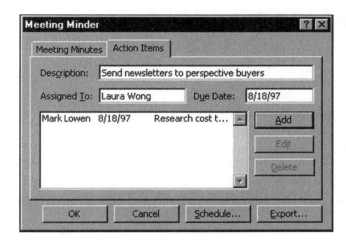

- If Microsoft Outlook is installed on your computer, you can click the Schedule button, which will send your action items to Outlook. Outlook is a program that helps you organize your schedule, manage items, as well as track billable time.

> *In this exercise, you will enhance a previously created presentation by adding slide transitions and animations to text and pictures. You will use Meeting Minder to create notations and use the Pack and Go feature to save your presentation.*

EXERCISE DIRECTIONS

1. Open ⌨ **LECTURE**, or open 💾 **33LECTURE**.

2. Display Rulers and Guides.

3. Display Slide 2 (Overview).
   - Change the slide layout to Clip Art & Text.
   - Insert three pictures: one relating to entertainment, one relating to athletics, and one relating to the literary or academic field. Use the Rulers to size each to approximately 2" high by 2" wide and position them as shown in Illustration A on the following page.
   - Animate each picture on mouse click using any desired effect.
   - Set the animation order as follows: 1. Entertainment picture; 2. Athletic picture; 3. Literary picture.

4. Create any desired transition effect for each slide.

5. Create a desired animation effect for bulleted text on each slide.

6. Change the animation order for the pictures on Slide 2 as follows: 1. Athletic picture; 2. Entertainment picture; 3. Academic picture.

7. Display Slide 6.
   - Insert a comment: Check to see if there is a family discount for five or more in a family.
   - Hide the comment. Save the changes to the presentation.

8. View the presentation. When Slide 5 displays, access Meeting Minder and add the following notes to the Meeting Minutes box.
   - Met with Janice Robbins and her daughter. They are available to be guests at the upcoming lecture.
   - Wendy Blackwell and her daughter, Cameron, are also available to be guests. Ms. Howell approves.

9. If Microsoft Word is installed on your computer, export your notes to Word and print a copy of them.

10. Save the presentation using Pack and Go, and make the following selections when prompted:
    - Save the active presentation.
    - Copy the files to the A drive.
    - Include the linked files.
    - Don't include Viewer.

11. Close the presentation window.

Illustration A

KEYSTROKES

PACK AND GO

1. Click **File**................................ Alt + F
2. Click **Pack and Go**............................ K
3. Follow prompts and click **Next** ..... Alt + N
   to move ahead.

ADD MEETING MINUTES

1. Click **Slide Show View** button .... 🖥
   OR
   a. Click **View** .... Alt + V
   b. Click **Slide Show**........................ W
2. Display slide on which to add meeting minutes.
3. Right-click the mouse.
4. Click **Meeting Minder** .... T
5. Click the **Meeting Minutes** tab.
6. Type ideas, notes, etc. in box.
7. Click the **Export** button........... Alt + E
   to send minutes to Word template.
   OR
   Click **Schedule** button .... Alt + S
   to add minutes to Outlook schedule.

ADD ACTION ITEMS

1. Click **Slide Show View** button......... 🖥
   OR
   a. Click **View** .... Alt + V
   b. Click **Slide Show**........................ W
2. Display slide on which to add action items.
3. Right-click the mouse.
4. Click **Meeting Minder** .... T
5. Click **Action Items** tab.
6. Insert desired information.
7. Click the **Export** button........... Alt + E
   to send minutes to Word template.
   OR
   Click **Schedule** button .... Alt + S
   to add minutes to Outlook schedule.

Exercise 34

■ Summary

In this exercise, you will get a presentation ready for a slide show. You will add transitions and timings, and prepare audience Handouts and Notes pages. You will use the Notes Page Master to add information to all notes pages.

EXERCISE DIRECTIONS

1. Open 🖮 **GYM**, or open 🖫 **34GYM**.

2. Switch to Slide Sorter view.

3. Apply a desired transition effect, a transition speed, and a sound to each slide in the presentation.

4. Switch to Slide view.

5. Apply any desired animation effect to bulleted text on Slides 2, 3, and 5. Dim previous points in any color.

6. Display Slide 6 (Graph slide). Animate the chart by element in a series and add a sound effect.

7. Save the changes to the presentation; do not close the file.

8. View the slide show.

9. Use the Annotator to circle the highest bar on the graph.

10. Switch to Notes Master view.

11. In the Page Setup dialog box, change the Notes and Handouts orientation to portrait.

12. Using the Text Box button, create the company name and date in Arial 24 point as shown in Illustration A on the following page.

    a. Position and size the text box to span the width of the bottom of the Notes Area placeholder as shown.

    b. Tab the date to the 3" mark on the horizontal Ruler.

    c. Use the Line tool on the Drawing toolbar to create the horizontal line. Position it below the name and date text and size it to span the Notes Area placeholder.

    d. Delete the footer and date placeholders.

    e. Move the number placeholder to the upper right corner of the page.

    f. Insert a page number on the top right corner of the page.

13. Switch to Notes Page view.

14. Add the following notes to the slides indicated:

    Slide 1:
    - Introduce yourself and your position in the company.
    - Explain the purpose of today's presentation.

    Slide 2:
    - Review each feature of the New World Gym.
    - Emphasize personal training packages.
    - Outline boxing program.

    Slide 3:
    - Review membership benefits.
    - Emphasize value of each benefit.
    - Compare these benefits to benefits offered at competing gyms.

    Slide 5:
    - Introduce the membership team.

15. Switch to Notes Master view.

16. Using the Copy feature, copy the bottom (company name and date) text to the clipboard.

17. Switch to Handout Master view.

    a. Paste the company name and date text and position it on the bottom center of the page as shown in Illustration B on page 202.

    b. Create a horizontal line below the name and date as shown.

    c. Delete the header, footer, and date placeholders.

d. Move the number placeholder to the upper right corner of the page.

e. Insert a page number on the top right of the page as shown in Illustration B.

18. Print one copy of each Notes Page in Black and White.

19. Print one copy of the presentation as Handouts (3 slides per page) in Black and White.

20. Switch to Slide Sorter view.

21. Add slide transition timings to each slide and change the advance method to advance automatically.

22. Set the slide show to run continuously and view the slide show again.

23. After viewing the entire presentation, stop the presentation.

24. Close the file; save the changes.

Illustration A

Introduce yourself and your position in the company.
Explain the purpose of today's presentation.

New World Gym   January 1998

Illustration B

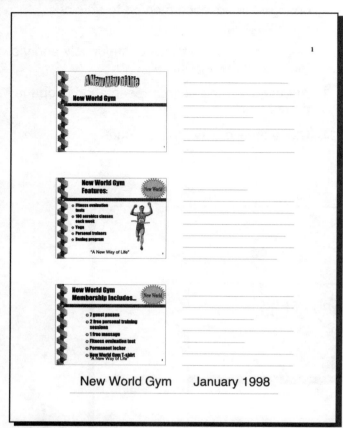

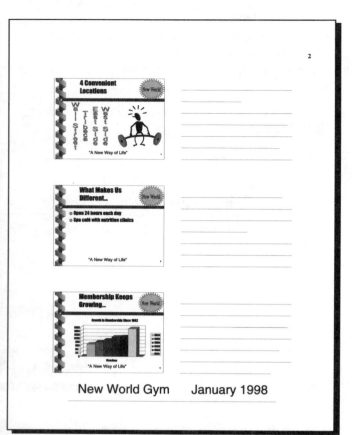

NEXT EXERCISE

Exercise 35

■ Summary

In this exercise, you will prepare a slide show presentation for college-bound students. Your presentation will explain to them how to apply to college. You will add transitions and animations to text, add slide transition timings, and prepare Handouts and Notes pages.

EXERCISE DIRECTIONS

1. Create the presentation shown in Illustration A on pages 206 and 207. Use the Whirlpool template, the appropriate slide layouts and relevant clip art.

2. Use the following data to create the chart on Slide 6:

	1994	1995	1996	1997	1998
Private College	$13,000	$17,000	$23,000	$25,000	$28,000
Public College	$4,000	$5,000	$6,000	$9,000	$11,000

3. Switch to Slide Sorter view.

4. Apply a desired transition effect, a transition speed, and a transition sound effect to each slide in the presentation.

5. Switch to Slide view.

6. Apply a desired custom animation to bulleted text on Slides 2, 3, 4, 5, and 7 using any desired effects. Dim bulleted items to any color after animation.

7. Display Slide 6 (Chart slide).
    *   Animate the chart by element in category.
    *   Add a sound effect.

8. Save the presentation; name it **COLLEGE**. Do not close the file.

9. View the slide show.
    *   On Slide 3, use the Annotator Pen to circle the Things to Consider paragraph.
    *   On Slide 6, circle the bar representing the private college tuition cost in 1998.

10. Switch to Slide Sorter view.

11. Add any desired slide transition timings to each slide and change the advance method to automatically.

12. Set the slide show to run continuously.

13. View the slide show again.

14. After viewing the entire presentation, stop the presentation.

15. Switch to Notes Master view.
    a. Insert a page number in the bottom right corner of the page.
    b. Delete the footer and date placeholders.
    c. Using the WordArt of your choice, insert the words "Off to College!" in a 36-point sans serif font. Position it in the bottom left corner of the page as shown in Illustration B on page 207. Size it to approximately 1" high by 4" wide.

16. Switch to Notes Page view.

17. Add the following notes to the slides indicated:

Slide 1:
*   Introduce yourself.
*   Explain the purpose of today's presentation.

Slide 2:
*   Explain how to register for the SAT and how the exam is graded.
*   Explain how to identify suitable colleges.
*   Explain how to send away for college applications.
*   Explain where to seek financial aid.

Slide 6:
*   Review the growth in tuition each year.

18. Switch to Notes Master view.

19. Copy the WordArt text to the clipboard.

20. Switch to Handout Master view.
    a. Delete the footer and date placeholders.
    b. Insert a page number in the bottom right corner of the page.
    c. Paste the WordArt on the bottom left corner of the page.

21. Switch to Slide Sorter view.

22. Compare your presentation with Illustration A on the following two pages. Make adjustments to placeholders and font sizes, if necessary, so that slide contents fit properly on each slide.

23. Print one copy of each Notes Page in Black and White.

24. Close the file; save the changes.

Illustration A

How to Plan for College

Simpson College Advisors
March 1998

1

Planning for College Doesn't Have to Be Complicated...

- Take the scholastic aptitude test (SAT)
- Identify colleges that best suit you
- Send in application forms
- Choose between admissions offers
- Investigate financial aid sources

2

Finding the College That Is Right for You...

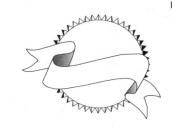

- Things to Consider:
  - your abilities
  - your interests
  - your values
  - your career interests
  - your geographic preferences
  - cost

3

Use the Web to Help You Make Choices

- Peterson's Education Center, www.peterson.com
  - offers detailed information on college programs
- CollegeNet, www.collegenet.com
  - helps you research schools according to region, cost and programs
- CollegeEdge, www.collegeedge.com
  - full of fun facts about college
- FastWeb, www.studentservices.com/fastweb/
  - offers financial aid information
- Financial Aid Information, www.finaid.org
  - ultimate financial aid source

4

How to Complete an Application...

- Type or neatly print all application forms
- Describe your interests, talents and hobbies
- Offer the admissions staff reasons you are well suited to the school

5

Tuition Rises Every Year...

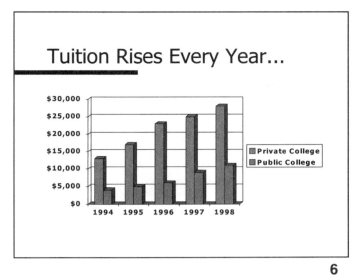

Apply for Financial Aid...

- College Work-Study
- Tuition Assistance Program
- Educational Opportunity Program
- Aid for Part-Time Students
- Higher Education Opportunity Program

6

7

Illustration B

How to Plan for College

Simpson College Advisors
March 1998

Introduce yourself.
Explain the purpose of today's presentation.

Off to College!

1

NEXT LESSON

Lesson 6
PowerPoint and the Web

Exercise 36

- ■ **Internet Basics**
- ■ **Using PowerPoint 97 to Access the Internet**
- ■ **Search the Internet Using a Search Engine**
- ■ **Search the Internet Using a Uniform Resource Locator (URL)**
- ■ **The Favorites Folder**

Web Toolbar

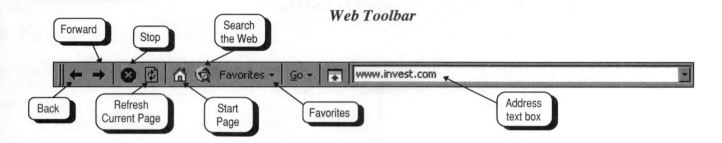

NOTES

Introduction

■ This lesson will introduce you to accessing the Internet directly from within PowerPoint 97. You will also learn how to use information gathered from various Web site searches in your PowerPoint presentation. If you are not connected to the Internet, you can use the Internet Simulation CD-ROM, published by DDC, to simulate Internet searches for some of the exercises in this lesson.

Internet Basics

■ The Internet is a worldwide network of computers. These computers may be located in businesses, schools, research foundations and/or individuals' homes. Those who are connected to this network can share information with each other, communicate via e-mail and search for information.

■ The World Wide Web (www) is a service of the Internet in which pages, created by companies, individuals, schools and government agencies around the world, are linked to each other.

■ In order to access the Internet, you (or your company, or school) must sign up with an Internet service provider (ISP). Some popular service providers include America Online, Microsoft Network (MSN), and CompuServe.

■ A Web browser is a program on your computer that displays the information you retrieve from the Internet in a readable format. The most popular Web browsers are Internet Explorer and Netscape Navigator. Some service providers give you a Web browser when you sign up. If your service provider does not give you a Web browser, you will need to purchase and install one.

Using PowerPoint 97 to Access the Internet

■ Microsoft PowerPoint 97 provides easy access to the Internet through menus and toolbar buttons. When you click the Web Toolbar button 🌐 on the Standard toolbar, the Web toolbar, illustrated above, displays.

Search the Internet

   ✓ *Note:*   *If you are using Microsoft Office 97, Internet Explorer is probably already set up on your computer. The exercises in this lesson assume you are accessing the Internet using Internet Explorer.*

■ The Internet gives you access to information, graphics, animation and sounds that you can add to a PowerPoint presentation.

■ To begin searching the Internet from within PowerPoint 97, click the Web Toolbar button on the Standard toolbar to display the Web toolbar. Then, click the Search the Web button 🔍 on the Web toolbar; this will bring you to the General Search page of Internet Explorer. The Internet Explorer window, illustrated below, replaces the PowerPoint window.

Internet Explorer Window

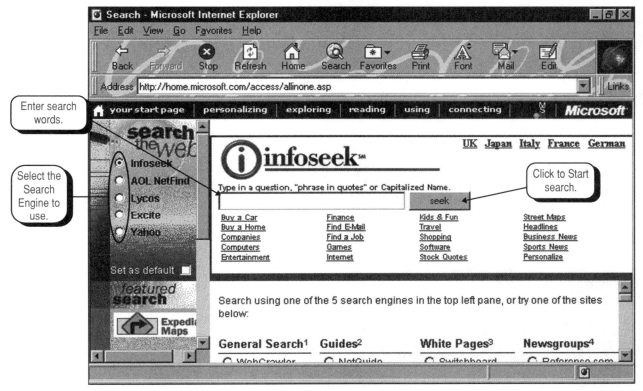

■ A search text box and a list of search engine names (Yahoo!®, InfoSeek℠, AltaVista™, Lycos®, Excite, etc.) display on the page. A search engine searches databases around the world for results of your search topic. Some search engines return more results than others.

■ To start a search, first select the search engine you want to use. Then, enter the search word(s) in the search text box, and click the appropriate button (Submit, Search, Go Get it) to start the search.

■ Search sites are updated constantly, so results can vary from day to day. For best results:

  • Always check for misspelled words and typing errors.

  • Use descriptive words and phrases to narrow the search.

  • Use synonyms and variations of words.

  • If you do not find what you are looking for, use a different search engine and try again.

■ When a site is contacted, its address of that site displays in the Address text box (for example: http://www.denverpost.com). A Web address is also referred to as a URL—Uniform Resource Locator.

Search the Web Using a Uniform Resource Locator (URL)

- A Uniform Resource Locator, frequently referred to as a URL, is a World Wide Web address. A URL address provides a direct link to a particular Web site.

- To access a Web page from PowerPoint 97 using a URL address, type the address in the Address text box on the Web toolbar *(see illustration of Web toolbar on page 210)* and press Enter.

- To access a specific Web site when you are in Microsoft Explorer, enter the URL address in the Address text box below the Internet Explorer toolbar *(see illustration below)* and press Enter. Or click File, Open.

- In the Open dialog box that follows, enter the URL address, and click OK.

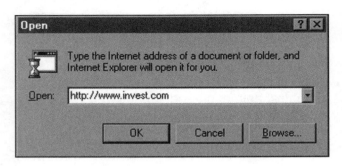

- Once you have contacted a site, some words appear in a different color, underlined, or both. Clicking on one of these hyperlinks takes you to a new page with related information. Illustrated below is the result of a search for clip art. Note the hyperlinks.

Sample Search Results

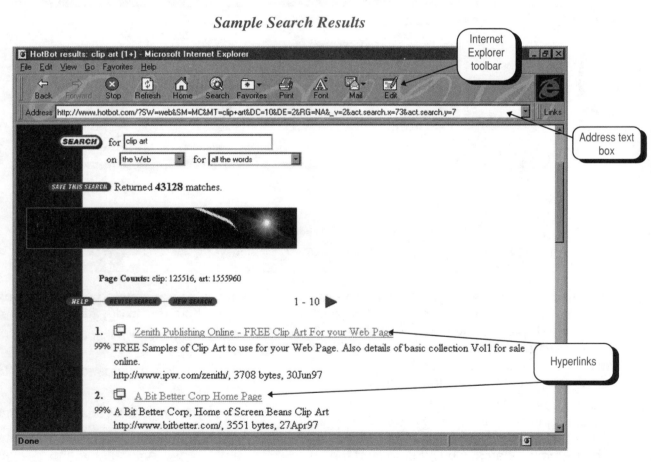

- Each time you click a hyperlink, you will be brought to a new page. To move back and forward among the links (pages) you have accessed in the current session, click the Back and Forward buttons ← → on the Internet Explorer toolbar.

- If the page seems to take too long to access, click the Refresh button 🔁 on the Internet Explorer toolbar. If you decide to take a different action, click the Stop button ⊗ on the Internet Explorer toolbar.

Favorites Folders

- If you find a site that you like and to which you wish to return, or if there is a site that you visit frequently, you can save the address of the site in the Favorites Folder. To do so, go to the Web site that you want to add to your Favorites folder, click the Favorites button [≡▾ Favorites] on the Internet Explorer toolbar, and select <u>A</u>dd to Favorites.

- In the Add to Favorites dialog box that follows, the name of the Web site you are currently visiting appears in the <u>N</u>ame box. Click OK to add the web address to the Favorites folder.

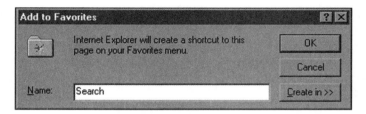

- To open a Web site from the Favorites folder in PowerPoint, click the Favorites button [Favorites ▾] on the Web toolbar and click Open <u>F</u>avorites from the submenu that appears. Then, select the site to which you wish to return. Internet Explorer will open at the selected Web site.

In this exercise, you will launch the Internet from within PowerPoint 97 and search the Web for information. If you have a live Internet connection, follow Directions A. If you plan to use the DDC Simulation, follow Directions B.

EXERCISE DIRECTIONS

Directions A

1. Create a new Blank Presentation.

2. Display the Web toolbar.

3. Move the mouse pointer over each button on the Web toolbar and note the ScreenTip that displays for each one.

4. Click the Search the Web button on the Web toolbar.

5. Select the Excite Search Engine on the General Search Page in Internet Explorer.

6. Type Clipart Collection in the search text box and click the Search button.

7. Scroll down through the list of hyperlinks. Click on the hyperlinks you want to go to until you find a site containing graphics you like.

8. Add this site to your Favorites Folder.

9. Click the Back and Forward buttons to move among the links.

10. Close Internet Explorer.

11. Close PowerPoint.

Directions B

✓ *If you make a mistake as you go through the simulation, click Menu and start the exercise again.*

1. Create a new Blank Presentation.

2. Display the Web toolbar.

3. Move the mouse pointer over each button on the Web toolbar and note the ScreenTip that displays for each one.

4. Launch the DDC Simulation.
   a. Click Go, Open on the Web toolbar.
   b. Type C:\DDCPUB\PPT97INT.IMR.
   ✓ *Be sure that the simulation has been installed on your hard drive. If files are on a drive other than C, replace C with the correct letter.*
   c. Click OK to launch the simulation.
   d. Select Exercise 1: Clipart Search.

5. Follow the on-screen prompts to find the clip art.

6. Add this site to your Favorites Folder.

7. Exit the DDC Simulation.

8. Close PowerPoint.

KEYSTROKES

DISPLAY WEB TOOLBAR

Click **Web Toolbar** button ....[🌐]
on the Standard toolbar.

OR

1. Click **View** .... [Alt]+[V]
2. Click **Toolbars** .... [T]
3. Select Web toolbar.

   ✓ *To hide Web toolbar, click the Web Toolbar button or deselect the toolbar from the toolbar list in the View menu.*

ACCESS INTERNET EXPLORER GENERAL SEARCH PAGE FROM POWERPOINT

1. Display the Web toolbar (see above).
2. Click **Search the Web** button ....[🌐]

PERFORM A SIMPLE SEARCH

1. Display the Web toolbar (see above).
2. Click **Search the Web** button ....[🌐]

   OR

   a. Click **Go** .... [Alt]+[G]
   b. Click **Search the Web** .... [W]
3. Click the Search engine you wish to use.
4. Type the search word(s) .... *text* in the search text box.
5. Click **Search** .... [Search] (or Submit, Go Get It, etc.).

ADD WEB ADDRESSES TO FAVORITES FOLDER

-FROM MICROSOFT INTERNET EXPLORER-

1. Display the site you want to add to the favorites folder.
2. Click the **Favorites** button .... [Favorites]

   OR

   Click the **Favorites** menu .... [Alt]+[A]
3. Click **Add to Favorites** .... [A]
4. Type the name .... [Alt]+[N], *name* of the site if not indicated.
5. Click **OK** .... [Enter]

OPEN A WEB ADDRESS FROM THE FAVORITES FOLDER

-FROM POWERPOINT-

1. Display the Web toolbar (see above).
2. Click **Favorites** button .... [Favorites ▾]
3. Click **Open Favorites** .... [F]
4. Double-click the site to open.

OPEN A WEB SITE FROM POWERPOINT

1. Type the URL .... *address* in the Address text box.
2. Press **Enter** .... [Enter]

   OR

1. Click **Go** .... [Alt]+[G]
2. Click **Open** .... [O]
3. Type the URL .... *address*
4. Click **OK** .... [Enter]

<table>
<tr><td>**Exercise**
37</td><td>■ **Get Help from the Microsoft Web Site**
■ **PowerPoint Central**</td></tr>
</table>

NOTES

Get Help from the Microsoft Web Site

■ In addition to the Help features that you have learned about earlier in this book, you can also get help from Microsoft Web sites. To do this, select Microsoft on the Web from the Help menu. A submenu displays several links to Microsoft support and information.

■ For example, if you click Microsoft Office Home Page, you will go to a page on the Microsoft Web site that displays information about MS Office products.

Microsoft Office Web Site

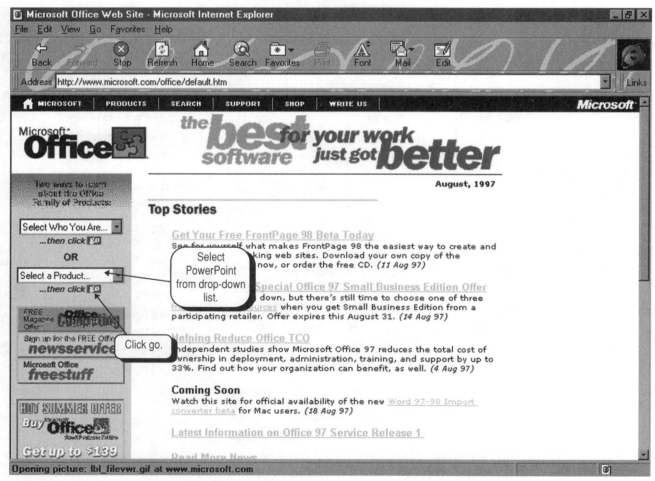

- To access information about PowerPoint, select PowerPoint from the Select a Product drop-down list on the Office Home Page and click go. This will link you to the Microsoft PowerPoint Home Page. Click on desired link.

Microsoft PowerPoint Home Page

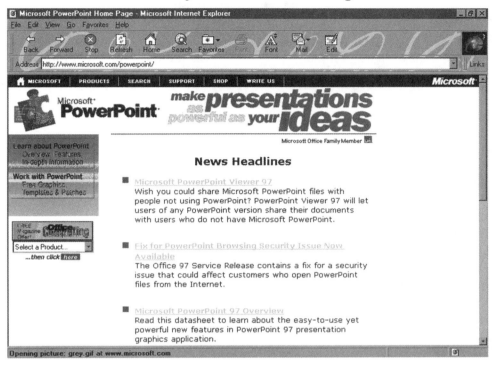

PowerPoint Central

- PowerPoint Central is a slide show presentation that contains information as well as tips and tricks about using PowerPoint. To access PowerPoint Central, select PowerPoint Central from the Tools menu.

- This presentation, created by Microsoft, includes hyperlinks that take you to Internet sites for additional clip art, video clips, sound clips, graphic effects, templates, etc., which you can use in your presentation.

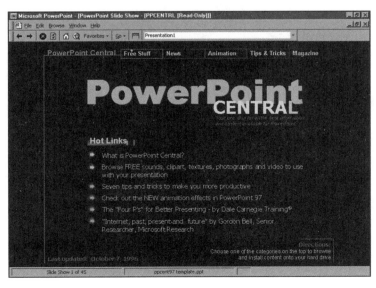

> *In this exercise, you will explore PowerPoint Central and access the Microsoft Help site. If you do not have a live Internet connection, skip steps 5-9.*

EXERCISE DIRECTIONS

1. Create a new Blank Presentation.

2. Access PowerPoint Central.

3. Select each of the following topics and review the contents of the slides within that topic.
   - News
   - Animation
   - Tips and Tricks
   - Magazine

4. Close PowerPoint Central.

5. If you have a live Internet connection, do the following:
   - Access PowerPoint Central.
   - Select Free Stuff.
   - Click the hyperlink to the Microsoft web site to access more free stuff.
   - Click on hyperlinks in the PowerPoint web site until you find a site that interests you.
   - Add this site to your Favorites Folder.
   - Return to PowerPoint.

6. Select Microsoft on the Web from the Help menu.

7. Click Frequently Asked Questions.

8. Click the link to Microsoft PowerPoint 97.

9. Add this site to your Favorites Folder.

10. Close Internet Explorer.

11. Close PowerPoint.

KEYSTROKES

GET HELP FROM MICROSOFT ON THE WEB

1. Click **Help** .... `Alt`+`H`
2. Click **Microsoft on the Web** .... `W`
3. Make desired selection:
   - **Free Stuff** .... `F`
   - **Product News** .... `P`
   - **Frequently Asked Questions** ...... `Q`
   - **Online Support** .... `S`
   - **Microsoft Office Home Page** ...... `O`
   - **Send Feedback** .... `K`
   - **Best of the Web** .... `B`
   - **Search the Web** .... `W`
   - **Web Tutorial** .... `T`

ACCESS POWERPOINT CENTRAL

1. Click **Tools** .... `Alt`+`T`
2. Click **PowerPoint Central** .... `R`
3. Follow prompts and make desired selections.

Exercise 38

■ **Copy Text, Images, Media and Sound Clips from the Web onto a Slide**

NOTES

Copy Text, Images, Media and Sound Clips from the Web

■ It is possible to copy text, images and media from the Web onto a slide.

■ To copy Web text, highlight the text you want copied, and click the Copy button or right-click and select <u>C</u>opy. Text is copied to the clipboard. Switch to your PowerPoint presentation, locate the slide on which you wish to copy the text, and click the Paste button on the Standard toolbar.

■ To copy an image or media clip from the Web, you must first download it. Microsoft provides a Web site called Clip Gallery Live, which provides additional clip art, pictures, sounds and video clips that are free. When you download these clips, they are automatically added to the Clip Gallery within Office 97.

■ To access the Clip Gallery Live Web page, select <u>P</u>icture, <u>C</u>lip Art from the <u>I</u>nsert menu. In the Microsoft Clip Gallery 3.0 that follows, click the Connect to Web button.

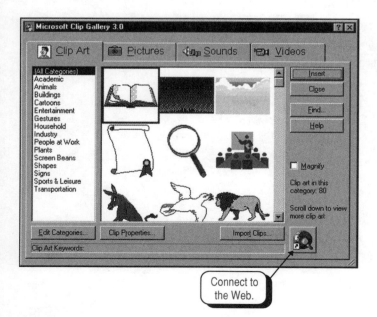

■ Internet Explorer automatically displays the Microsoft Clip Gallery Live page.

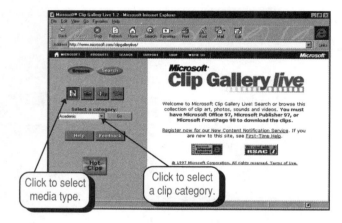

■ Click the media type you want: Clip Art, Pictures, Sounds or Videos, select a category of clips to view and click Go.

■ To download the clip, click the hyperlink below the clip and follow the prompts to download it. The clip will be added to your Clip Gallery.

■ To insert the clip in your slide, select an appropriate slide layout (Clip Art & Text, Media Clip & Text). When you double-click the placeholder, Microsoft Clip Gallery 3.0 will display with the new clips. Select the clip you want and click <u>I</u>nsert.

■ You can also access other Web sites that have clips other than the Microsoft clip site. If you visit a site that has a picture you want, right-click the picture and select <u>C</u>opy. The picture is placed on the clipboard. Display the slide on which you wish to copy the image and click the Paste button. Or, to download the image, right-click and select <u>S</u>ave Picture As, and save it to your hard drive *(see the Keystrokes on page 223 for specific steps)*.

EXERCISE DIRECTIONS

Directions A.

1. Open ⌨ SILVER, or open 💾 38SILVER.

2. Insert a new slide using the Clip Art & Text layout.
   - Enter the text as shown in Illustration A on the following page. Adjust the title placeholder or font size so that text does not overlap the logo.
   - Double-click the clip art placeholder.
   - Click the Search the Web button in the Microsoft Clip Gallery dialog box.
   - Select a relevant category and click Go.
   - Download the desired clip art (this will be added to your Clip Gallery).
   - Insert the new clip art into the clip art placeholder. Resize the picture, so it does not overlap the logo, as shown in Illustration B on the following page.

3. Switch to Slide Sorter view. Move this slide to become Slide 7.

4. Insert a new slide using the Title Only layout.
   - Use the Background dialog box to omit the Silver Age logo from this slide.
   - Switch to Slide view.
   - Enter the title text as shown in Illustration C on the following page; center the text in the placeholder.
   - Click the Search the Web button on the PowerPoint Web toolbar.
   - Use the following URL to go to a Web site that contains pictures of San Francisco: http://www.computersamerica.com/ mousing_around/gatecam/gatecam_gallery.cfm.
   - Right-click on any desired picture and save it as **SANFRAN.** Note the folder to which you are saving this file.

5. Switch to PowerPoint.
   - Insert the picture on the new slide.
   - Size the picture to fill the slide below the title. Position it so that it is centered on the slide as shown in Illustration D on the following page.
   - Create a text box and enter the address information in a 20-point bold, sans serif font. Center the text in the text box and position it at the top middle of the picture as shown in Illustration D.

6. Print one copy of each new slide. Close the file; save the changes.

7. Close PowerPoint.

8. Exit the Internet.

Directions B.

1. Open ⌨ SILVER or 💾 38SILVER.

2. Insert a new slide using the Clip Art & Text layout.

3. Enter the text as shown in Illustration A on the following page. Adjust the title placeholder or font size so that text does not overlap the logo.

4. Launch the DDC simulation.
   - Click Go, Open on the Web toolbar.
   - Type C:\DDCPUB\PPT97INT.IMR.
   - ✓ Be sure that the simulation has been installed on your hard drive. If files are on a drive other than C, replace C with the correct letter.
   - Click OK to launch the simulation.
   - Select Exercise 1: Clipart Search.
   - Copy the flower clip art (follow the prompts at the bottom of the screen to do this).

5. Switch to PowerPoint.

6. Paste the flower in the clip art placeholder. Size it so that it does not overlap the logo, as shown in illustration B on the following page.

7. Switch to Slide Sorter View. Move this slide to become Slide 7.

8. Insert a new slide using the Title Only layout.
   - Use the Background dialog box to omit the Silver Age logo from this slide
   - Switch to Slide view.
   - Enter the title text as shown in Illustration C on the following page; center the text in the placeholder.

9. Launch the DDC Simulation.
   - Select Exercise 2: San Francisco.

10. Use the following URL to go to a Web site that contains pictures of San Francisco: http://www.computersamerica.com/ mousing_around/gatecam/gatecam_gallery.cfm.

11. Follow the on-screen prompts to copy the sunset picture.

12. Close the DDC Simulation and switch to PowerPoint.

13. Paste the picture on the new slide.

- Size it to fill the slide below the title.
- Position it so that it is centered on the slide as shown in Illustration D, below.
- Create a text box and enter the address information in a 20-point bold, sans serif font as shown. Center the text in the text box and position it at the top middle of the picture as shown.

14. Print one copy of each new slide.

15. Close the file; save the changes.

Illustration A

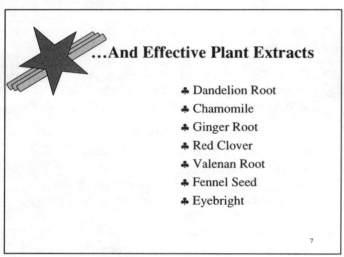

Illustration B

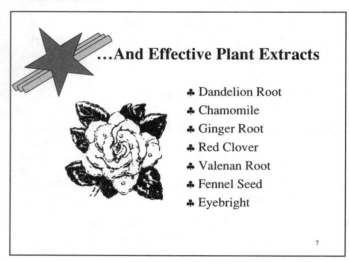

Illustration C

Visit Us in San Francisco

Illustration D

Visit Us in San Francisco

KEYSTROKES

COPY TEXT FROM THE WEB

1. Select the text you wish to copy from the Web.
   a. Right-click the mouse.
   b. Click **Copy** C
2. Switch to PowerPoint .... Alt + Tab
3. Display the slide on which you want to paste the text.
4. Click the **Paste** button .... 🖼
   OR
   a. Click **Edit** .... Alt + E
   b. Click **Paste** .... P
   OR
   a. Right-click the mouse.
   b. Click **Paste** .... P

COPY IMAGES, MEDIA OR SOUND CLIPS FROM THE WEB

1. Locate the image from the Web you wish to copy.
   a. Right-click the mouse.
   b. Click **Copy** C
2. Switch to PowerPoint .... Alt + Tab
3. Display the slide on which you want to paste the image.
4. Click the **Paste** button .... 🖼
   OR
   a. Click **Edit** .... Alt + E
   b. Click **Paste** .... P
   OR
   a. Right-click the mouse.
   b. Click **Paste** .... P

DOWNLOAD IMAGES, MEDIA OR SOUND CLIPS FROM THE WEB

1. Locate the image from the Web you wish to copy.
   a. Right-click the mouse.
   b. Click **Save Picture As** .... S
   c. Click **File name** text box ... Alt + N
   d. Type a filename .... *name*
   e. Click **Save in** .... Alt + I
      and select drive and folder in which to save the image.
   f. Click **Save** .... Alt + S
2. Switch to PowerPoint .... Alt + Tab
3. Display the slide on which you want to paste the clip.
4. Click **Insert** .... Alt + I
5. Click **Picture** .... P
6. Click **From File** .... F
7. Click **Look in** .... Alt + I
   and select drive and folder containing image or clip to insert.
8. Double-click filename of picture to be inserted.

DOWNLOAD IMAGES, MEDIA OR SOUND CLIPS FROM THE MICROSOFT WEB SITE TO THE CLIP GALLERY

1. Click **Insert** .... Alt + I
   a. Click **Picture** .... P
   b. Click **Clip Art** C
   OR
   a. Click **Movies and Sound** V
   b. Click **Movie from Gallery** .... M
   OR
   Click **Sound from Gallery** .... S
2. Click the **Connect to Web** .... 🔍
   for additional clips button.
3. Click the icon .... 🗗 🖼 🖼 🖼
   for the media type you want.
4. Click the **Select a category** drop down arrow.
5. Click a category .... ↓ ↑ , Enter
6. Click the **Go** button.
7. Click the hyperlink below the clip you want to download.
8. Follow the prompts to download the clip into your Clip Gallery.
   OR
   If a virus warning dialog box appears:
   a. Select **Save it to disk** .... Alt + S
      to save the clip to an external disk.
   b. Click **OK** .... Enter
   c. Click in the **File name** .... Alt + N
      box and type a name for the clip.
   d. Click the **Save in** box .... Alt + I
      and select a drive and folder in which to save the clip.
9. Click **Save** .... Enter

Exercise

39

- **Create a Hyperlink to Another Slide in a PowerPoint Presentation**
- **Create a Hyperlink to a File or Web Site**

NOTES

Create a Hyperlink to Another Slide in a PowerPoint Presentation

- A hyperlink is a shortcut that allows you to jump to another location. You can create a hyperlink on a slide to link to another slide within the same presentation, to a slide in another presentation or to another software program. A hyperlink can also be created to link to a Web site.

- A hyperlink can be applied to text or objects. When a hyperlink is applied to text, the text appears colored and underlined. When the mouse pointer is positioned over a hyperlinked object or text in Slide Show view, the mouse pointer changes to a hand. Clicking on a hyperlink will activate the link and bring you to the linked slide or program.

- For example, the first slide in your presentation might be a contents page. Each item on the contents page could be hyperlinked to a particular slide in the presentation containing information that relates to the contents page topic.

- To create a hyperlink, select the text or object on which to create a hyperlink. Then, select Hyperlink from the Insert menu. If you have not yet saved your document, you will be prompted to do so. The Insert Hyperlink dialog box displays.

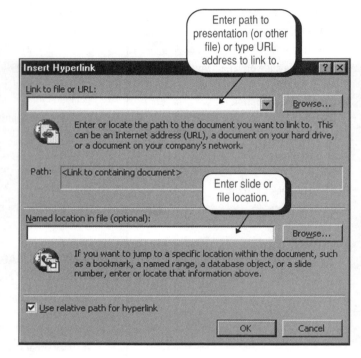

- **To link to another slide in the current presentation**, click the Browse button next to the Named location in file text box in the Insert Hyperlink dialog box.

- The Hyperlink to Slide dialog box appears. Select the Slide Title of the slide you wish to link to and click OK.

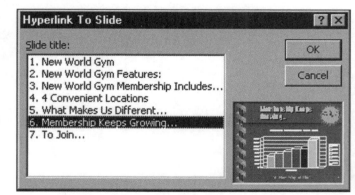

- The Insert Hyperlink dialog box reappears, with the slide location inserted in the Named location in file text box. Click OK to accept this link.

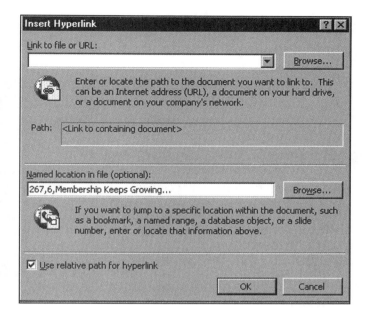

- **To link to a specific slide in another presentation,** enter the presentation you wish to link to in the Link to File or URL text box or click the Browse button next to the Link to File or URL text box and select the presentation to link to. Then click the Browse button next to the Named location in file text box. The Hyperlink to Slide dialog box appears. Select the specific slide you wish to link to and click OK. The Insert Hyperlink dialog box reappears with the selected slide title in the Named location in file text box. Click OK.

- The text on which you have created the hyperlink will now appear colored and underlined. To activate this link, you must be in Slide Show view.

- After you activate a hyperlink that links to another slide in a presentation, you must right-click the mouse and select Go, Previously Viewed. This action will allow you to return to where you left off in your original slide show.

Create a Hyperlink to a File or Web Site

- To create a hyperlink that links to another file or to a Web page, select the text or object on which to create the hyperlink and select Hyperlink from the Insert menu. If you have not yet saved your document, you will be prompted to do so. The Insert Hyperlink dialog box displays *(see illustration to the left).*

- **To link to another file,** click the Browse button next to the Link to file or URL text box, and select the file.

- **To link to a web page,** type the URL address in the Link to file or URL text box (see above). Then click OK. You must be in Slide Show view to activate this link.

- After you activate a hyperlink to another file, you must right-click and select Go, Previously Viewed to return to where you left off in the original slide show. To return after activating a link to a Web site, click the Go menu and select Back.

In Part I of this exercise, you will create a hyperlink to a slide in another presentation. In Part II of this exercise, you will create a hyperlink to a Web site. If you have a live Internet connection, follow Directions A. If you plan to use the DDC Simulation, follow Directions B.

EXERCISE DIRECTIONS

PART I

1. Open 🖮 **PLAN**.

2. Display Slide 3 (The Team).
    *   Apply a hyperlink to the title text, "The Team," as shown in Illustration A on page 228, and link it to the organizational chart slide in the FOOD presentation created in Exercise 21.

3. Display Slide 7 (Competition).
    a. Apply a hyperlink to the title, "Competition" as shown in Illustration B on page 228, and link it to either the Chart or Table slide in the FOOD presentation created in Exercise 21 (whichever contains related information).
    b. Change all bulleted text to light yellow.

4. Apply a desired transition effect for each slide.

5. Use any desired preset animation for bulleted text on all slides.

6. View the slide show and activate the hyperlinks.

7. Print one copy of slides as Handouts (6 slides per page) in Black and White.

8. Close the file; save the changes.

9. Close the presentation window.

PART II

> ✓ *If you have a live Internet connection, follow Directions A. If you plan to use the DDC Simulation, follow directions B.*

Directions A

1. Open 🖮 **WEDDING**, or open 💾 **39WEDDING**.

2. Insert a new slide using the 2 Column Text layout.

3. Enter the slide title text as shown in Illustration C on page 228.
    a. Use a decorative font for the words "COUPLE OF THE MONTH." Center the text in the placeholder.
    b. Adjust the title placeholder and or font size so that the text fits as shown.

4. Enter "Innsbruck, Austria" and "Bressanone/Brixen, Italy" in the columns as shown.
    a. Use the same decorative font as used for "COUPLE OF THE MONTH."
    b. Remove the bullets from these two column headings.
    c. Enter the first bulleted item in each column as shown. Use a 28-point Times New Roman font.
    d. Move bulleted list placeholders, if necessary, so that the title text does not overlap list headings.

5. Insert a relevant picture and position and size it to fit in the bottom left corner of the slide as shown.

6. Switch to Slide Sorter view. Move this slide to become Slide 8.

7. Switch back to Slide view.

8. Click the Search the Web button on the PowerPoint Web toolbar.

9. Use the following URL to go to a Web site on European ski resorts: http://www.ski-europe.com/resorts.html. Add this site to your Favorites Folder.
    a. Click the hyperlink for Innsbruck, Austria.
    b. Scroll down to the "Mountain Facts" section.
    c. Find three facts about Innsbruck.
    d. Copy the first fact, switch back to PowerPoint and paste it as a bulleted item below "Innsbruck, Austria." Repeat for the second and third facts.
    e. Reduce font sizes as necessary so that all text fits properly on the slide and does not interfere with the logo.

10. Open the ski resorts page from the Favorites Folder on the PowerPoint Web toolbar.
    a. Click the hyperlink for Bressanone/Brixen, Italy.
    b. Scroll down to the "Mountain Facts" section.
    c. Find three facts about Bressanone/Brixen, Italy.
    d. Copy the first fact, switch back to PowerPoint and paste it as a bulleted item below "Bressanone/Brixen, Italy." Repeat for the second and third facts.
    e. Reduce font sizes as necessary so that all text fits properly on the slide and does not interfere with the logo.

11. Close Internet Explorer.

12. Hyperlink the words "Innsbruck, Austria" on Slide 8, and link it to http://www.ski-europe.com/factsheets/Innsbruck.html.

13. Hyperlink the words "Bressanone/Brixen, Italy" on Slide 8, and link it to http://www.ski-europe.com/factsheets/bressanone.html.

14. Set up the slide show to advance the slides manually on mouse click.

15. Apply the Split Vertical Out transition effect to this new slide.

16. Apply the Spiral animation effect to the bulleted text on this slide.

17. View the slide show and activate the hyperlinks.

18. Print one copy of the new slide.

19. Close the file; save the changes.

Directions B.

1. Open ⌨ **WEDDING**, or open 💾 **39WEDDING**.

2. Insert a new slide using the 2 Column Text layout.

3. Enter the slide title text as shown in Illustration C.
   a. Use a decorative font for the words "COUPLE OF THE MONTH."
   b. Adjust the title placeholder and/or font size so that the text fits as shown.

4. Enter "Innsbruck, Austria" and "Bressanone/ Brixen, Italy" in the columns as shown.
   a. Use the same decorative font as used for "COUPLE OF THE MONTH."
   b. Remove the bullets from these two column headings.
   c. Enter the first bulleted item in each column as shown. Use a 28-point Times New Roman font.
   d. Move the bulleted list placeholders if necessary so that the title text does not overlap list headings.

5. Insert a relevant picture and position and size it to fit in the bottom left corner of the slide as shown.

6. Switch to Slide Sorter view. Move this slide to become Slide 8.

7. Switch back to Slide view.

8. Launch the DDC simulation.
   a. Click Go, Open on the Web toolbar.
   b. Type C:\DDCPUB\PPT97INT.IMR
   ✔ *Be sure that the simulation has been installed on your hard drive. If files are on a drive other than C, replace C with the correct letter.*
   c. Click OK to launch the simulation.
   d. Select Exercise 3: Skiing Europe.

9. Follow the prompts at the bottom of the screen.

10. Write down three facts about Innsbruck, Austria.

11. Write down three facts about Bressanone/ Brixen, Italy.

12. Switch to PowerPoint.

13. Enter the three facts for each ski resort as bulleted items. Reduce font sizes as necessary so that all text fits properly on the slide and does not interfere with the logo.

14. Hyperlink the words "Innsbruck, Austria" on Slide 8, and link it to: C:\ DDCPUB\PPT97INT.IMR.
    ✔ *You cannot link directly to the Web site using the simulation.*

15. Hyperlink the words "Bressanone/Brixen, Italy" on Slide 8, and link it to: C:\DDCPUB\PPT97INT.IMR.

16. Set up the slide show to advance the slides manually on mouse click.

17. Apply the Split Vertical Out transition effect to this new slide.

18. Apply the Spiral animation effect to the bulleted text on this slide.

19. View the slide show and activate the links.

20. Print one copy of the new slide.

21. Close the file; save the changes.

Illustration A (sample solution content)

The Team

▼ Patsy Maher, Chairperson and CEO
▼ James Rogen, President
▼ Robert Hein, Vice Chairman
▼ Rachel Wu, Chief Operating Officer
▼ Frank DiGenaro, Chief Financial Officer
▼ Jennifer Freehold, Treasurer

9/30/97

Illustration B (sample solution content)

Competition

▼ The Food Giant is the only supermarket of its peers to have net sales growth from 1996 to 1997.
▼ The Food Giant's earnings have grown each year for the past 5 years.
▼ In these years, the Company's competitors have suffered from higher operating costs and lower revenues.

9/30/97

Illustration C

Say Yes...

Our *COUPLE OF THE MONTH* Wins a Free Honeymoon to Ski Europe

...and Leave the Rest to Us!

Innsbruck, Austria

❤ Maximum elevation: 7810 feet
❤ Vertical drop: 4780 feet
❤ Lifts: 49 (9 cable-cars/railways; 14 chairlifts; 26 T-bars)

Bressanone/Brixen, Italy

❤ Maximum elevation: 10,035 feet
❤ Vertical drop: 5630 feet
❤ Total gradient covered: 413,642 feet

8

KEYSTROKES

TO CREATE A HYPERLINK TO ANOTHER SLIDE IN THE CURRENT PRESENTATION

1. Select the text or object on which to create a hyperlink.
2. Click **Insert** .... `Ctrl`+`I`
3. Click **Hyperlink** .... `I`

   ✓ *You will be prompted to save your document if you have not already done so.*

4. Click **Browse** .... `Alt`+`W`
   (Next to the Named location in file text box).
5. Select the **Slide Title** .... `Alt`+`S`
   of the slide to link to.
6. Click **OK** .... `Enter`
7. Click **OK** .... `Enter`

CREATE HYPERLINK TO A SPECIFIC SLIDE IN ANOTHER PRESENTATION

1. Select the text or object on which to create a hyperlink.
2. Click **Insert** .... `Ctrl`+`I`
3. Click **Hyperlink** .... `I`

   ✓ *You will be prompted to save your document if you have not already done so.*

4. Click **Browse** .... `Alt`+`B`
   (Next to the Link to file or URL text box).
5. Select the File to link to.
6. Click **Browse** .... `Alt`+`W`
   (next to the Named location in file text box).
7. Select the **Slide Title** .... `Alt`+`S`
   of the slide to link to.
8. Click **OK** .... `Enter`
9. Click **OK** .... `Enter`

TO CREATE A HYPERLINK TO ANTOHER FILE

1. Select the text or object on which to create a hyperlink.
2. Click **Insert** .... `Ctrl`+`I`
3. Click **Hyperlink** .... `I`

   ✓ *You will be prompted to save your document if you have not already done so.*

4. Click **Browse** .... `Alt`+`B`
   (Next to the Link to file or URL text box).
5. Select the file to link to.
6. Click **OK**. .... `Enter`
7. Click **OK** .... `Enter`

CREATE A HYPERLINK TO A WEB PAGE

1. Select the text or object on which to create a hyperlink.
2. Click **Insert** .... `Ctrl`+`I`
3. Click **Hyperlink** .... `I`

   ✓ *You will be prompted to save your document if you have not already done so.*

4. Click the **Link to file** .... `Alt`+`L`
   or URL text box.
5. Type the URL address .... *address*
6. Click **OK** .... `Enter`

ACTIVATE A HYPERLINK AND RETURN TO ORIGINAL SLIDE SHOW

1. Click the **Slide Show View** button... 🖳
   OR
   a. Click **View** .... `Alt`+`V`
   b. Click **Slide Show** .... `W`
   OR
   a. Click **Slide Show** .... `Alt`+`D`
   b. Click **View** .... `V`
2. Click the hyperlink in your presentation.
3. Right-click the mouse (on the linked page).

   If hyperlink is to another slide in a PowerPoint presentation:
   a. Click **Go** .... `G`
   b. Click **Previously Viewed** .... `P`

   If hyperlink is to a web page:
   Click the **Go** menu .... `Alt`+`G`

4. Click **Back** .... `B`

Exercise
40

- **Save a Presentation as a Web Page (Save as HTML)**
- **Use an Online Template to Create a Web Page**

NOTES

Save a Presentation as a Web Page (Save as HTML)

- You can save any presentation you create in PowerPoint as a Web page. To do so, you must save the presentation in an HTML format. HTML is a programming language that Internet browsers use to interpret and display Web Pages. PowerPoint provides a Save As HTML option on the File menu. When you save your presentation using this option, PowerPoint automatically converts your presentation into HTML language.

- To use your presentation as a Web page, complete your presentation and select Save As HTML from the File menu. This will activate the Save As HTML Wizard. Follow the prompts in the Save As HTML Wizard to set up your Web page.

Save as HTML Wizard Dialog Box

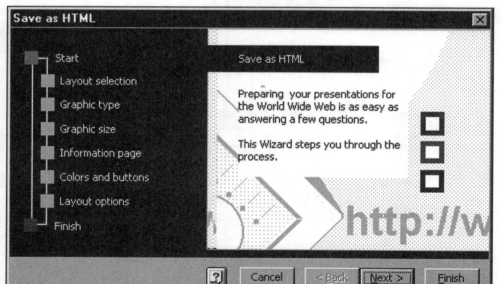

■ Below and on the following pages is an illustration and explanation of the options on each Wizard screen. Make desired selections and click the Next button until the last Wizard screen appears. Then, click the Finish button and follow the prompts to save your presentation in HTML format.

Screen   **Options**

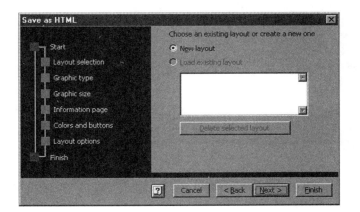

Click to create New Layout or Load Existing Layout. Select Load Existing Layout if you have already saved a layout you wish to use.

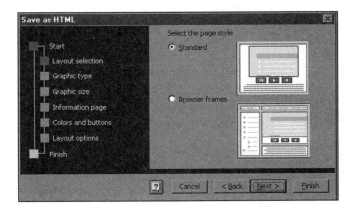

Click Standard to display the slide only; click Browser frames to create a Web page that uses frames.

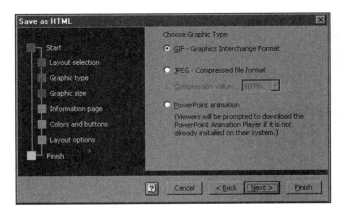

Click the graphics type. Both GIF and JPEG files are image types supported by the World Wide Web. JPEG compresses your files. Select PowerPoint animation if your presentation contains animation and/or special effects. To view a presentation with animation, you will need to install PowerPoint Animation Player. You can download the latest version of Animation Player from the PowerPoint Web page: (http://www.microsoft.com/powerpoint/internet/player/default.html).

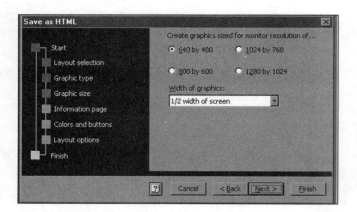

Click a monitor resolution and width for your graphics. Higher resolution values create larger graphics. *Caution: Larger graphics can take longer to load.*

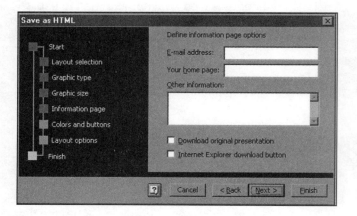

Enter information page options such as your e-mail address and your home page Web address (URL). You might want to include other information such as your business address, city, state and zip code. Make the desired check box selection to download the original presentation or to download the latest version of Internet Explorer along with your presentation.

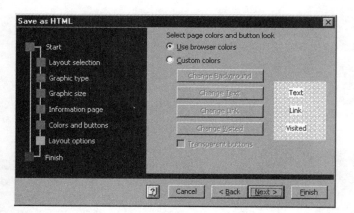

Select Web page colors. Click Use browser colors to apply default browser color scheme. Or, to apply custom colors, click the command button for each item to change (Change Background, Change Text, Change Link, Change Visited) and choose a desired color from the palette that displays. Select Transparent buttons if you want the buttons to appear that way. The button refers to the Next button that appears on the Web page (see next screen). Note the results of your selection in the preview window.

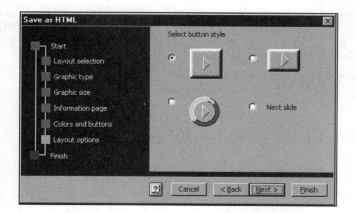

Select the button style you wish to use to indicate Next Page.

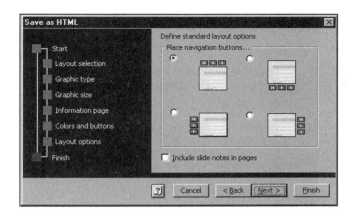

Select a placement option for navigation buttons on your Web page. Indicate whether you wish to include slide notes on each page

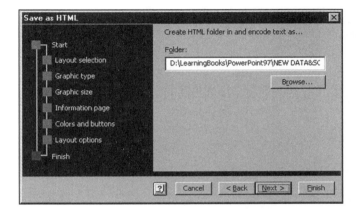

Indicate the folder in which PowerPoint will save the files for your Web page presentation.

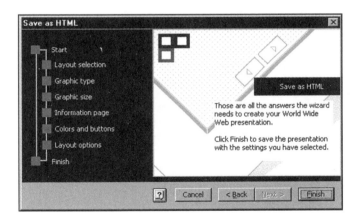

Click the Finish button to create your Web page with the settings you selected.

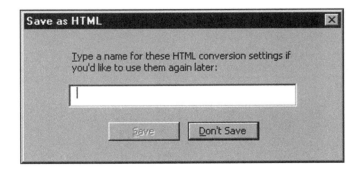

Type a name for all of the settings you selected if you want to use them again and click Save.

Use an Online Template
to Create a Web Page

■ PowerPoint provides specially designed templates that make it easy for you to design a presentation to be published on the Web.

■ Online templates contain items on the first slide that are hyperlinked to related slides in the presentation, so you can jump to a related section in your presentation and then automatically return to the home page slide.

■ To access Web templates, select New from the File menu. Select the Presentations tab and select one of the online presentations.

■ To publish an online template presentation, save it in HTML format *(see Save Presentation as a Web Page on page 230)*.

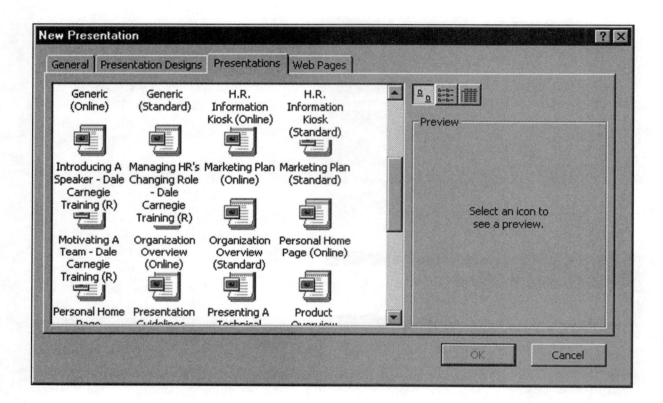

You work for the Trilogy Production Company. They are producing a new film called Space Adventures. In this exercise, you will create a home page to advertise their movie using the Personal Home Page template. This presentation will be saved in HTML format so that it can be viewed on the Internet.

EXERCISE DIRECTIONS

1. Create a new presentation; use the Personal Home Page (Online) template.

2. Delete the sample text and enter the information on each slide as shown in Illustration A, below. Click on the fifth bullet to select it and press Delete.

3. Insert any relevant graphic on Slide 2.

4. Display Slide 3.
   - Change the slide layout to 2 Column Text.
   - Remove bullets from the first item in each column as shown.

5. Display Slide 4.
   - Change the slide layout to Bulleted List.

6. Display Slide 5.
   - Delete the sample hyperlink.
   - Insert a decimal tab at 5" and enter the currency amounts as shown.

7. Apply any desired transition effect to each slide.

8. Apply any desired animation effect to bulleted text on each slide.

9. Apply a 5-second transition timing to each slide and set the slides to advance automatically.

10. Spell check.

11. Save the file; name it **SPACE**. Then save it again, this time in HTML format.

Illustration A

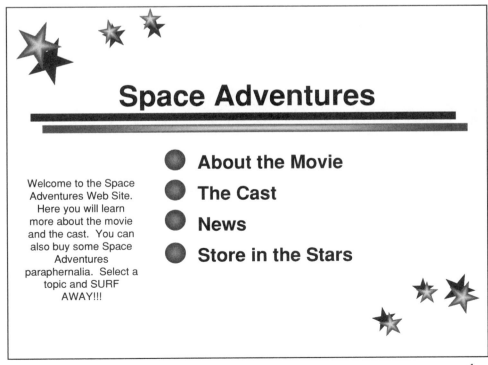

1

About the Movie

- Currently filming in Houston, Texas
- Film to be released in June 1998
- Budget: $100,000,000
- Premiere Party in New York City on May 10, 1998--Click for contest info (you can go!)

2

The Cast

Actors in order of importance
- Peter Michaels
- Jonathan Clipper
- Jamal Mitchell
- Warren Lettem
- Darrell Parker

Actresses in order of importance
- Sandy Weber
- Louise Martinez
- Wendy Billatto
- Sara Kinder
- Yvette Saunders

3

News

- 10/9/97--Janet Marino, lead female, was replaced by Sandy Weber
- The cast will make an appearance at the Dallas Mall on December 20, 1997
- 10/25/97--Peter Michaels and Sandy Weber signed a contract to star in ABC Productions' upcoming film, *Walk On*

4

Store in the Stars

- **Space Adventures**
  - Pen $2.50
  - Hat $12.95
  - T-Shirt $17.95
  - Sweatshirt $24.99
  - Shorts $17.99
  - Gym bag $29.99

5

KEYSTROKES

SAVE A PRESENTATION AS A WEB PAGE (SAVE AS HTML)

1. Click **File**.............................. `Alt`+`F`
2. Click **Save as HTML**........................ `H`
3. Follow prompts.
4. Click **Next to move forward** ... `Alt`+`N`
5. Click **Finish**............................ `Alt`+`F`

CREATE A WEB PAGE USING A WEB TEMPLATE

1. Click **File** .... `Alt`+`F`
2. Click **New**.. `N`
3. Click the **Presentations** tab.
4. Double-click an online presentation.

- **Copy Presentation Files to a Server on the Web**
- **View a Presentation in a Browser**
- **View a Presentation on the Web**

NOTES

Copy Presentation Files to the Server

- In the previous exercise, you saved your presentation in HTML format, a programming language that Internet browsers use to interpret and display Web Pages. In order for others to view your HTML presentation on the Internet, however, you must place your presentation on a Web server where it can be accessed.

- To do this, you must copy your presentation files from your computer to the Web server. You must know the name of the Web server and the directory on the server where your presentation will be saved before starting the copy process. If you do not know this information, contact your Internet Service Provider.

- To copy files to the Internet, it is easiest to use the Microsoft Web Publishing Wizard. The Web Publishing Wizard is located in the ValuPack folder on the Office 97 CD-ROM and requires a separate installation from the PowerPoint program or the Office 97 Suite. To install the Web Publishing Wizard from the CD-ROM, double-click on the Webpost icon in the Webpost subfolder (WEBPOST.EXE) of the ValuPack and follow the prompts.

- You can also download the Web Publishing Wizard from Microsoft's Web site at http://www.microsoft.com/windows/software/webpost/. When you reach the Microsoft Web Publishing Wizard Web site, scroll down and follow the download instructions to install the program.

Microsoft Web Publishing Wizard Web Site

- After you have installed the Web Publishing Wizard, open the program. In the Web Publishing Wizard dialog box that follows, click the Next button to begin copying your presentation to the Web.

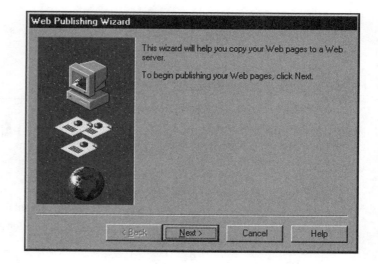

- In the second Wizard dialog box, click the Browse Folders button, select the folder containing the HTML presentation that you want to publish to the Web, and click Next.

  ✓ Note: *Remember that in order to publish a presentation to the Web, you must first save it in HTML format (see Exercise 40). When a PowerPoint presentation is saved in HTML format, each slide and image is saved separately and stored in one folder. You must select the entire folder to publish the complete presentation to the Web.*

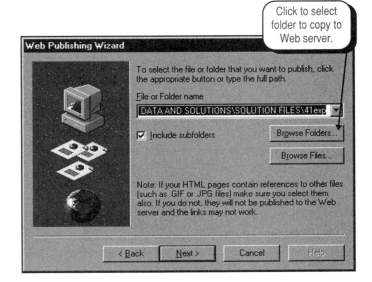

- In the third Wizard dialog box, click the drop-down arrow and select the name of the Web server to which you wish to save your presentation. (The URL address of the selected server displays below the drop-down box.) Click the Next button to continue.

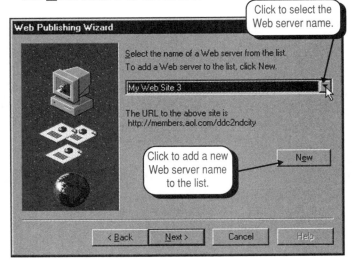

- Or, to add a new Web server name to the list, click the New button. In the dialog box that follows, type a name to describe the new server in the text box. Then select or enter the name of your Internet Service Provider in the drop-down list box and click Next.

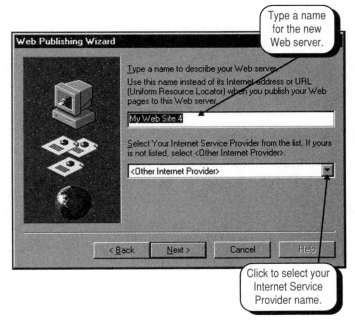

- In the dialog boxes that follow, enter the Web server URL address and/or other user information requested by the prompts and click Next.

  ✓ Note: *If you do not know the URL for the Web Server to which you can publish personal Web pages, or any other user information, contact your Internet Service Provider.*

- Click Finish when you reach the final Wizard screen. The Wizard will then copy your presentation to the Web server. This process may take several minutes to complete.

View a Presentation in a Browser

- Before publishing your presentation to a Web server, you can test it by viewing it in your Web browser (Internet Explorer, Netscape Navigator, etc.). To do so, access your Web browser and select Open from the File menu.

- In the Open dialog box that follows, click <u>B</u>rowse and locate and select the folder containing your Web presentation. Click <u>O</u>pen and select the Index file. Click <u>O</u>pen and then click OK.

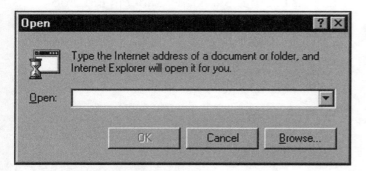

- The Index page of your presentation displays. Click the "Click here to start" hyperlink to view the first slide.

Index Page

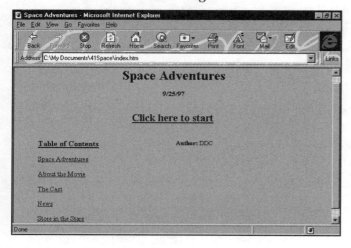

- The presentation will display just as it would on the Web, with navigation buttons that you can use to move from page to page.

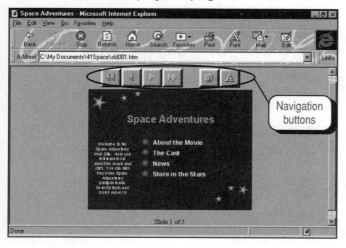

View a Presentation on the Web

- After you have run a test viewing of an HTML presentation in a browser and have saved the presentation to a Web server, you can view it on the Web, just as you would any other Web site. To do so, enter the URL address for your presentation in the Address text box on the Web toolbar and press Enter.

- The Index Page appears first, displaying hyperlinks to each slide in the presentation. Click on the "Click here to start" hyperlink to view the first slide in the presentation. From there you can click on the navigation buttons to move from slide to slide.

In this exercise, you will use your Web browser to view a presentation you created previously. If you have a live Internet connection, follow Directions A. If you plan to use the DDC Simulation, follow Directions B.

EXERCISE DIRECTIONS

Directions A

1. Launch your Web browser.

2. Click File, Open and type the file path to the folder containing the HTML version of **SPACE** that you saved in Exercise 40 (**41SPACE.html** on data disk). Then click OK.

3. Open the presentation Index page (index.htm) and click "Click here to start" to view the first slide in the presentation.

4. Click the hyperlink, "The Cast."

5. Use the navigation buttons to view the remaining slides in the presentation.

6. Close the presentation.

7. Exit the Web browser.

Directions B

1. Launch the DDC Simulation.
   a. Click Go, Open on the Web toolbar.
   b. Type C:\DDCPUB\PPT97INT.IMR.
   ✓ *Be sure that the simulation has been installed on your hard drive. If files are on a drive other than C, replace C with the correct letter.*
   c. Click OK to launch the simulation.
   d. Select Exercise 4: Web Browser.
   e. Follow the prompts to open the HTML presentation in Internet Explorer.

2. Access the first slide in the presentation.

3. Click the hyperlink, "The Cast."

4. View the remaining slides in the presentation.

5. Exit the DDC simulation.

KEYSTROKES

COPY PRESENTATION FILES TO A SERVER ON THE WEB

1. Open the Microsoft Web Publishing Wizard.
2. Click **Next**.................................... Enter
3. Click **Browse Folders**............. Alt + O
   and select the folder containing the presentation you want to copy.
4. Click **Next**.................................... Enter
5. a. Click the **Select the** .... Alt + S
      name of a Web Server from the list drop-down list box and select a server.
   b. Click **Next**.............................. Enter
   OR
   To add a new Web Server to the list:
   a. Click **New** .... Alt + E
   b. Click in the **Type**...... Alt + T, *name* **a name to describe your Web Server** text box and enter a name.

c. Click **Select your Internet** .... Alt + S
   Service Provider from the list drop-down list box, and select your provider.
d. Click **Next**................................ Enter
6. Enter the appropriate URL and user information as prompted in the remaining dialog boxes.
7. Click **Finish**................................. Enter
   when you reach the final dialog box.

VIEW A PRESENTATION IN A BROWSER

1. Launch your Web browser
2. Click **File**.............................. Alt + F
3. Click **Open** ....O
4. Click **Browse** and open the folder containing your Web presentation.
5. Double-click on the **Index** file icon to open the Index page.
6. Click the navigation buttons to move from slide to slide.

VIEW A PRESENTATION ON THE WEB

1. Type the URL address............... *address* for your presentation in the Address text box on the Web toolbar.
2. Press **Enter** .... Enter
3. Click on the "Click here to start" hyperlink to view the first slide.
4. Click on navigation buttons to move from slide to slide.

Exercise 42

■ Summary

You work for the Universal Football League in their marketing department. In this exercise, you will prepare a presentation that will be shown to prospective sponsors of the 1998 All-Star game.

EXERCISE DIRECTIONS

1. Create a new presentation; apply the Dad's Tie template design.

2. Accept the default Title Slide layout for the first slide.

3. Switch to Outline view.

4. Enter the slide information as shown in Illustration A on page 244.

5. Switch to Slide view.

6. Display Slide 1.
    a. Insert a relevant clip art image. Size it to approximately 2" high by 2" wide and position it in the bottom left corner of the slide as shown in Illustration B on page 244. Copy the image and position the copy in the lower right corner of the slide as shown.
    b. Change the color of the sub-title text to dark blue to match the title text. Center the sub-title text.

7. Switch to Slide Master view.

8. Create a WordArt object that says, "All-Star Game '98." Use a 2-dimensional WordArt design and any font face, sized to 36 point.
    a. Size the WordArt to approximately 4" wide by 1" high.
    b. Apply the 3-D-12 design to the WordArt.
    c. Color the 3-D design dark blue.
    d. Color the WordArt yellow.
    e. Position the WordArt object at the bottom center of the slide as shown in Illustration C on page 244.
    f. Insert a slide number in the bottom right corner of the slide.
    g. Change the first-level bullet to a blue 5-pointed star; change the second-level bullet to a yellow-filled circle.

9. Switch to Slide view.

10. Display Slide 2 (The Basics).
    a. Set a right-aligned tab at 8" in the body text placeholder.
    b. Enter the information as shown in Illustration D on page 245.
    c. Link the words, "Texas Stadium," to the following URL: http://www.usatoday.com/sports/football/sfn/sfn07sta.htm.
    ✓ *If you have a live Internet connection, you can link to the URL by clicking on the hyperlink in Slide Show view. If you do not have a live connection, your presentation will not open to the URL Web site. You may, however, create the link to practice the procedure.*

11. Display Slide 3 (Pre-Game Events).
    a. Change the layout to 2 Column Text.
    b. Enter the information shown in Illustration E on page 245.
    c. Center, italicize, and remove the bullet from the first line of each column, as shown.

12. Display Slide 4 (We're Still Looking…).
    a. Create a text box and enter the sub-title as shown in Illustration F on page 245. Resize the text box so that the text fits on two lines and position it below the title as shown. Decrease the font size if necessary.
    b. Change the layout to Table Slide.
    c. Create the table as shown in Illustration F.
    d. Use four columns and seven rows.
    e. Size the columns as follows: Column 1: 2.5"; Columns 2-4: 1.8".
    f. Change the font size to 20 points.
    g. Left-align and italicize the data in the first column; center-align the data in columns 2-4.

h. Bold the first-row headings and underline the word "Package" in each.

i. Reposition and/or resize the table and the sub-title placeholder so that text does not overlap.

13. Display Slide 5 (Have a Heart...).
   a. Change the layout to Clip Art & Text.
   b. Insert relevant clip art.
   c. Resize and/or reposition the image, if necessary, so that it does not overlap the WordArt.

14. Display Slide 6 (Attendance Is Expected...).
   a. Change the layout to Chart Slide.
   b. Enter the following data to create a pie chart:

1994	1995	1996	1997	Expected 1998
25,256	39,265	37,381	42,879	55,251

   c. Create the following chart title: "Number of People in Attendance."
   d. Display the legend.
   e. Resize and/or reposition the chart, if necessary, so that it does not interfere with the WordArt.

15. Display Slide 7 (Meet the Executives).
   a. Change the layout to Organization Chart Slide.
   b. Enter the information shown in Illustration G on page 246.
   c. Resize and/or reposition the chart as necessary.

16. Display Slide 8 (Warm Up Until Kick-Off).
   a. Change the layout to Clip Art & Text.
   b. Insert relevant clip art.
   c. Resize and/or reposition the image as necessary.
   d. Enter the information shown in Illustration H on page 246. Link the subbullet text to the URL shown.

17. Insert a new slide; apply the Bulleted List layout.
   a. Omit the Slide Master background graphics from this new slide.
   b. Enter the information as shown in Illustration I on page 246.
   c. Move this slide to become Slide 2.
   d. Link each bulleted item to its related slide.

e. Create a WordArt object that says: "All-Star Game 1998" as shown in Illustration I. Use a 2-dimensional WordArt design and a 36-point sans serif font in all caps.
   • Color the WordArt blue.
   • Size the WordArt to approximately 1" high by 3½" wide.
   • Apply the 3-D-Style 19 effect. Color the 3-D effect yellow.
   • Position the WordArt in the upper right corner of the slide and rotate it so that it appears as shown in Illustration I.

18. Apply the Random Transition effect to all slides.

19. Apply the following animations to the slides indicated:
   a. All slides except Slide 1: Animate all titles to fly in from the right.
   b. Slide 1: Use any desired effect to animate the sub-title and add a sound effect.
   c. Slide 2: Use the Fly From Top Right effect to animate the WordArt. Use the Spiral effect to animate the text.

20. Apply any desired text and/or object animation for the remaining slides.

21. Spell check.

22. Save the file; name it **FOOTBALL**.

23. View the slide show.

24. Print the presentation as Handouts (6 slides per page) in Black and White.

25. Close the presentation window.

Illustration A

1 ⊒ Universal Football League
All-Star Game
1998

2 ⊒ The Basics

3 ⊒ Pre-Game Events

4 ⊒ We're Still Looking for Sponsors

5 ⊒ Have a Heart Is Our Charitable Partner
   ■ 10% of all revenue will go to Have a Heart
   ■ Players will make hospital visits 2 weeks before the game

6 ⊒ Attendance Is Expected to Be the Highest Ever

7 ⊒ Meet the Executives

8 ⊒ Warm Up Until Kick-Off

Illustration B

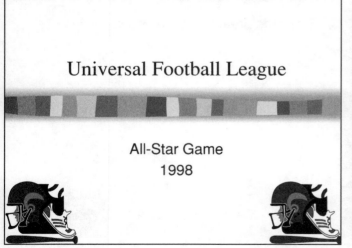

Illustration C

Illustration D

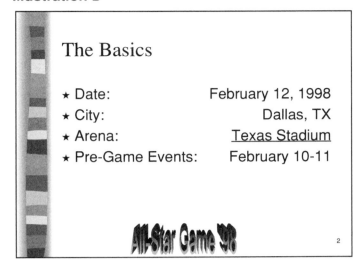

The Basics

★ Date: February 12, 1998
★ City: Dallas, TX
★ Arena: <u>Texas Stadium</u>
★ Pre-Game Events: February 10-11

All-Star Game '98

2

Illustration E

Pre-Game Events

February 10
★ Touch Football Game
★ Player/Celebrity Appearances
★ UFL Luncheon

February 11
★ Fan Jam
★ UFL Golf Tournament
★ Kids' Clinic

All-Star Game '98

3

Illustration F

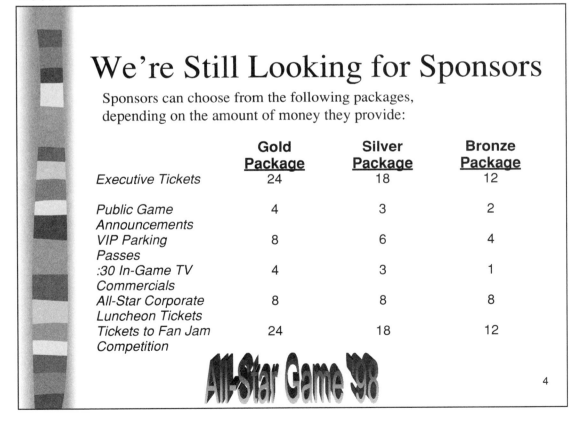

We're Still Looking for Sponsors

Sponsors can choose from the following packages, depending on the amount of money they provide:

	Gold <u>Package</u>	Silver <u>Package</u>	Bronze <u>Package</u>
Executive Tickets	24	18	12
Public Game Announcements	4	3	2
VIP Parking Passes	8	6	4
:30 In-Game TV Commercials	4	3	1
All-Star Corporate Luncheon Tickets	8	8	8
Tickets to Fan Jam Competition	24	18	12

All-Star Game '98

4

Illustration G

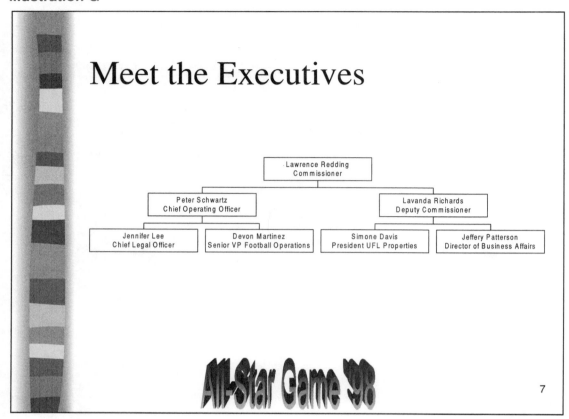

Illustration H

Illustration I

Agenda

ALL-STAR GAME 1998

★ The Basics
★ Pre-Game Events
★ Sponsors
★ Our Charity
★ Expected Attendance
★ Meet the Executives
★ Play Virtual Football

NEXT EXERCISE

Exercise

43

■ **Summary**

In this exercise, you will create a presentation for Stone Cinema Productions, a company that produces television and cinema productions. This presentation will be shown to prospective clients of the company. You will create a link to another presentation and to a Web site so that the viewers can further understand some of the business dealings and resources of this company. If you have a live Internet connection, follow Directions A. If you plan to use the DDC Simulation, follow Directions B.

EXERCISE DIRECTIONS

Directions A

1. Create a new presentation. Do not apply a template design.

2. Accept the default Title Slide layout for the first slide.

3. Create a logo as follows:
   a. Using the rectangle tool on the Drawing toolbar, create a square; size it to approximately 2½" high by 2½" wide and fill it black. Position it in the upper left corner of the slide as shown in Illustration A on page 250.
   b. Using the rectangle tool, create another square; size it to approximately ½" high by ½" wide and fill it white. Position it on the top left corner of the black square as shown.
   c. Copy and paste the white square to create four more white squares. Place the copies along the left side of the black square as shown.
   d. Use the Align or Distribute feature to distribute the five white squares vertically and center-align them.
   e. Create a rectangle away from the present logo; fill it black. Size it to approximately 1" wide by 2½" high.
   f. Create four more copies of the white square and place them inside the black rectangle as shown to create a filmstrip.
   g. Distribute the four white squares vertically and center-align them.
   h. Group the filmstrip.

   i. Rotate the filmstrip and place it over the upper right corner of the black square as shown in Slide 1 of Illustration B on page 251.
   j. Group the entire logo.

4. Copy the logo to the clipboard.

5. Switch to Slide Master view.
   a. Paste the logo and position it in the lower right corner of the slide as shown in Illustration B. Resize it to approximately 1½" high by 1½" wide.
   b. Change the first- and second-level bullets to any two desired symbols in any two desired colors.

6. Switch to Slide view.

7. Create the remaining presentation as shown in Illustration B, applying the appropriate slide layouts.

8. Omit the Slide Master background graphics from Slide 1.

9. For Slides 2, 3 and 4, apply the Clip Art & Text layout.
   a. Delete the text placeholder.
   b. Move the clip art placeholder to the center of the slide.
   c. Insert any desired clip art.

10. Display Slide 5.
    a. Link the words, "Canyon Productions," to the following URL: http://www.canyon.org.
    b. Run the slide show.

c. When Slide 5 displays, activate the hyperlink. After you access the Web site, scroll down and click on the "Services" hyperlink. Locate five services. Copy the first service, switch to PowerPoint, and paste it into Slide 5 as a second-level bulleted item in the second column as shown in Illustration B. Repeat for the four other services.

d. Reduce the font size of the text in each column so that all text fits properly on the slide and does not interfere with the logo.

11. Display Slide 9.
    - Link the words, "Promotion of UFL's '98 All-Star Game," to the **FOOTBALL** presentation created earlier.

12. Change the font color of each slide's title to a different color.

13. Switch to Slide Sorter view. Compare your presentation to Illustration B. Make any necessary adjustments to placeholders and/or font sizes so that all text fits properly on each slide.

14. Apply any desired slide transition to each slide. Apply a sound effect to the title slide.

15. Apply any desired animation to clip art objects.

16. Apply any desired animation to bulleted text.

17. Spell check.

18. Apply a 5-second slide transition timing to each slide and set the slides to advance automatically.

19. Save the file; name it **TV**.

20. View the presentation.

21. Print one copy as Handouts (6 slides per page) in Black and White.

22. Close all files.

Directions B

1. Create a new presentation. Do not apply a template design.

2. Accept the default Title Slide layout for the first slide.

3. Create a logo as follows:
   a. Using the rectangle tool on the Drawing toolbar, create a square; size it to approximately 2½" high by 2½" wide and fill it black. Position it in the upper left corner of the slide as shown in Illustration A on page 250.

b. Using the rectangle tool, create another square; size it to approximately ½" high by ½" wide and fill it white. Position it on the top left corner of the black square as shown.

c. Copy and paste the white square to create four more white squares. Place the copies along the left side of the black square as shown.

d. Use the Align or Distribute feature to distribute the five white squares vertically and center-align them.

e. Create a rectangle away from the present logo; fill it black. Size it to approximately 1" wide by 2½" high.

f. Create four more copies of the white square and place them inside the black rectangle as shown to create a filmstrip.

g. Distribute the four white squares vertically and center-align them.

h. Group the filmstrip.

i. Rotate the filmstrip and place it over the upper right corner of the black square as shown in Slide 1 of Illustration B on page 251.

j. Group the entire logo.

4. Copy the logo to the clipboard.

5. Switch to Slide Master view.
   a. Paste the logo and position it in the lower right corner of the slide as shown in Illustration B. Resize it to approximately 1½" high by 1½" wide.
   b. Change the first- and second-level bullets to any two desired symbols in any two desired colors.

6. Switch to Slide view.

7. Create the remaining presentation as shown in Illustration B, applying the appropriate slide layouts.

8. Omit the Slide Master background graphics from Slide 1.

9. For Slides 2, 3 and 4, apply the Clip Art & Text layout.
   a. Delete the text placeholder.
   b. Move the clip art placeholder to the center of the slide.
   c. Insert any desired clip art.

10. Launch the DDC Simulation.
    a. Click Go, Open on the Web toolbar.
    b. Type C:\DDCPUB\PPT97INT.IMR.
    ✓ *Be sure that the simulation has been installed on your hard drive. If files are on a drive other than C, replace C with the correct letter.*

c. Click OK to launch the simulation.

d. Select Exercise 5: TV.

e. Follow the on-screen prompts to locate the list of services. Write down five services.

11. Switch to PowerPoint.

12. Display Slide 5.

a. Enter the five services as second-level bulleted points in the second column as shown in Illustration B.

b. Reduce the font size of the text in each column so that all text fits properly on the slide and does not interfere with the logo.

13. Display Slide 9.

• Link the words "Promotion of UFL's '98 All-Star Game" to the **FOOTBALL** presentation created earlier.

14. Change the font color of each slide's title to a different color.

15. Switch to Slide Sorter view. Compare your presentation to Illustration B. Make any necessary adjustments to placeholders and/or font sizes so that all text fits properly on each slide.

16. Apply any desired slide transition to each slide. Apply a sound effect to the title slide.

17. Apply any desired animation to clip art objects.

18. Apply any desired animation to bulleted text.

19. Spell check.

20. Apply a 5-second slide transition timing to each slide and set the slides to advance automatically.

21. Save the file; name it TV.

22. View the presentation.

23. Print one copy as Handouts (6 slides per page) in Black and White.

24. Close all files.

Illustration A

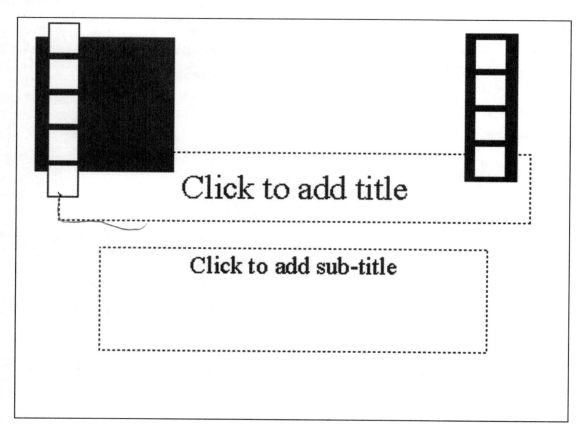

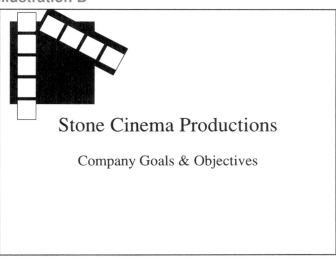

Stone Cinema Productions

Company Goals & Objectives

1

Television

2

Licensing & Merchandising

3

Marketing/Sponsorship

4

Studio Resources

- ➢ Product Placement in Stone Movies
- ➢ Product Placement in Stone TV Programs
- ➢ Advertising in Stone Videos
- ➢ Promotion at Stone Live Events
- ➢ Promotion on Stone Interactive Ventures

- ➢ Affiliated with <u>Canyon Productions</u> in Washington, DC, whose services include:
  - ▤ Documentaries
  - ▤ Video News Releases
  - ▤ Electronic Press Kits
  - ▤ Marketing & Communication Videos
  - ▤ Internal Employee Communication Videos

5

Building Successful Franchises

➢ Diversity of Properties
➢ Long-Term Focus
➢ Integrated Approach
➢ Edgy, Alternative Sensibility

6

Resources and Capabilities

➢ Relationships with Leading Networks
➢ Success with Football-Themed Entertainment
➢ Unique Creative Sensibility
➢ Expertise in Young Adult Franchises

7

Licensing Strategy

➢ Focus on Distinctive Merchandise; Establish Point of Difference for League
➢ Partner with Specialty Retailer(s) for Initial Roll-Out
➢ Integrate Merchandising into Television and Sponsorship Activities

8

Key Strategic Issues

➢ Exposure for UFL Football Games
  ▤ Number of Games Broadcast
  ▤ Time Periods and Ratings of TV Outlet
  ▤ Willingness to Broadcast Other Programming in Addition to Games

➢ Promotion of UFL's '98 All-Star Game

9

NEXT EXERCISE

Exercise
44

■ **Summary**

You work for the Ministry of Finance of Ukraine and are making a presentation to a group of investors about the history and economic health of your country. In this exercise, you will create an 8-slide presentation using the features learned throughout this book. You will add information to one of the slides from a Web site to which the slide is linked. If you have a live Internet connection, follow Directions A. If you plan to use the DDC Simulation, follow Directions B.

EXERCISE DIRECTIONS

Directions A

1. Refer to the report shown in Illustration A on pages 256-257.

2. Create an 8-slide presentation based on the information contained in the report.

3. Use any desired template design and slide layouts; however, use the default Title Slide layout for the first slide in your presentation.

4. Include the following elements on the Slide Master:
   - a logo design using AutoShapes and WordArt. Use "UKRAINE" as the WordArt text. Position the logo in the upper left corner of the slide.
   - a slide number. Position it in the bottom right corner of the slide.
   - a new bullet design for the first-level bullets in any desired color.

5. Include the following slide layouts in your presentation:
   - one Table Slide layout
   - one or two Chart Slide layouts
   - one Clip Art & Text layout

6. Spell check.

7. Apply any desired slide transitions.

8. Apply any desired animation to bulleted lists.

9. Apply any desired animation to the clip art and chart(s).

10. Insert a new Text & Clip Art slide to become Slide 9. Enter the slide title text and relevant clip art as shown in Illustration B on page 258.
    a. Search the Web for trade opportunities in the Ukraine by entering the following URL address in the Address text box on the Web toolbar: http://www.pcg.kiev.ua.
    b. When you reach the Web site, click the "Trade Opportunities" hyperlink.
    c. Locate two trade opportunities. Copy the first trade opportunity and paste it as a bulleted item on Slide 9. Repeat for the second trade opportunity.
    d. Adjust the text placeholder and/or font size so that text fits properly on the slide.
    e. Link the word "Trade" in the slide title to the following URL address: http://www.pcg.kiev.ua/trade.html.

11. View the slide show.
    - On Slide 9 click the hyperlink and allow the audience to read the information below each trade opportunity.

12. Print one copy as Handouts (6 slides per page) in Black and White.

13. Save the presentation in HTML format; name it **UKRAINE**.

14. Close all files.

Directions B

1. Refer to the report shown in Illustration A on pages 256-257.

2. Create an 8-slide presentation based on the information contained in the report.

3. Use any desired template design and slide layouts; however, use the default Title Slide layout for the first slide in your presentation.

4. Include the following elements on the Slide Master:
   - a logo design using AutoShapes and WordArt. Use "UKRAINE" as the WordArt text. Position the logo in the upper left corner of the slide.
   - a slide number. Position it in the bottom right corner of the slide.
   - a new bullet design for the first-level bullets in any desired color.

5. Include the following slide layouts in your presentation:
   - one Table Slide layout
   - one or two Chart Slide layouts
   - one Clip Art & Text layout

6. Spell check.

7. Apply any desired slide transitions.

8. Apply any desired animation to bulleted lists.

9. Apply any desired animation to the clip art and chart(s).

10. Insert a new Text & Clip Art slide to become Slide 9. Enter the slide title text and relevant clip art as shown in Illustration B on page 258.

11. Launch the DDC Simulation.
    a. Click Go, Open on the Web toolbar.
    b. Type C:\DDCPUB\PPT97INT.IMR.

    ✓ *Be sure that the simulation has been installed on your hard drive. If files are on a drive other than C, replace C with the correct letter.*

    c. Click OK to launch the simulation.
    d. Select Exercise 6: Ukraine.
    e. Follow the on-screen prompts to locate trade opportunities. Write down two of them.

12. Switch to PowerPoint.
    a. Enter the two trade opportunities as bulleted items on Slide 9.
    b. Link the word "Trade" in the slide title to the following site: C:\DDCPUB\PPT97INT.IMR.

    ✓ *You cannot link directly to the Web site using the simulation.*

13. View the slide show.

14. On Slide 9 click the hyperlink to open the DDC Simulation.

15. Return to PowerPoint.

16. Print one copy as Handouts (6 slides per page) in Black and White.

17. Save the presentation in HTML format; name it **UKRAINE**.

18. Close all files.

Illustration A

Ukraine: Its People, History and Economy

Background
Ukraine is located in Eastern Europe and is bordered by Belarus and Poland to the north, the Slovak Republic and Hungary to the west, Russia to the east and the Black Sea to the south. It is the second largest of the former Soviet republics after Russia, with a population of 52 million people. Ukraine attained its independence in August 1991, following the collapse of the Soviet Union. Kiev is the capital and largest city in Ukraine.

People
About 75% of the people of the Ukraine are Ukranians, a Slavic nationality group with its own customs and language. Russians, a separate group that speaks the Russian language, make up about 20% of the population. Each region of the Ukraine has its own dialect, although many urban Ukrainians speak Russian a majority of the time. Schools such as the universities of Kiev, Lvov and Odessa teach a standardized form of Ukranian.

History
During the 1200s, Mongol tribes, later known as the Tartars, conquered the Ukrainian region. In the early 1300s, Lithuania and Poland gradually took control of the Ukraine. Under Polish-Lithuanian rule, Ukrainian peasants were bound to the land as serfs. During the 1400s, many discontented peasants joined bands of independent soldiers called Cossacks. The Cossacks occupied the territory that lay between the Poles and the Tartars. The region became known as Ukraine, which is a Slavic word meaning borderland.

Most of the Ukraine remained under Polish rule until the 1600s, when Russia gained control of the region. In 1917, the Bolshevik Revolution led to the establishment of a Communist government in Russia. Ukraine became known as the Ukrainian Soviet Socialist Republic. Ukraine gained its independence in 1991, when the Soviet Union collapsed.

Economy
Ukraine is one of the countries of the former Soviet Republic that is currently undergoing transition to a market economy. In doing so, Ukraine is experiencing severe economic contractions. Prior to independence, whole towns and regions of Ukraine were developed around a single industry. The disruption of the Soviet trading system in 1991 devestated the Ukraine economy, which still has yet to recover fully. The economy today, however, is increasingly more diversified than it was under Soviet rule. The share of 1995 GDP in Ukraine was as follows:

Industry	30%
Construction	10%
Agriculture & Forestry	15%
Trade & Services	40%
Others	5%

Economic indicators have improved since independence:

	1992	1993	1994	1995	1996
Total nominal GDP ($bln)	20	33	37	36	46
GDP per capita ($)	383	629	705	689	890
Inflation (%)	1310	4735	891	377	80
Unemployment rate	0.3	0.4	0.4	0.6	1.6

Exports are weighted toward commodities:
Share of 1996 merchandise exports

Food & Beverages	20%
Iron, Steel & Aluminum	30%
Petroleum products	5%
Chemicals	10%
Machinery	10%
Transport equipment	5%
Others	20%

Illustration B

NEXT EXERCISE

Exercise 45

■ Summary

Westin College, to which you are applying, requires its applicants to create a presentation about themselves rather than submit a college application. In this exercise, you will create a presentation about yourself. For the purpose of the exercise, you live at 275 Madison Avenue, New York, NY 10016. If you have a live Internet connection, follow Directions A. If you plan to use the DDC Simulation, follow Directions B.

EXERCISE DIRECTIONS

Directions A

1. Create a new presentation.

2. Apply any desired template design and use any desired slide layouts.

3. Create a slide for each of the following topics and enter relevant information about yourself that relates to each topic.

   - Name, address, phone number, fax number, e-mail address.
   - Hobbies
   - Talents
   - Honors
   - Community service
   - Academic interests
   - Extra-curricular activities

   ✓ *Include additional topics or omit those topics that do not relate to you. You might want to include a picture of yourself. This may be accomplished by scanning your photograph or taking your photo with a digital camera and downloading the image on your computer. Then, you can use Insert, Picture and include your scanned or digital picture.*

4. On the Slide Master, create your own logo and insert a slide number.

5. Create a hyperlink on any word in your address to the following URL: http://www.mapblast.com/ yt.hm?CMD=FILL&FAM=mapblast&SEC=start.

6. View the slide show.

   a. When the slide containing the hyperlink displays, activate the hyperlink.

   b. When you get to the Web site, scroll down and enter "My House" in the Location Label text box, "275 Madison Avenue" in the Address text box, and "New York, New York 10016" in the City and State text box.

   c. Click the Blast me a Map! button and view the map.

   d. Right-click on the map and save it as **MAP.** Note the folder to which you are saving this file.

7. Switch to PowerPoint.

   a. Insert the map (Insert, Picture, From File) on the address slide.

   b. Resize and/or reposition the map as necessary.

8. Apply any desired transition effect to each slide.

9. Apply any desired animation effect to bulleted text and/or clip art.

10. Apply a 5-second slide timing to each slide and set the slides to advance automatically.

11. Print one copy as Handouts (6 slides per page) in Black and White.

12. Save the presentation; name it **ME.**

13. View the presentation.

14. Use Pack and Go and save your presentation to a disk.

15. Close the presentation window.

Directions B

1. Create a new presentation.

2. Apply any desired template design and use any desired slide layouts.

3. Create a slide for each of the following topics and enter relevant information about yourself that relates to each topic:

   - Name, address, phone number, fax number, e-mail address.
   - Hobbies
   - Talents
   - Honors
   - Community service
   - Academic interests
   - Extra-curricular activities

   ✓ *Include additional topics or omit those topics that do not relate to you. You might want to include a picture of yourself. This may be accomplished by scanning your photograph or taking your photo with a digital camera and downloading the image on your computer. Then, you can Insert, Picture and include your scanned or digital picture.*

4. On the Slide Master, create your own logo and insert a slide number.

5. Launch the DDC Simulation.

   a. Click Go, Open on the Web toolbar.

   b. Type C:\DDCPUB\PPT97INT.IMR.

   ✓ *Be sure that the simulation has been installed on your hard drive. If files are on a drive other than C, replace C with the correct letter.*

   c. Click OK to launch the simulation.

   d. Select Exercise 7: City Maps.

   e. Follow the on-screen prompts to locate the map of 275 Madison Avenue and copy it to the clipboard.

6. Switch to PowerPoint.

7. Paste the map onto the address slide. Resize and/or reposition the map as necessary.

8. Apply any desired transition effect to each slide.

9. Apply any desired animation effect to bulleted text and/or clip art.

10. Apply a 5-second slide timing to each slide and set the slides to advance automatically.

11. Print one copy as Handouts (6 slides per page) in Black and White.

12. Save the presentation; name it **ME.**

13. View the presentation.

14. Use Pack and Go and save your presentation to a disk.

15. Close the presentation window.

INDEX

Note: Entries listed in all caps indicate listings for keystrokes.

D

FREE CATALOG
AND
UPDATED LISTING

We don't just have books that find your answers faster; we also have books that teach you how to use your computer without the fairy tales and the gobbledygook.

We also have books to improve your typing, spelling and punctuation.

Return this card for a free catalog and mailing list update.

275 Madison Avenue,
New York, NY 10016

☐ Please send me your catalog and put me on your mailing list.

Name

Firm (if any)

Address

City, State, Zip

Phone (800) 528-3897   *Fax (800) 528-3862*

SEE OUR COMPLETE CATALOG ON THE INTERNET @: http://www.ddcpub.com

---

FREE CATALOG
AND
UPDATED LISTING

We don't just have books that find your answers faster; we also have books that teach you how to use your computer without the fairy tales and the gobbledygook.

We also have books to improve your typing, spelling and punctuation.

Return this card for a free catalog and mailing list update.

275 Madison Avenue,
New York, NY 10016

☐ Please send me your catalog and put me on your mailing list.

Name

Firm (if any)

Address

City, State, Zip

Phone (800) 528-3897   *Fax (800) 528-3862*

SEE OUR COMPLETE CATALOG ON THE INTERNET @: http://www.ddcpub.com

---

FREE CATALOG
AND
UPDATED LISTING

We don't just have books that find your answers faster; we also have books that teach you how to use your computer without the fairy tales and the gobbledygook.

We also have books to improve your typing, spelling and punctuation.

Return this card for a free catalog and mailing list update.

DDC Publishing

275 Madison Avenue,
New York, NY 10016

☐ Please send me your catalog and put me on your mailing list.

Name

Firm (if any)

Address

City, State, Zip

Phone (800) 528-3897   *Fax (800) 528-3862*

SEE OUR COMPLETE CATALOG ON THE INTERNET @: http://www.ddcpub.com